BROADCAST
BLUES

BROADCAST BLUES

Dispatches From the Twenty-Year War
Between a Television Reporter
and His Medium

Eric Burns

Aaron Asher Books
HarperCollins*Publishers*

FIRST EDITION

Designed by George J. McKeon

Library of Congress Cataloging-in-Publication Data

Burns, Eric.
   Broadcast blues:dispatches from the twenty-year war between a television reporter and his medium/Eric Burns.
      p.   cm.
   ISBN 0-06-019032-9
   1. Burns, Eric.   2. Television journalists—United States—Biography.   3. Television broadcasting of news—United States.   I. Title.
PN4874.B846A3   1993
070'.92—dc20   92-54715
[B]

93 94 95 96 97 ❖/RRD 10 9 8 7 6 5 4 3 2 1

For Dianne, Toby, and Cailin
and
Lydia Yacovoni Burns

RÉSUMÉ

FOREWORD

I LOOK AT MY RÉSUMÉ and marvel at how it has compressed the time. A few numbers stand for a year, a few lines of type for hundreds of assignments, a few pages for an entire career. The incredible shrinking decades. I feel my head shake: bemusement or regret or the latest addition to my collection of tics.

Before the résumé officially began, I dabbled. Was a student teacher whose own students found literature irrelevant, a newspaper reporter whose work did not leap off the page, a seldom-watched talk show host whose topics were never the stuff of headlines. Nothing very satisfying here, just some ways to earn money during my last summers of college and the first years out. No sense of direction, no hurry to find one; the sixties had sputtered to a close, and the seventies were off to a sluggish start.

In retrospect, though, I can make of the early jobs an overture to the eventual career. I can imagine myself, at some level of consciousness, wanting to combine the erudition of the schoolteacher with the newspaper reporter's grasp of occurrences and transmit the results via television signal into millions of homes. I can imagine myself inside the homes, an indispensable presence. Vacuum cleaners pick up dirt, washing machines launder clothes, but television sets are appliances of a higher cultural order. They do not save labor; they bond societies. They inform and enlighten, provide the raw materials that the citizens of a democracy convert into the wisdom imputed to them by the Founding Fathers. I want to help matters along. Somebody plug me in.

I can imagine my relationship to the citizens, and it is one of many sides. I am the parent and they are the children who depend on me for guidance in times of trial. I am the doctor and they the patients who cannot go on without my diagnoses of social ills. I am the soloist and they the concertgoers who applaud my verbal virtuosity.

It will be several years before I see myself as a three-card monte dealer, simultaneously delighting and impoverishing the people at home by my clever shuffling of events.

I remember my first news director. A thoughtful man, moodier than most of his rank, irascible even on his better days. But always caring, always making his own brand of sense. He told me once that the journalist has a distinction unique among members of the American salaried classes: he is the only one of them who cannot explain his product. Attorneys can define the law, and roofing contractors know what shingles are, and butchers can close their eyes and offer perfect descriptions of a side of beef or whole dressed fowl. But ask a journalist to spell out news for you and what do you get?

"A blank stare or windy phrases," the news director said, cleaning his fingernails with a pocketknife. "Maybe both."

"Do *you* know what news is?" I asked cautiously, afraid of exposing my own ignorance.

He shook his head. "It's like the judge said when the fellow asked him about obscenity. I know it when I see it, and sometimes I'm not even sure then."

Within a year of this conversation, the news director did something about his indecision. He quit his job, stole off to a cabin on a small Wisconsin lake, and supported himself by making fishing lures for the locals out of plastic and wood and feathers. Painted them bright colors, gave them clever names. Strange little things. Easily definable, though.

I have also come to believe that at even deeper levels of consciousness, my choice of career was influenced as much by my insecurities as by my interests. Was I afraid of leading a colorless life? I would attach myself to stirring events. Did I think I lacked a certain panache? I would seek the company of esteemed men and women. Was there a chance the world would find me unworthy of notice? Not if I stood in front of a camera and pretended to feel at ease. Whatever I lacked inherently, I would gain by association.

And I associated with the best of them, or at least the best known: Jimmy Carter and Alan Alda and Alan Greenspan and Tom Cruise and Tom Wolfe and Farrah Fawcett and Henry Kissinger and Gerald Ford and Kirk Douglas and Pete Rose and Pierre Trudeau and Bob Hope.

To Yasir Arafat, from whom I was separated by hundreds of jubilant members of the Palestine Liberation Organization, I shouted questions across a Tunis tarmac.

To Richard Daley, from whom I was separated by the bulletproof window of a limousine, I waved as he acknowledged my question about the twilight of machine politics in Chicago by mouthing an expletive.

And to Dewey Bogart, from whom I was separated by two generations, I merely listened that night in Athol, Massachusetts, as he coaxed such a mournful rendition of "Beautiful Dreamer" from his musical saw that I can still hear it on occasions when the moon is clouded over and my soul is more than usually restless.

I have reported on civil rights and women's rights and gay rights and drug abuse and environmental abuse and tax reform and political campaign reform and the federal budget deficit and the profligacy of military spending. I have tracked swine flu and legionnaire's disease and cancer and AIDS. I was in London when Prince Charles and Lady Diana Spencer took their ill-fated vows; in Tennessee when James Earl Ray escaped from Brushy Mountain State Prison; at Three Mile Island when the nuclear power plant reopened after its almost catastrophic accident; and in Colorado when Claudine Longet went on trial for murdering the ski instructor who had been her lover, and her former husband, singer Andy Williams, showed up all blue-eyed and crewneck-sweatered and warbled a few bars of testimony on her behalf, leaving the female members of the jury in a swoon and the concept of blind justice in serious disrepair. Claudine was sentenced to two months for manslaughter. She served one.

I have been to a toga party and an Edsel farm and a Nebraska bathroom with a toilet seat that said, "Go, Big Red!" I have been to conventions of Democrats, Republicans, and romance novelists, to Academy Award presentations and baseball All-Star games. I sat in on a rehearsal with John Cougar Mellencamp and his band; I skipped lunch with the perpetually fasting Dick Gregory. I delivered obituaries for Arthur Godfrey, Tennessee Williams, and Hubert Humphrey. I covered strikes by football players and coal miners and ballet dancers and auto workers. I reported on nature at its most inimical to humankind: hurricanes in Illinois and droughts in Kansas and floods in Missouri and so much snow in Minnesota that it was called "the blizzard of the century." There was another one a few years later.

In the heavily Jewish community of Skokie, Illinois, I watched Nazis march through the streets, as the Supreme Court ruled was their right. In western Pennsylvania I saw steel mills turn out their lights and padlock their gates and shut down their towns as effectively as they had closed themselves. In Ames, Iowa, I went to the first International Conference on Iceberg Utilization, the topic of which was towing the title mass to Saudi Arabia as a source of fresh water.

I reached my various destinations by foot, car, truck, jeep, tractor, station wagon, bicycle, motorcycle, bus, train, ferry, steamer, dinghy, DC-3, DC-9, 707, 727, 737, 747, 767, L-1011, Lear, Cessna, Piper Cub, chopper, crop duster, and seaplane. I carried a notebook in one hand and a tape recorder in the other and proceeded in lockstep with a field producer and a cameraman and a soundman, ever observing, ever sniffing out the atypical and elevating it to undue notice. I have worked all night and slept all day and awakened with concentric circles around my eyes and bags under my bags. Once able to fly from New York to London and hit the ground running, I eventually reached the point of feeling jet-lagged when I turned the clock ahead an hour for Daylight Savings Time.

I would rather have done things differently. I would rather have been Theodore Roosevelt's man in the arena, "whose face is marred by dust and sweat and blood … who does actually strive to do the deeds." But I performed no deeds well enough to pack an arena. The best I could do was decide where to sit for the triumphs and follies of others.

I chose the first row. I took out pen and pad and recorded my impressions. I cleared my throat and slicked back my hair and entered the homes of the citizenry, another face on the appliance.

I lived the first lines of my résumé, in innocence and enthusiasm, twenty years ago.

1973   Anchorman, Newswriter

WNOW-TV, Parkersburg, West Virginia

IT IS SIX-THIRTY ON A SUMMER EVENING and I am alone in a small, dark room. In my hand is a thirty-minute reel of videotape, just recorded, still warm; I am tapping it against the opposite palm. In a few moments I will put it back on the machine and look at it and bring myself under its spell as I do every night at this time. But I always proceed slowly, always have to shake off the layers of reluctance. It is not my nature to be so self-indulgent, to think of a television screen as the electronic version of a reflecting pool and myself as Narcissus. But it is a condition of employment, a necessary means to the end. No matter how important my stories are, viewers will ignore them if my appearance puts them off; no matter how perceptive I am in the telling, they will change channels if my mannerisms grate on their nerves. Style is the spoonful of sugar that makes the substance go down, and although the latter can be mastered simply through diligence, the former is a more nebulous thing. Style is less what I am than what the viewer perceives: one may call me authoritative while another says arrogant; what this viewer considers easygoing that viewer finds insipid. Somehow, by watching tapes of myself, I have to divine the thoughts of the unseen audience, reinforce the positive, refurbish the negative, and meld the potentially disparate elements into a single acceptable package.

Simple as that.

I sip some ice water from a styrofoam cup, kick off my shoes, breathe deeply in the manner suggested by books on Eastern meditative techniques.

Before me are two television monitors. One, above a hand-lettered sign that says AIR, is showing a rerun of *Yancy Derringer*: Jock Mahoney as a New Orleans cowboy all in white, his stock-in-trade the smallest gun ever toted by a western hero on television.

The other monitor, designated LINE, is blank. Extending from a console between the two screens is a microphone; a headset hangs over it, and on the tip, acting as a cap to keep out dust, is a foil condom wrapper. Trojan. Midnight blue and ribbed for extra satisfaction.

To the left of the AIR monitor is an audio board with the capacity for eight channels but only enough knobs for three, the rest having been yanked off by the director in moments of rage at his ineptitude. Two of the knobs fell victim to a single swipe a few weeks ago when I read on the air a story about the death of former Cuban dictator Fulgencio Batista and the director cued a slide of Secretariat over my shoulder. Batista appeared later in the program in place of the gypsy moth caterpillar as I explained that the insect's five-month reign of tree-stripping terror in several Mid-Atlantic states was over. The caterpillar itself popped up during a report on the crew of Skylab. And off went the knobs, with fuses crackling and wires uprooting.

To the right of the LINE monitor is the tape machine on which my thirty-minute reel was recorded and to which it will soon return. Condition of machine: critical and worsening. The plastic shield over the VU meter is so yellow with age that it is almost opaque; one has to guess at the position of the needle. The rewind button, having been scavenged from the coffee maker in the sales department, is neither the same shape nor color as the other buttons. Taped to the wall nearby is a picture of Edward R. Murrow, but it is irony, not inspiration.

I flip the tape reel over in my hand, continuing to tap.

The room is a few degrees cooler than a sauna. Beads of sweat bubble at my hairline and run down my cheeks, turning my makeup to mud and leaving a damp brown ring inside my collar. I loosen my tie, unbutton my shirt, and run a finger around my neck, tugging fabric away from skin. I pluck at my pants to separate the strands of double-knit material from my leg hairs, but they do not want to part; the bond is like Velcro. There is a fan on the floor next to me—the newest, least damaged piece of equipment in the entire control room—but it is not plugged in for fear of overloading the circuits and blowing WNOW-TV in Parkersburg, West Virginia, clean off the air.

All right, I decide, the time has come. I slap the reel onto the tape machine, fastening it over the spool and then winding the tape through the playback heads and into the takeup reel on the other side. I jiggle the reels a few times to get the proper tension. There is a switch beneath the two monitors, and I flip it from AIR to LINE. *Yancy Derringer* becomes a memory, and LINE makes a soft growling sound. I hit the play button; the machine chugs and wheezes. Then a few seconds of bars and tone, a few seconds of theme music, and half an hour less commercials of a young man on the move in one of America's most glamorous professions.

> Good evening, everyone. I'm Eric Burns, and this is the early edition of *Action News.*
>
> Our top story tonight is another bombshell from the nation's capital. Federal judge John Sirica has ordered President Nixon to turn over to him tape recordings of Watergate-related conversations that took place in the Oval Office.
>
> Presidential aides, however, say that Mr. Nixon—and I'm quoting here—"will not comply with the order under any circumstances."

There is so much to notice.

How comprehensible am I? Am I enunciating clearly, emphasizing the right words, reading at a rate that is comfortable for viewers? Am I bobbing my head enough to appear animated but not so much that I resemble one of those toy chihuahuas that people of dubious taste display in the back windows of their Pintos and Chevettes? Am I making eye contact, conveying a mastery of my material, giving the impression of being wiser, or at least older, than my years? I am half Italian; do I look too swarthy? I am half English; do I look too bleached?

I slide my chair as close to the monitor as it will go. I crane my neck. I squint, looking at myself closely, then more closely, and begin to feel lightheaded, as if in motion, spiraling down into a fugue state, a booze-on-an-empty-stomach kind of giddiness. The room outside the screen vanishes, sucked into darkness. I wiggle my toes into the floor, grab the arms of my chair, trying for purchase in the real world—to no avail. I am losing myself in the thousands of dots that make up the hundreds of lines of resolution that make up the electronic version of my face. I am floating away.

But the result of this self-absorption, curiously, is distance. Just as a familiar word repeated too many times loses its meaning, so does a familiar visage too intently observed lose its identity. The parts no longer add up to the accustomed whole. The sense of separation between myself on the screen and myself in the control room increases so dramatically that the one might be on a train and the other on the platform left behind. Is this how schizophrenics get their start?

> Meanwhile, there is more trouble on the horizon for Vice President Spiro Agnew. According to reports today, a Bal-

timore financier who has been a friend of Agnew's since the sixth grade is ready to assist the U.S. Attorney's office in its investigation of the vice president on charges of bribery, extortion, and tax fraud.

Am I blinking too much or too little? Am I slouching or sitting up too straight? Is my tie centered under my shirt collar and hanging at a precise perpendicular to my belt, and have my collar points stayed flat under the jacket lapels? Are my glasses even, the front-piece parallel to the line of my eyebrows? Is the angle of my head low enough so that the reflection of the studio lights on my lenses is not too distracting? Should my glasses be a different style? A different color? Should I wear contacts?

In local news, preparations are in full swing for the annual Art Fair at Parkersburg Community College, and this year's event promises to be bigger and better than ever.

And my overbite. As if I don't have enough to worry about, enough reason to doubt my eventual success as an electronic newsman, there is the fact that my upper lip extends over my lower lip almost far enough to cast a shadow on my chin—or so a former girlfriend once announced. The result is that my face, in repose, appears to be frowning, which is not inappropriate if I'm telling of Arab gunmen killing three and wounding fifty-five in the lounge of the Athens airport, or of Idi Amin's decision to kick the Peace Corps out of Uganda before he eats them. But if a lost dog has been safely returned to its owner or a three-hundred game rolled at the Valley Lanes, an adjustment is mandatory. I have to stick out my lower jaw, clench it, and the sensation is so unnatural that I feel like the model for the smile button.

Any chance I'm overdoing all this?

I fast-forward through the commercials.

Taking a look now at sports ...

What is that shadow on my cheek? Is it the lighting in the studio, or do I have to start shaving later in the day? Would a little more makeup or a lighter shade solve the problem?

... the United States Open tennis championships got underway today at Forest Hills in the New York borough of Queens ...

Is my hair neat?

> ... and there were no bans, no counter-bans, no boycotts.

Are my shoulders properly angled to the camera?

> There had been fears ...

Eyebrows arched?

> ... that such top-ranked players as Billie Jean King and John Newcombe ...

Eyes sincere?

> ... would not play the Open this year ...

Teeth clean?

> ... because they had signed contracts with the fledgling World Team Tennis league.

Fingernails clipped, zipper zipped?

> But the disputes have been resolved, and first-round matches were played today as scheduled.

Car locked, apartment lights out, college loans paid back, problems of early childhood resolved, position on afterlife settled?

> In matches already completed involving seeded players ...

When the director cuts to a wide shot at the end of each segment, do the pointless scribbles I am making on the pages of my script appear to be notes of consequence, somehow related to the day's events and my grasp of them? Or are they obvious busywork, just something to do when there is nothing to say? Years from now, I will read an essay by the television critic Ron Powers in which he reduces to their essence the mannerisms of the television news anchorman. He finds them absurd. He calls them "functions not previously stressed in the human evolutionary chain."

> Turning our attention now to the weather ...

I am trying to find a personality but cannot settle on the specifics. Personality is an individual repeating himself, which is to some extent desirable and to a greater extent unavoidable. But whether the person is full-time flesh and blood or part-time dots and lines on a screen, it is crucial that he achieve a balance. Too little personality and he is anonymous, too much and he is a caricature. The latter seems the more frightening prospect, for it means that the core of individuality has become a tool of trade, a commodity. The human being loses what is spontaneous in him, turns mechanical; he stops *being* himself and starts *doing* himself—perhaps not even as well as others do him. In 1937 a radio station in Washington, D.C., held a Zasu Pitts impersonation contest. As a joke, the real Zasu Pitts entered. She finished second.

> ... inviting you to join me again later for *Action News* at
> ten. Until then ...

I hit the stop button, then rewind, and the tape begins to spin backward, the machine rattling like a sloppily assembled erector set, Edward R. Murrow continuing to look down dubiously.

It occurs to me that I could stand a less formal delivery, varying my cadences to sound quirkier, not so predictable. Also that I should lean into the camera a little more, show the folks at home I am their confidant as well as their parent and doctor and soloist, not so much announcing the news as letting them in on it. And I go on.

Perhaps my hair is *too* neat, plastered.

Perhaps I should wear it in a different style.

Longer.

Shorter.

Curlier.

Straighter.

More conservative ties.

Battery-powered ties that light up and blink.

A Nehru jacket with a turtleneck and love beads.

Is this what Rich Little goes through when he develops a new character?

The tape finishes rewinding and slaps around on the spool a few dozen times. I turn the machine off and the reel stops, but the echo of the slapping hangs in the air in the empty building, not so much a sound as a tingling on the ears, almost a weight, fading away so gradually I cannot say when it is finally gone. I glance behind me at the clock on the corridor wall. Seconds before seven. I take a last sip of ice water, crinkle the cup, and toss it into a rusty wastebasket. I turn the switch beneath the monitors from LINE to AIR and change the channel selector from WNOW-TV to the *CBS Evening News* from the affiliate in Charleston.

"Good evening," says Walter Cronkite in that rolling basso profundo of his, and he too begins his program by telling of Judge Sirica's demand for the Watergate tapes. I keep my chair pushed close to the monitor, hunkering in. I will now watch Cronkite even more raptly than I watched Burns—if that is possible—and in the course of the next half-hour will flip the dial back and forth and pay similar attention to John Chancellor on NBC and Howard K. Smith and Harry Reasoner on ABC. It is one thing to learn from your mistakes, another to take instruction from those who, by reason of their stature in the business, seem not to make any.

Cronkite introduces a report from Phil Jones on Capitol Hill.

I go back to junior high.

Most days I would race home from school without either of the detours my friends most commonly made: the playground to smoke cigarettes without inhaling or the dairy store for pinball and sexual speculation. I would dash up one street and down another, through an alley and across a neighbor's backyard, and would end the sprint by crashing through the front door of my house and lunging for the television as if it were a finish line. It was a Crosley with a thirteen-inch screen, if I remember correctly: black-and-white, tinny speakers. I would turn it on with a snap, but it came to life slowly, the living room taking on the blue-gray glow that suggested to children of my age a hatch opening on an alien spacecraft in a bad movie. A shade of unreality. The dial was already set to the station that carried *American Bandstand,* and I would drop to my knees before it with receptors wide open.

I suppose I was already afraid that no one would notice me. My father seldom did: too drunk. My mother did as often as she dared, but there was a distracted quality to her attentiveness, the fear that too much of it would jump-start one of my father's rages. "Quit pampering the kid!" he would bellow, tongue thick, currents of boozy breath escaping, the scent of an old Zippo. "You'll turn him into a mama's boy."

I had no brothers or sisters, no friends or relatives my own age who lived on the block, no adult acquaintances willing to unbend for the sake of a child. I lived alone, and in the way of such children took nothing for granted. I never felt approval was my due; it never came naturally to me, seemed as difficult to earn as good wages for menial work. As a result, I got into the habit of looking wistfully at strangers. Their very remoteness was an attraction; they had fewer reasons to withhold approval than people in my orbit. Of course, I had to catch their eye first, win them over.

I thought maybe if I danced well enough ...

"Here we go, guys and gals," I can still hear Dick Clark saying, leaning over his podium, the top ten hits of the week posted beneath him, "with Danny and the Juniors and 'At the Hop.'"

> *Bah, bah, bah, bah,*
> *Bah, bah, bah, bah,*
> *Bah, bah, bah, bah,*
> *Bah, bah, bah, bah,*
> *At the hop!*

And the drums kicked in and the bass laid down a backbone and the piano started thumping, and I watched enthralled as Frank Spagnuola and Dottie Horner did the jump. They would twirl each other around with what appeared total abandon, Dottie ducking under Frank's outstretched arms, Frank flinging Dottie away from him and then whipping her back like a yo-yo at the end of an especially taut string. Then out again and back, out again and back, Dottie grinning at Frank as she went whirling by, Frank grinning at her, and both of them, when they sensed the camera pointing their way and zooming in for a closeup, flashing their grins into the living room at me. Their faces were sweaty, but the sweat was a sheen, a polish, and it made their cocky, flaunting expressions gleam through the ether. They were gone with the music, on another plane entirely. I was along in the rumble seat.

"All the cats and chicks can get their kicks at the hop," Danny and the Juniors sang, and Frank's and Dottie's lips were moving and so were mine. "Let's go!"

Everybody!

"Let's go to the hop. Let's go to the hop, oh baby ..."

I would watch Bob Clayton and Justine Carrelli do the stroll. They would lock their elbows at their sides as they held hands, and drag their feet on the floor as they shuffled down the line of fellow strollers, dipping their shoulders first one way and then the other to the reluctant beat. "Well, blessa muh so-ul," moaned the Diamonds, "how uh love to strolllll." No smiles here; the music called for poutiness and the kind of herky-jerky motions that Dr. Frankenstein's monster made in the movies. The stroll was music and dance as sheer attitude, and the attitude was exaggerated cool. It said something about you, being able to pull off the stroll, and I took notes on it and all the rest of what I saw and heard on *American Bandstand*.

The program was my homework, not algebra or history or geography, and I was the most diligent of students. Put right hand on hip when swinging girl out, was the kind of thing I might have jotted down. Keep head high, don't look at feet, stay loose as goose. Sometimes I would draw little diagrams of the steps that were especially tricky, diagrams I could never decipher the next day but nonetheless kept locked in the jewelry box I had made in woodworking class.

During commercial breaks, in the eerie light of that television set from the early days, I would get up and practice with an imaginary partner. I would coil her around like Dottie and make her jiggle like Justine, and in some corner of my adolescent mind I would not be a pretender in a living room in western Pennsylvania, but one of the actual kids on the real *American Bandstand* at the other end of the state in Philly. The camera would zoom in on *me*. The music would course through *my* central nervous system. *I* would be its televised embodiment, giving it expression with *my* dazzling steps. Other kids in other places, kneeling in front of their own televisions in a state close to supplication, would be envying *me*.

Or so I dreamed as a kid in junior high, on those afternoons almost a decade and a half ago, when what the television showed seemed the best that life could offer, almost magical in its perfection, such an improvement on the world as I knew it. It was a powerful dream, easily recalled despite the passage of years and despite the fact that a new dream, equally powerful, has taken its place. Now it is mental, not physical, agility that I prize. Now it is the top stories of the day, not the top hits, with which I want to be associated. Now at stake is professional, not social, success. It is inevitable that a child who is ignored will withdraw, and that a child who withdraws will plot a comeback. In junior high, I did not care how it happened; I would as soon have sung as danced, as soon have stood on my head as either. Now, though, I have standards. I may be hollering for attention, but my tones are well modulated and my grammar precise. I may be exposing myself, but I hold my body at a modest angle. I am attracting the spotlight while maintaining my dignity, and am smug about the combination.

But there are times when I fear I am fooling myself, when I wonder whether in essence I am behaving at twenty-seven precisely as I did at thirteen: studying the moves of the people on television and copying them so I can make a good impression. I cannot help thinking, in the close, damp darkness of the WNOW-TV control room, that I should have come further in all this time.

But I do not persist with doubts like this. I have a more immediate concern. None of the network news anchormen, it turns out, is an appropriate role model for me. Just as I could not duplicate all the gyrations of Frank and Bobby and the rest of the *Bandstand* regulars, neither can I assume the speech patterns and facial tics of the men behind the national anchor desks. I am too chortly, for example, when I try Cronkite; too professorial when I try Chancellor; too prissy when I try Smith; too laconic when I try Reasoner.

So I have begun to examine more closely the newscasts' bit players, the correspondents, men and the very occasional woman flung here and there at the whim of occurrence, some of whom will be the next generation of network anchors. I watch them as they do their standups in battlefields and cornfields and the corridors of government buildings. I memorize their images, apply myself to their inflections, practice my own versions of them during commercials. They are closer to me in age and outlook than the anchors and should be easier to simulate. But none of them works for me either.

ABC's Peter Jennings, reporting from the Middle East, has the style to which I most aspire. Natty in appearance, dignified in bearing, Jennings brings to the presentation of his material a cosmopolite's sensibilities rather than a journalist's. But try though I do, I cannot reproduce his delivery. I come across as uncaring, snooty, like a butler announcing dinner to a group of guests for whom he has no particular regard.

CBS's most visible correspondent this summer is its man at the White House, the robotically menacing Dan Rather. One night, on the late edition of *Action News*, I made a stab at the man. I steeled my eyes, clamped my back teeth, read my copy with what I thought was crisp authority. But when I looked at the tape the next day, I found that I had been growling, snapping off my words as if I had a distaste for them, a personal grudge. And when I tried my rendition of the loopy grin that always freezes on Rather's face when he says something he thinks is clever, I looked like a mental patient who has just been told something he does not understand, but is afraid to let on lest the people who run the asylum delay his release. I have not attempted Rather since. I cannot imagine he has a future.

NBC's man at the White House, Tom Brokaw, poses a different problem. His personality is not as clearly defined as that of Rather or Jennings, which is probably a compliment in that it means he is less affected. He is also, for the same reason, harder to emulate. Is there a certain tucking of the chin, a wryness to the set of the lips, when he relates the news? I am not certain. Does he hitch his head at times, rearing back slightly for additional emphasis? Brokaw is like the kids who danced in the background on *American Bandstand*, the ones whose names I never knew and whose steps, although perfectly acceptable to the eye and in time with the music, were never engaging enough to copy.

There are others, of course, correspondents introduced by the anchors with fanfare, dramatic presences who seem the stars of their events, not mere chroniclers. But Marvin Kalb is too assertive for me, and Sander Vanocur too pompous, and Daniel Schorr too full of himself. Fred Graham is too down-home, Bob Schieffer too stuffy, Irv Chapman too earnest. I cannot even consider Mike Wallace because I lack the cunning, and Irving R. Levine is out because I am so thin that when I wear a bowtie I risk being mistaken for a swizzle stick.

I punch off the LINE monitor a few minutes before the network news programs end. The picture disappears in an instant, but a white dot remains in the center of the screen, fading away only gradually as the monitor continues to hum from somewhere deep within its tubes and circuits. Other machines in the control room make sounds of their own: clicks and buzzes and muted grumblings. I can only assume, the public appetite for television being what it is, that the equipment in even a small-time control room is never able to achieve perfect tranquility. Only the fan, upon which I have propped my feet to watch the last few minutes of *NBC Nightly News*, remains dormant.

I wipe the sweat from my forehead with the back of my hand and from my cheeks with my palms. I slide my chair away from the screens, finally disengaging, blinking to bring into focus objects other than the monitor. Slipping back into my shoes, I stand with due caution, needing a few moments to recover from the low-altitude vertigo of my intense concentration. Then I proceed down the hall to the bathroom in the sales department to wash off my makeup. Since there are no paper towels in the dispenser, I have to rub away the layers of pancake with soaking balls of toilet tissue that leave billions of tiny scraps of white in my stubble. I pluck out a few here and there but do not have time to get them all. I will just have to look like this, oddly freckled, at dinner. It hardly matters.

I retrace my steps through sales, past the control room and studio, and stop at the newsroom, which is barely the size of the efficiency apartment I have taken on a Parkersburg side street. I check the wire machine, another piece of hardware that never sleeps, to find out whether anything important has happened since *Action News* went on the air at six. Nothing. The machine clacks away peaceably, no bells chiming or rows of asterisks printing to signify a bulletin. The Associated Press can think of nothing better to do than run old stories with new leads. I rip a long scroll of paper out of the machine, stuff it into a huge cardboard box in the corner, exit through the back door of the station, and climb into my car.

Ahead of me, as I drive down Route 7 toward the business district of Parkersburg, is the Little Kanawha River. Plumes of acrid gray smoke twist into the twilight sky from the factories that line its banks and fuel the local economy: Parkersburg Iron and Steel; the old Viscose plant, which makes synthetic fibers; and O. Ames, one of the country's leading manufacturers of shovels. But I do not go far enough to see them. A few blocks north of the main drag and an equal distance south of the shitkicker bar district, where male patrons sit on stools on the sidewalk, drinking beer from bottles and wolf-whistling at cars that are raked and lowered, chopped and channeled, I turn into the parking lot of Kentucky Fried Chicken. It is the only restaurant I can afford on the salary of a television news anchorman in the 196th largest market in the United States.

As I enter, I see my director, who bolted from the station the instant *Action News* ended and has now finished his meal, dumping the leavings from his tray into a large wastebasket next to the front counter.

"Left the tape for ya," he says, as he does two or three times a week when we meet like this; the other nights he dines at a sales department desk a la brown bag. "Look at 'er?"

I nod.

"What'd ya think?"

A shrug. It embarrasses me to discuss my immersion in self, even with someone like the director, who would understand. I suppose he is one of those strangers I want to impress.

"Anything new for the ten?" He removes a mint-flavored toothpick from his shirt pocket, tears the wrapper off, and begins dislodging kernels of corn from his teeth. The Colonel's kernels, as he said one night with a grin.

"Doesn't look that way. It'll just be a rearranged six, I suppose."

He turns up his palms. "Hey, if that's all there is, that's all there is."

"Be back in half an hour," I say.

"I see we're outta paper towels again. I'll leave a note for Becky."

"Thanks."

"Later, pard." Stuffing his fists into the front pockets of his jeans, the director shuffles out the door to the pickup truck he uses not only to drive to and from WNOW-TV, but for his weekend job as a plasterer's apprentice in Marietta, Ohio.

I step up to the counter and order the special: two pieces of regular, mashed potatoes, and cole slaw. I would prefer white meat only but do not want to spend the extra quarter. The girl slides a full tray at me before the money is out of my pocket. She says nothing about my white-flecked stubble.

I take a seat in the back of the restaurant and continue my deliberations as Merle Haggard wails on the jukebox about confusions in his own life.

I know what I want to be when I grow up.

I just haven't figured out who.

1974–1976   Reporter, Substitute Anchorman

KMSP-TV, Minneapolis, Minnesota

THE ASSIGNMENT EDITOR sits behind a horseshoe-shaped desk in the middle of the newsroom in market number fourteen. He tugs at his mustache, at once a nervous gesture and a random pruning of prematurely gray hairs. On the desk before him are press releases and newspaper articles and wire copy and handwritten notes from the dispatcher. He looks down at them. He looks up at the reporters who anxiously surround him. He considers the pairings. He yanks so hard at a particularly stubborn hair that his whole upper lip pops forward.

"Selfridge!" he finally barks, and the green flag is waved on the day.

A young woman grabs her purse and steps out of her cubicle, metal-tipped heels tap-tapping on the tile floor. She is blinking away tears caused by the insertion of contact lenses too early in the morning but is otherwise raring to go. Shoulders flung back, chin upraised: she could be posing for a hood ornament.

"Warehouse fire in Eden Prairie," the assignment editor says, handing her a scrap of paper from a small yellow tablet.

"Big?"

"What else."

"Injuries?"

"Gotta be."

"Fatalities?"

"Who's the reporter?"

Military cadences. That kind of briskness at this hour of day.

"Who've I got?"

"Unit three."

"Jess," she translates with a nod, satisfied that the cameraman with whom she will cover the fire is up to the demands of the shoot.

"Went for gas half an hour ago," the assignment editor says. "Ought to be waiting for you in the lot."

"I'm gone," she says, and cuts a ninety-degree turn on those metal heels, clattering out of the newsroom like a small herd of purposeful animals.

"McNair!"

"Yo," unenthusiastically, from a middle-aged man in a shapeless jacket and a tie that does not match. His eyes are as watery as Selfridge's, but the problem in this case is bleariness, not corrective lenses. McNair has been awake too short a time, in the television news business too long. He pads over to the horseshoe-shaped desk, feet never leaving the floor.

The assignment editor holds out a press release. "Red Owl news conference at the Radisson at ten."

"What for?" He takes the paper but does not look at it.

"New program to hire more minorities in upper management."

"Oh," he says. "Wow."

"Spokesman from one of the black groups'll be there for a react."

"Journalist's dream."

"Then you're cleared for B-roll in the Edina store."

"Could be Emmy time." McNair balls the press release in his fist and stuffs it into the side pocket of his jacket, still not making eye contact with it or the man who gave it to him.

"Piece of cake," the assignment editor says, "so I want you to do something else for me too."

"There's a surprise."

"Weather video."

McNair is somehow able to roll just one eye. The other remains half lidded, as if unwilling to watch his retreat from the horseshoe-shaped desk. To the younger reporters at KMSP-TV, McNair is a kind of ghost. We look at him questioningly. We wonder which of us will grow up to be like him, going through the motions, apathetic.

"High's supposed to be in the thirties today, some flurries."

"Lordy," McNair says, "and only December."

"So you swing by the Nicollet Mall, get some shoppers buttoning up their overcoats as they come out of the stores. Fussing with their scarves. I don't know, whatever they're doing."

"Who?"

"Unit one." An alcoholic with a permanent case of the shakes and so unyielding a belief in his steadiness that he refuses even to pack, much less use, a tripod. His name is Stewart. He is known to one and all as Cinema Verité.

"Why me?" McNair wonders, as he does about one thing or another five mornings a week. He slides his feet the rest of the way out of the newsroom before he can be told anything else not to his liking.

"Gunderson!" And the pace picks up.

Hearing on controversial redistricting proposal at Government Center, B-roll in affected neighborhoods to follow.

Unit seven.

"O'Reilly!"

City Hall protest against cutbacks in social services budget. Invue protesters and councilmen who support cutbacks.

Unit five.

"Lewinski!"

Follow-up on mood in small town north of Twin Cities four days after funeral of prominent citizen who killed wife and Scottish terrier and then turned shotgun on self.

Unit four.

"Leeds!"

Feature on man who has learned to ski despite amputated leg and today appears in sporting goods department of Dayton's to promote new line of athletic apparel.

Unit two.

Assignment editor stops.

Picks at a few more hairs.

Does not call Burns.

And with the departure of Leeds, muttering angrily that reports on one-legged skiers hawking neon shades of Spandex are not why he went to journalism school, no one remains in the newsroom except the assignment editor and me.

The clock on the wall behind him shimmies with each jerk of the second hand. I glance at it. Nine-fourteen. Through the window next to me comes a shaft of cold blue winter sun. A few bare branches of oak and elm are visible on France Avenue, vibrating in the wind.

"Got one for you," the assignment editor says after what seems a period of intense deliberation, "but you gotta play along with me."

I wait.

He is tapping a fingernail on a front tooth. "Had a couple drinks with Selfridge the other night, and we were talking about this. What I did, I sorta promised I'd give her first crack when it finally happened. She finds out I gave it to you, she'll have her period."

I am sitting in my cubicle, getting a feel for the day by reading the metro section of the *St. Paul Pioneer Press*, which is open across my lap. "Gave what to me?"

"So here's the plan. We'll tell her I didn't get wind of it till she was gone."

"Get wind of what?"

"Yeah. You were about to head out on some kind of turkey"—he riffles through the papers on his desk—"like this thing," and he holds up a press release announcing the annual open house at the University of Minnesota School of Veterinary Medicine. "Star is this cow with a hole in its stomach. About the size of a basketball. And there's a piece of clear plastic over the hole, stitched into the side of the cow. So it's like a window, really. Or a porthole."

"What's the point?"

"Study how the stomach works. The vets look through the plastic and watch the cow's digestive juices do their thing on a bellyful of grass. It's pretty interesting, actually. We covered it last year. Maybe I'll shoot it for the weekend. Anyhow, we say this is what you were gonna do today, but then the call came in on the other thing and you were the last one left in the newsroom, so I had to give it to you. Selfridge'll still raise holy hell, but at least I'm covered."

"Okay, but what's the story?"

The assignment editor bites the eraser on his pencil stub, then mouths the words broadly. "The Rainwater girl."

Adrenaline surges in me like water from a burst dam. A charge of electricity, voltage off the meter. My head jerks up; fingertips, needing to tap, start on the desktop. "Really?"

"Kid you not, pal."

The Rainwater girl. The specter that has hovered over Twin Cities newsrooms for eleven days: the name in the headlines, the face on the front pages and in the little boxes over the shoulders of the television anchors. She was abducted by person or persons unknown in broad daylight in front of her school. Everyone saw her get in the car. No one saw the driver. The police have been without a clue, and even the most hopeful have written the little girl off.

"They found her?"

"Yep."

"Murdered?"

"Brutal."

An intake of breath.

"Story is it's the grisliest scene the cops've come across in years."

"Suspect?"

"Don't think so, not yet." The assignment editor leans back in his chair and laces his fingers behind his neck. "They just turned up the body at dawn. Actually, some joggers came across it near Lake of the Isles. Shallow grave, piece of her clothing nearby. Sweater, I think. It's like whoever planted the kid didn't give a damn whether she was found or not. Shouldn't've taken a week and a half, you ask me."

"Do the wires have it?"

The assignment editor's lips turn up. "My own private source in the Minneapolis PD," he says. "Guy owes me big-time. Still, it's not the kind of thing you can keep under wraps for long. We got half an hour, maybe an hour, before everybody else in town starts breathing down our necks."

Now my lips turn up, and it occurs to me that there is something extraordinary in a journalist's smile at a time like this, something that surpasses anticipation and pride and even possessiveness. What is in the journalist's smile when the big story breaks is paternalism; the story is a baby, and it is *his* baby. He will raise it, nurture it, see that it is dressed up properly and sent out to the world. Although he will not admit it and possibly is not aware of the fact himself, somewhere in his heart he believes the story would not even exist without his role in the transmission: a tree falling in the forest and not a soul to hear. So the journalist has rights with the story, a relationship to it; in the most extreme cases, he may even secretly fear that *he* would not exist without *it*. An insurance agent does not feel this way about a policy he writes, nor does a stockbroker about an order he places. But those are merely occupations. Journalism, like parenthood, is a calling.

"You want me to head out to Lake of the Isles?" I ask.

"The hell for?" The assignment editor leans forward, frowning, elbows descending to the desk and one hand gripping his chin. "I'll have Leeds drop over after his Dayton's shoot and pick up some B-roll for you—not that there's much to see at this point. Everybody's pretty much cleared out by now. Few strips of crime scene tape around some trees, maybe." He rips another small yellow sheet from his pad and stands.

The assignment editor is a large man, energetic and perspiring; it is twenty after nine in the morning and he has already generated the underarm stains of someone coming off an eight-hour shift. He extends the sheet of paper and I rise to take it. On it are an address and phone number.

"Mrs. Rainwater?"

"The lady herself." And he sits back down, the cushion of his chair wheezing upon impact.

I look at the paper longer than necessary, resisting the urge to gulp. What had I been thinking of? A visit to the burial site, obviously, but what else? Interviews with cops and conversations with neighbors and the reflections of teachers and playmates of the little girl? Shots of the house and the school and a casket sure to be closed? Was I thinking as well of how nicely Nancy Rainwater's fate would lend itself to some darkly poetic lines of narration about evil lurking in the recesses of the human soul? Was I eager for the chance to write indignantly for a change, rather than dispassionately, as journalism usually requires? In my enthusiasm at having been assigned the big story, how had I managed to ignore its fundamental component, the interview with the next of kin? I would have to intrude upon another human being at the moment when her grief was at its freshest. I would have to interrogate her, poke and prod, make of her sorrow the raw material of a day's work. And although I would not feel her pain, there would be my own discomfort to contend with, the result of imposing the will of my profession on someone so terribly vulnerable. The story might be my baby; the child was hers.

I suddenly wish my subconscious had tried to dazzle my besotted old man some other way.

"Could we wait a little?" I ask the assignment editor, knowing how weak and impractical I sound. But nothing else comes to mind.

"Wait?"

"The woman just found out."

"Officially, maybe, but c'mon. Girl's been missing a week and a half, and she was grabbed off the street in one of the shittiest parts of town there is. You don't think Mrs. Rainwater already knew, way down deep?"

"Still ..."

"Burns!" He is the drill sergeant again, demanding the recruit snap to. "I gave this to Selfridge, she'd be in the car by now, you know that? Be drooling, foaming at the mouth. Invite friends over to watch the piece on her audition tape, sell tickets."

And in that instant I understand. The assignment editor is not rewarding me with the Rainwater story, not signaling my progress, letting me know that I have come far enough during my four months in Minneapolis to be trusted with the big one. No, what he is really doing is testing me. Selfridge has been at the station for three years and has shown her mettle on numerous occasions, whereas this is the first time a blockbuster, demanding such reportorial indelicacy, has come along on my shift. Which means my turn for a rite of passage, my turn to prove that in addition to having a journalist's skills, I am equipped with the requisite fortitude. I have resolved my Parkersburg dilemma by choosing to stop imitating others; although it seems more an act of default than of courage, I have decided to be myself. I thought it would be enough. Now the assignment editor is raising the possibility that it isn't.

That's one way to look at it. Another is suggested by novelist E. L. Doctorow in *The Book of Daniel*. Doctorow tells of a boy who invades the private moments of the people closest to him. He spies on his mother and father making love, and creeps up on his aunt in the bathroom, once observing that "her eyes were shut and her head was tilted back and her teeth were bared as she sat on the pot with her bloomers around her knees arching her back in an ecstasy of defecation." The boy refers to himself not as a possessor of fortitude but as "a small criminal of perception." I know how it is. I am about to become one myself.

I dial the number on the sheet of paper the assignment editor gave me. The phone is answered on the second ring.

"Hello, Mrs. Rainwater?"

"Who's this?"

"Eric Burns."

"Who?"

"Well, I'm a reporter and—"

"Television?"

"Pardon me?"

"Television reporter?"

"Yes. KMSP, Newsnine."

"Oh."

"And I know that this is the worst possible time to be calling, but—"

"I think I heard of you. You do the crime stories."

"Not really."

"Sure you do."

"Some of them. Are you Mrs. Rainwater?"

"I'm her friend Glory."

"Is Mrs. Rainwater there?"

"She's here," but Glory gives no indication that she will summon her. For the moment all I hear is Glory's breathing, and there is something odd about it; it seems a struggle.

"Well, the reason I'm calling is that I'm wondering whether it would be possible for me to do an interview with her."

"For the television?"

"Yes."

"When?"

"Now, actually."

"Now?"

"As soon as possible. We could get there in half an hour, maybe less."

"I don't know," Glory says, "she's pretty shook up," and that is my cue. Doubts about my inner resources notwithstanding, I take it. Somewhere inside me a gear shifts or an override mechanism kicks in or an automatic pilot takes over. Something. Something journalistic. I start in on a spiel that comes naturally to reporters at times like this, even though we are not born with it and it is not taught in schools or handed down within the industry from veteran to rookie. Its source is a mystery to me. I only know that the teacher I used to be could not have spoken such words and that the newshound I have now become cannot avoid them. I remind myself of a used-car salesman who tells a customer, in response to complaints about a particular vehicle's rusted undercarriage and dented fenders, that there are no rips in the upholstery and no smudges on the chrome.

"As I said, I know the timing must seem awful to you, Glory," is the opening refrain, complete with mention of customer's name, "but I was thinking that maybe Mrs. Rainwater might feel better if she had someone to share her feelings with this morning. And I don't mean just me. I mean the television audience, the people who would be watching our interview tonight on the news, because when you get right down to it, the TV audience is really a kind of community, and connecting with it might be just the thing Mrs. Rainwater needs to make her feel less alone, maybe even less troubled, although I know that seems like a tall order right now. And it might work the other way around too. Mrs. Rainwater might be able to do something for the TV audience in return."

How it flows; unrehearsed, even unbidden, the words simply pour forth, a casual ooze.

"See, there are probably other parents who watch our news who've had something like this happen to them or know someone who's had something like this happen to them or at least have been afraid of this kind of thing. Mrs. Rainwater could be an example for them, an inspiration. She could give them some support and even some hope, just by her very presence. Now, you're probably thinking that Mrs. Rainwater isn't worrying about other people at a time like this, and I'm the first to admit she doesn't owe anybody anything. But it just could be that by sharing her sorrow with others, Mrs. Rainwater might lighten her own load a bit, get some of the poison out of her system. I don't have to tell you what a wonderful thing that would be."

And the odometer hasn't been touched and the tires still have thousands of miles of tread on them.

On the other end of the phone, silence: thick and judgmental. Silence as well in the newsroom. The assignment editor is staring at me through eyes not totally focused, patting his upper lip as if to make amends for extracting too many hairs with too much force for too long a time. And he is not alone. Standing next to him is the Lance man, who comes to our newsroom once a week to fill the vending machine by the dispatch office with vanilla-cream cookies and peanut-butter-and-cheese crackers. He wears a muddy brown uniform and a muddy brown baseball cap. He has leaned his hand truck against the horseshoe-shaped desk, folded his arms atop it, and rested his chin on his arms. He too is gripped by the unfolding drama, despite his ignorance of particulars.

"Hold on, will you?" Glory says.

"Of course." I set the receiver down on my desk for a moment and test my forehead with the back of my wrist. Cool and dry. Inside, my brain is burning and damp.

"What's happening?" the assignment editor says.

"It's a friend of Mrs. Rainwater's. She's checking with her."

The Lance man straightens up.

The assignment editor nods. "Should work," he says. "You're sounding good."

"I'm not so sure." I return the phone to my ear, tucking the mouthpiece under my chin. "Would you do it? Look at it that way. If you were the father of a little girl whose dead body had just been found in the woods and some television reporter called and gave you the line of bullshit I just unloaded, would you go on camera?"

"Holy smokes," says the Lance man, suddenly enlightened.

Assignment editor: "Of course not."

"Well?"

"But I'm not the one you're asking." He sneezes, then pulls a handkerchief from his pants pocket and squeezes the tip of his nose. "The folks out there in Televisionland are different from you and me, pal. You'll see."

"Us versus them?"

"What versus? There's no versus. We're on the same side. We give them what they want and they take it, a commercial transaction. Business. We're just different kinds of people."

"We know better?"

"We know different. Let's leave it there."

A few seconds later Glory is back on the line. "Mr. Burns?"

"Yes, ma'am."

"You said about half an hour to get here?"

"About that."

"You know the address?"

"I have it."

"Come on, then. We'll be waiting," and she hangs up before I can either thank her or question her sanity.

I drop the phone into the cradle. The assignment editor raises his eyebrows. I flash him a thumbs-up.

"All *right!*" he says, and shoots both arms into the air, allowing an unobstructed view of his underarm stains. He stamps his feet on the floor. "Great job, great job, you reeled her in like a pro!" He pounds the desktop a time or two, then grabs the edge with both hands and spins himself around in his plastic-castered chair. "Gonna make some history tonight, ladies and gentlemen, I *feel* it!"

The Lance man is nodding and smiling, seeming no less pleased, if considerably more restrained.

I reach for an imitation-leather bag on a shelf above my desk. In it are some tools of the trade: an audio tape recorder, a pack of spare batteries, a notepad, several pens, a street atlas, maps, telephone directories of local government personnel, and a hairbrush. I clip my beeper to the strap and sling the bag over my shoulder.

"Who've I got?"

"Six."

"Check."

"But let me tell you about that." The assignment editor is pushing all the papers on his desk into a single stack, almost ceremoniously: another day successfully orchestrated. "Donny's a good man, a real humper, you know that. But he has a tendency to frame his interviews a little on the loose side. I want you to make sure he doesn't do that today. I want the Rainwater woman's face to fill the screen." He holds one hand horizontally at his forehead, the other horizontally at his chin. "Just like this I want to see her face. Bigger than life. You read me?"

"I do."

"Another thing." The assignment editor glances at the Lance man, seeming suddenly uneasy. All innocence, the Lance man returns the look but makes no move to leave, even though the empty boxes on his hand truck testify to the fact that the vending machine has already been filled and his business at Newsnine concluded.

"Like I said, we're gonna have at least a half-hour jump on the competition, but they'll probably be lined up outside the Rainwater place when you wrap, like a goddamn parade. Think about planting a little seed with Mrs. R. before you split."

"Seed?" I would like to spare him the embarrassment of the Lance man's eavesdropping, but am without a clue.

"Yeah, you know, about how you gotta watch out for the other stations, can't really trust 'em the way you can trust ol' Newsnine. You say they don't always get the facts right, and even when they do, they have a tendency to play things up too sensationally, like the supermarket tabloids. And what might work even better is—you paying attention?"

"Yeah. Yes."

"Just as you're leaving, you say something about how much your interview must've taken out of Mrs. Rainwater. You're sorry you had to put her through all that, and you can't believe she's going to go through it all again for CCO and then again for STP and maybe even one *more* time for the damn indie. Not to mention the radio and the papers. You say to her: What's the point? It's too much, especially on a day like this. Tell her you really believe that, you've gotten to like her a lot in your brief time together, so you want to give her a little friendly advice. For her own good. She's talked to us, she's done her duty to the media. Of course, you put it in your own words. Read?"

"Sure."

The assignment editor steals another look at the Lance man and is absolved.

"Hey," the eavesdropper says, "competition."

Assignment editor: "Buzz me when you wrap."

"Ten-four."

"Good luck," he says.

"Good luck," says the Lance man.

I thank them both, and depart from the newsroom in a state of high dubiety.

Sharon Rainwater lives on the outskirts of downtown Minneapolis in a brick bungalow so small that it seems a dwelling from a fairy tale, the home of a kindly old woman in the forest. And so run-down that she has obviously run afoul of a wicked witch. The house sags in the middle, lists to one side, does not appear firmly anchored. The paint is blistered around the windows, planks are missing from the front steps, and there is no screen in the screen door, which hangs crookedly and would in all likelihood slap against the frame in a stronger wind than today's. The front yard is the size of a throw rug, the porch not much bigger. A green awning with yellow stripes at each end provides the house with its lone splash of color but also gives a feeling of disproportion; it looks like a very large visor on a very small head.

"What's the drill?" says Donny as we pull up at the curb. The top stories of the IDS Center rise behind the house, mirrored surfaces reflecting what remains of the morning's fading sunlight. The temperature seems cooler than it was when we left the station, the breeze more brisk.

"I'll go in alone."

"Want me to unload?"

"Let me make sure no one's rattled." I open the passenger door of unit six and get out.

I feel the eyes upon me before I actually see them, feel them bore into me like rays of malevolent intent. I look around. An old woman in a down parka is sweeping the porch next door. Two teenage girls are emerging from a house on the other side of Mrs. Rainwater's. An elderly man in a ten-gallon hat is walking away from me on the opposite side of the street, looking over his shoulder. Eight eyes that I can make out, but I know there are more: peeking around corners or squinting through blinds or narrowing in disdain from other vantage points. They saw me drive down the street in my orange station wagon with the huge letters KMSP on the trunk and hood and the huge number nines on the doors. I have not been subtle. They know what I want.

If it is true that the South has never forgotten the Civil War, it is equally true that parts of the Midwest have never gotten over the Indian wars, and the presence of a white man in Native American territory still signifies no good. It still means the white man wants to take, still means he believes the Native American can be forced to give. Even if he is a journalist. Or especially if he is a journalist, scheming to deprive the Native American not of land or trinkets but of dignity, taking the measure of his misfortune and crafting it into segments for a television news program. The journalist is looking for tales of alcohol and drug abuse, of sadness and dislocation, of the longing that these urban misfits feel for a different life in a different place, far from skyscrapers and crowded streets and inhospitable settings for the exercise of tradition. He wants to retail some tragedy, does the journalist, and he knows that here, in the largest native American enclave of any city in the United States, he can pick it up cheap.

Several months ago, when an old man was murdered in another Native American neighborhood, a spokesman for a local civic group complained about the media's descent. He said to reporters:

Your great-great-grandfathers slaughtered the Indians; your great-grandfathers herded the survivors onto reservations; your grandfathers decided they wanted the land for themselves and drove the Indians into the stone and steel canyons; your fathers ignored our pleas; and now you come around with your notebooks and cameras and wonder if there's anything bothering us.

So well do I remember the man's words.

The woman has stopped sweeping and simply holds the broom. The teenage girls are standing on their porch. The man in the ten-gallon hat leans against a tree with his hands behind his back. All are looking down now, but they are masters of the angle and their terrible rays ricochet. I feel them no less acutely; I am not a man to them but a type, and they despise it. They also yield to it. In neighborhoods like this, journalists are the new cavalry.

I knock on Sharon Rainwater's door, listen. There is no indication of movement within. On the porch railing are a dozen or more jars with holes poked in the lids and dead insects inside. A child's collection from last summer. Rings of dirty ice have formed in most of the jars.

Then I hear footsteps and the turning of a latch, and a moment later the front door opens.

"Mr. Burns?"

The woman before me is wearing blue corduroy slacks and a Minnesota Twins sweatshirt with the sleeves pushed up and bunched at the elbows. She is short and wide and has recently been beaten. Her left eye is purple and her nose swollen, one nostril appearing to be out of service entirely and the other operating with only marginal efficiency. There is a cut at the corner of her lip, and her forearm bears the stripes of bruises inflicted at different times. She looks at me with less wariness than I would have expected.

"I'm Glory," she says. Affable enough, but she does not offer a hand and does not open the screen door. Her eyes flit, lids blink rapidly. "Who's that?" She is gesturing beyond me.

"Oh. My cameraman."

"What's he doing?"

"Just waiting."

"Bring him in."

"Are you sure?"

She is.

I turn and wave toward the station wagon. Donny gets out and walks around to the back to begin assembling the gear.

Glory tells me to come in. I wipe my feet on the mat on the porch, and it splits into two pieces, WELC and OME.

Glory chuckles. "Don't worry."

"I'm sorry."

"It's been like that." She bends over and puts the pieces together as I step by her.

I find myself in a living room whose gloominess, however appropriate to the day, seems a permanent feature. Walls beige, furniture brown, upholstery solid tones of even darker colors. The shades are drawn; only a single lamp with a low-watt bulb is lit, and it is in the corner of the room farthest from the door, on a table at the foot of some stairs. There is a light fixture in the middle of the ceiling, but it does not work; black- and red-capped wires hang down from it, looking like the legs of a large spider.

Yet the room appears well cared for. The rug is so threadbare that the floor shows through in spots, but it is a clean floor with a scent of aerosol lemon. The tea towels that cover the arms of a small sofa and rocking chair are tattered but crisply ironed. The end table and the formica-topped table in front of the sofa are both chipped but shiny and free of dust or smudges. On the end table is a telephone, the receiver off the hook and wrapped in a blanket. I know what it means. The rest of the Twin Cities newsrooms are hot on Newsnine's trail.

The only other piece of furniture in the room is a rabbit-eared television on a wheeled stand. On top of it, in a cardboard frame, is a picture of a seven-year-old girl whose smile, all crinkly eyes and bunched cheeks, seems natural to her, not something called up at the bidding of the school photographer. I have seen the picture before. The television stations and newspapers have been running it for a week and a half, accompanying their daily speculations on the girl's fate.

"Pretty," Glory says, standing at my shoulder and breathing as best she can through her battered nose. She has tilted her head back and to the side, keeping the slightly open nostril higher than the other.

"Yes," I say.

"She never did nothing bad to nobody. Never would have. She was a princess."

"I can tell."

"I'm serious."

"So am I."

"She was all I had." It is a different voice, and it comes without warning from a place in the room I cannot immediately identify. I turn and make out the figure of Sharon Rainwater leaning in the doorway that leads to the kitchen. Her dress is black. Her arms are folded so tightly across her chest that she might be holding herself together. Her head is bowed, and she wears slippers of some sort. She is standing in darkness. My watch says it is not quite ten, but in this house of sorrow it might as well be midnight.

"Hello, Mrs. Rainwater."

"Hello."

"Thank you very much for seeing me. I know how hard it must be. I mean, I don't have any idea."

"I don't usually look like this."

I assume she means that her expression is forlorn or her eyes red from crying or that it is her custom to dress in brighter hues. But at that moment Sharon Rainwater glides toward me out of the shadows, pointing a finger at her face. "All of this. You know?"

I am astonished by my first clear look at her. She has not merely applied makeup; she has slathered it on so thickly that she might have used a trowel. I cannot even guess what her normal facial tone might be. There is a large dollop of rouge on each cheek, so much lipstick that her mouth seems a fresh wound, and so much mascara that her eyelashes droop. She looks less like a grieving mother than like one of the hookers who work Franklin Avenue, a few blocks to the west. I can only gape at her. I do not understand.

"But television," she says listlessly, "if you're on television you have to wear extra makeup because the lights are so bright and otherwise you don't look right. Isn't that true, Mr. Burns?"

"It depends."

Glory: "No, it don't."

"All the people on television wear lots of makeup," Sharon says. "I know that. I've read it. Besides, you can tell."

Yes. Usually. Always. But you have just learned of the death of your daughter, Mrs. Rainwater, and she was the only child you had, and there is no husband around to help you start on another. Your daughter was murdered, Mrs. Rainwater, and even by the standards of so bestial a crime, she was horribly treated. As later wire stories will report, and as you probably already know, she was beaten, slashed, and sexually abused. It would be all right for you to look less synthetic than a streetwalker this morning, Mrs. Rainwater. It would offend no sensibilities, start no tongues wagging.

So I find myself thinking, until I am suddenly jarred by my duplicity. It is as if I am eavesdropping on the mind of an evil twin, a small criminal of *mis*perception. Here I am, scolding Sharon Rainwater for doing what I urged her to do, finding her deficient because she apparently finds me trustworthy. True, I did not ask her to deplete inventories at Revlon on my behalf, but she would not look as she does if she did not believe it is what I and my medium require. I have made my pitch. The customer is buying, dented fenders and all. I am offended. Jesus, I say, I hope to myself.

Glory goes over to Sharon and takes her hand and leads her to a seat on the end of the sofa. "Maryanne Ten Brook," she says.

Sharon nods.

I remain standing a few feet inside the front door.

"It's a woman we know," Glory explains, "a woman from the neighborhood. Over on East Twenty-fourth, I think."

"Twenty-third."

"That's right, East Twenty-third." Glory is patting her forearm bruises. "Last month the house next to hers burned down and a little baby died. *Was* it last month?"

"I think so."

"Anyhow, what happened was they found out there was something wrong with the furnace, like it was too old. That's what started the fire. So Maryanne seen it start and watched it all, and when the TV people came by she was in the street and they asked her about it. They put this light right in her face, really bright, she said. She had to squint, and for a minute all she could see was these black dots in front of her eyes. And then she watched the story on the news program—"

"Not your station," Sharon says.

"No, not your station, but she watched it that night, and she said you could see all the lines. Even lines that wasn't there in real life. That was the thing that really blew her mind. Plus she said she looked all washed out. Paleface." Glory grins.

Sharon does not.

"She said she understood right then why you're always reading about the people on television wearing so much makeup and having special people around to do it for them."

Sharon: "She said if she's ever on TV again ..."

"That's right," says Glory, "that's right. If she's ever on TV again ..."

I understand the logic of a trivial conversation at a mournful time. The need for distraction is overwhelming; if the bereaved can pay attention to something other than the cause of the sorrow, at least for a few moments, it is less likely that raw nerves will be further inflamed. And the more trifling the topic, the greater the degree of safety. I have known survivors of bombings to go on to reporters about favorite television shows from childhood, and survivors of natural disasters to insist on discussing sports in which they normally have but a slight interest.

Sharon Rainwater's distraction is makeup, the words meant to hide her feelings as the substances do her face. Perhaps, like me, she has a kind of automatic pilot she can engage when circumstances dictate. I do it to get my story, she to ease her mind as best she can. But in the process both of us, employee and viewer of television alike, are admitting the medium's power. Surrendering to it. Feeding it. The power of the appliance's intimidating pervasiveness.

"And that's what people like me do, Mr. Burns, right? Talk to the television."

I take a step toward the sofa. I am close enough now to discern the features under Sharon Rainwater's mask, and they are what people sympathetic to the Native American like to call noble: pronounced brow, high cheekbones, strong chin. But the chin is quivering as she returns my gaze, and her red eyes are grimly vacant. Tears coat them like a glaze but do not fall.

"I've seen it all my life," she says, "ever since I was a kid. I never wanted it to be my turn, Mr. Burns, but now it is, and so I've just got to do it. Tomorrow it'll be someone else. But today ..." And a few of the tears come loose, sliding down her cheeks, caught at the chin by a tissue.

A knock at the door. Sharon starts. Glory pats her on the back, whispering in what I do not think is English, then gets up and admits Donny the loose-framer. He carries his CP-16 camera, already affixed to a tripod, on one shoulder; a battery belt hangs over the other, and in his hands are two canvas bags crammed with lights, light stands, microphones, cables, and spare cans of film.

"Living room?" he says.

"Anywhere in here," I tell him.

He looks around, picturing the shot in his mind. He proposes leaving Mrs. Rainwater where she is on the sofa and sliding the rocking chair around for me. "Unless it squeaks."

"I'll sit still."

Glory says, "It don't squeak."

"And we should pull up the shades," Donny adds. "If that's okay."

Glory tells him he may raise one or two only. The room is not to be bright this morning. The dreary winter daylight must be kept out.

"How long you figure?" Donny asks me.

"Twenty minutes after you're set up."

But we are finished with the interview in fifteen, possibly less. The topic is tragic, not complex; there are only so many questions to ask of a person in Sharon Rainwater's position, only so many variations on how do you feel, what kind of girl was Nancy, who do you think would have done such a thing, do you want to see the bastard fry, what about the future, *now* do you believe in a benevolent God?

Another five minutes and the cameraman and I have packed up the equipment, said our goodbyes, and repeated our thanks. Sharon nods to us in parting; Glory offers a hand. We tell them the story will be on the early and late news tonight, then walk out the front door of the Rainwater bungalow into a virtual convention of Twin Cities media.

"About fuckin' time!" a voice screeches.

"Two more minutes and we'd've knocked the door down on you!"

The KSTP van is parked behind our station wagon, followed by a van from WCCO television and a car from WCCO radio. Across the street is a variety of other vehicles, all sporting call letters and numbers or the names found on local mastheads. Reporters and cameramen infest the neighborhood, drinking coffee and checking their watches and cursing Newsnine for keeping them outside so long on so cold a morning. One radio reporter is pacing along the sidewalk, recording his impressions of the neighborhood in stream-of-consciousness fashion; another is interviewing a bewildered-looking mailman. A newspaper reporter and photographer sit among the jars of insects on the railing of the Rainwater porch; it was the photographer who threatened violence against the front door. A second reporter-photographer team squats on the steps, passing a bag of potato chips back and forth. No Native Americans are visible, though, and there is no sense of furtive eyes. Too much cavalry.

"First goddamn scoop *your* goddamn station *ever* got," one of the journalists says as Donny and I pick our way through the multitude to the station wagon.

"Somebody's screwin' somebody," is the analysis of one of the two women on the scene.

And from the reporter on the railing, "Now let the pros go to work," whereupon, en masse, like the countless molecules of a single unstable compound reacting to sudden stimulus, the ladies and gentlemen of the fourth estate descend on Sharon Rainwater's door. Fists rap and feet stomp and elbows are flung as my colleagues fight for position, now arguing with one another instead of Newsnine. "Fuck off" and "Move over" and "I was here first" rise over an undercurrent of snarling that sounds like the gathering of distant thunder. The guy from the railing pushes another paper's photographer; a television reporter swats at a radio stringer.

Yet when the door is answered, the whole batch of them will

transform, change demeanor completely, turn servile so suddenly that an onlooker might think he was watching TV and the channel had been changed without warning. They will apologize to Glory for intruding, beg for admittance, swear to be brief and accurate and as well-mannered as altar boys and candy stripers. Crassness will yield to courtesy, coats and ties to sackcloth and ashes; they will be, as journalists always are in situations like this, obsequious bullies.

Inside unit six, Donny turns the key in the ignition, simultaneously bringing to life the two-way radio. I overhear a conversation between the assignment editor and Selfridge; like me, she has just finished her story and is returning to the station. The assignment editor wants to know how it went.

"Fantastic."

"What'd you get?"

"Flames."

"Great," and he tells her she has two minutes and is a lock for the first segment.

"Two and a half."

"We'll talk about it."

A few seconds later, obviously still ignorant of the fact that Nancy Rainwater has been found and paternity granted to me, Selfridge signs off.

"Unit six to base, six to base."

"Come in, six."

"We're wrapped at the site and are ten-seven to shop."

"How'd it go?"

"Fine."

"What'd you get?"

"Tears."

Tears we got, in the ramshackle but well-tended house, and they testified to Sharon Rainwater's grief as powerfully as her makeup did to the influence of the medium she served so well. They smeared her mascara and cut tracks down her face and melted her rouge until her cheeks looked as if they had been bloodied in a fight. She wiped her eyes a few times during the interview and blackened them with shadow. She bit her lips and got chips of lipstick on her front teeth. She tugged at strands of hair, and some of them stuck to her jaw and forehead, glued on by the tears. It was as if Sharon Rainwater, in a horrible quandary about her role for the morning, had donned a clown's face over the traditional mask of tragedy, covering both bases.

Yet somehow, instead of being ludicrous, the sight of her was all the more poignant. The makeup called attention to the tears in dramatic fashion, a dark background highlighting the vivid display of grief; and the tears so grotesquely distorted the makeup that no viewer will find his eyes wandering tonight, either at five or at ten. Sharon Rainwater will magnetize people to their screens. In giving a public performance of so private an emotion, she contrived a face that could not more accurately have reflected her confusion, nor more certainly guaranteed a spellbound audience.

"Tears," I say one more time in the passenger seat of trusty old unit six, as much to myself as to the radio: what we got were tears.

"You lead the show tonight," the assignment editor says.

"Okay."

"Two minutes, two and a half, you name it."

"All right."

"Maybe we'll even put you on the set, you and Phil do a little cross-talk."

"Whatever."

"We'll see what Big Al thinks."

"Sure."

"ETA?"

"About twenty minutes."

"I'll get Jimmy to stoke up the processor, have it ready as soon as you're back. Nice going, Burns. I knew you could do it. Over and out."

I turn off the radio before Selfridge can call in with her questions.

We are driving south on Interstate 35W, away from downtown Minneapolis, past long walls of thick timber that shield neighborhoods more stylish than Sharon Rainwater's from the unceasing din of traffic. The sun has disappeared, and the sky is now a gunmetal gray, growing bleaker and more menacing by the mile. A light snow has begun but does not exactly fall; the flakes—more gray than white themselves—swirl in the air, the movement mostly horizontal. The forecast says they will not stick.

I turn up the heater, slide back my seat, and stretch my legs as much as the limited space will allow. Then, closing my eyes, I lean to the side and allow my head to tap lightly against the window as the orange station wagon makes its way back to the newsroom, where, with the single exception of Selfridge, people threaten to treat me like a returning hero.

1976–1983   Correspondent, NBC News

Cleveland, Chicago, New York

APRIL 1976

NEW YORK

THE CAN OF STERNO that warmed my room service dinner has long since gone out. The maids have finished turning down the beds and left their little droppings of foil-wrapped mints and tiptoed into the night. The corridors are silent. I can still hear the soft ringing of elevator bells, but the sounds are not as frequent as they were earlier, nor as urgent. Outside, the streets of Manhattan are as quiet as those of a small town in the Midwest. Easter Sunday is almost the Monday after.

My hotel is in midtown, ideally situated in place but not in time, as some of the appointments of the room suggest the era of gaslight and coach-and-fours. The wallpaper is flocked, the drapes heavy, the bed lumpy, the upholstery worn; the lamps illuminate no better than candles. There is a television that does not focus, with a built-in radio that emits a constant stream of static. The bathtub has a rubber stopper at the end of a chain, but it does not fit the drain properly, so that the water not only leaks out but makes a squeaky, whooshing sound in the process. If I fill the tub almost to the top and get in immediately, I can have a nice, relaxing soak of eight minutes.

But the hotel offers corporate discounts to employees of NBC News, and since that is what I am now, this is where I stay for my orientation to a world as far from Parkersburg, West Virginia, as my junior high living room was from the studios of *American Bandstand*. The orientation period is four weeks. I have completed three. Following is some of what I have learned:

There are more cigarette smokers in network news than in local. There are more nail biters. There are more noses with cracked veins at the nostrils and more distended pores and more hands that cannot stop shaking. There is more need for chewing gum and breath mints to mask the odors of luncheon beverages. There is more pencil chewing and cheek scratching. There are more stooped shoulders, no doubt the result of added responsibility; people in the service of the network have the weight of the world to carry, whereas those in local news bear only the burden of a single city.

There are more suits here, as opposed to the jacket-and-slacks combinations of local, and they are often Brooks Brothers suits of blue or gray. Wingtips outnumber moccasins, and they are brown and scuffed. Shirts are solid blue or solid white or blue-and-white stripes, but if the latter, the stripes are always narrow, unflashy. There is more starch in network shirts than in local shirts; there are more monogrammed pockets; the collars are less likely to be frayed. Ties are silk, not polyester, although the patterns in network and local are similar: diagonal stripes or those squiggly little raindrop shapes. There is greater use of aftershave lotion here, but the brands are relentlessly traditional: Old Spice and English Leather and Canoe.

There is less likelihood of interviewing a Sharon Rainwater at the network than there is in local.

As befits a place of such sobriety, the executive offices of NBC News have carpeting that not only covers the floors but runs halfway up the walls, assuring hushed tones for all but the most strident of conversations; and strident or not, conversations seldom reveal irreverence toward the company's bureaucratic structure, unwieldy though it is. A distinction made is a distinction observed. To wit: an associate producer and an assistant producer are of different castes; an executive vice president and a senior vice president and a mere vice president are of different species. As for people with engraved stationery and those whose paper is flat-printed, they might have to ride in the same elevator from time to time but are otherwise not inhabitants of the same planet. And the *NBC Nightly News* staff is of higher rank than the *Today* staff, the dayshift workers of higher rank than the night, the television employees higher than the radio.

All in all, I am not sure I belong in a place so rigidly stratified. But it is early in the game; I cannot tell whether I am uncomfortable because the network is inappropriate to me or simply new. I suppose it will take a while.

In addition to observing during my three weeks of orientation, I have listened, getting the following advice.

The executive producer of *Today* has told me he likes my light touch and hopes I will be able to do features for him occasionally.

The executive producer of *Nightly* has said I have a tendency to get cute from time to time and had better watch myself, especially when reporting shoulder-stooping events. My term, not his.

A news editor insists there is such a thing as an NBC way of writing a script and it is up to me to master it.

A woman on the domestic assignment desk believes that all NBC News correspondents sound alike and has encouraged me to find an original voice.

One vice president has instructed me to "go balls-out on every story. Take no prisoners."

Another has said, "You catch more flies with honey than with vinegar."

Several people have told me not to put up with any shit but have not explained further.

I am taking it all in.

And John Chancellor, the first of the people I tried to emulate in Parkersburg whom I was to meet in real life, allowed me into his office at the beginning of last week and told me how one progresses through the corps of correspondents. He lit a pipe, leaned back in his plush chair.

One starts, he intoned, by spending a year or two in a small domestic bureau. Then one moves to a larger bureau like Chicago or New York or Burbank for several more years, cutting one's teeth, getting one's feet wet. One next proceeds to Washington for an apprenticeship as a backup at a major government post like State or the White House or Pentagon. A few more years here, learning both the ropes and the lay of the land, and then one ships out for overseas duty and the development of a world view. The first stop is Frankfurt or Paris or someplace like that, and after a decent interval, reassignment to London, where, if one is up to it, one assumes the mantle of senior European correspondent. One keeps the mantle long enough to grow into it fully, Chancellor explained, and then returns to America for a first-string posting in Washington: State or the White House or Pentagon. A few more years pass and one is occasionally tapped to fill in at the anchor desk when Chancellor of *Nightly* or Brokaw of *Today* is sick or on vacation. A few *more* years and one is considered for an anchor position of one's own.

I listened to Chancellor for seven minutes. He dispensed with the next quarter-century of my life. One cannot help but mutter about vocational predestination as one staggers away from the man's office.

I have spent several days in the field with the established correspondents, hovering behind Robert Hager at a conclave of Moonies and Bob Jamieson at the United Nations and Betty Rollin in the home of a Queens family with six children—three sets of identical twins. They enlightened me with their methods, intimidated me with their efficiency. Jamieson never broke a sweat, and the only reason Hager did was that he combined the acumen of an ace reporter with the pace of a Keystone Kop. It would have been easier on my ego to have been sent out with another beginner.

Only once during my three weeks of orientation have I been assigned a story of my own. Today. The Easter Parade. I prepared for it as if it were the first landing of men on the moon.

Yesterday I went to the New York Public Library and dug through back issues of the local papers to learn what I could about previous parades: how long they had lasted, what complications had arisen, what the weather had been like. I read several versions of how the idea for the parade had come about in the first place. I looked up "Easter" in four encyclopedias and a religious reference book to find out more about the roots of the observance. I looked up "parade" to brief myself on the custom of human beings marching down thoroughfares lined with other human beings. I browsed through two general histories of New York and another devoted almost entirely to Fifth Avenue. I perused a couple of fashion histories. I even leafed through a biography of Irving Berlin.

Today I made yesterday look like a day off. I got up early and committed to memory all the notes I had taken at the library. I went to the *Nightly* newsroom before the producers had even arrived, to scan the parade previews that moved on the wires. I started patrolling the sidewalks of Fifth Avenue more than two hours before the event was scheduled to begin, picking up what intelligence I could from early arrivals and police setting up barricades at cross streets. I found one family that had driven down from Nova Scotia for the festivities, found a cop who had been assigned to the parade for seventeen consecutive years and swore there were tales to tell. I jotted down the location of each for later shooting.

When the parade started, I walked alongside it for much of the route, getting a marcher's-eye view, feeling a participant's vibes. I took notes on everything I saw. What struck me most of all was the difference between what people were wearing this year and what I had come to think of as traditional for the occasion. There were few parasols, few top hats and canes, few skirts with bustles. No man wore spats, no woman a high, lacy collar. Instead there were miniskirts and muscle T-shirts and bare midriffs; there were men sporting earrings and women with vinyl boots up to their kneecaps; there were fishnet stockings and cowboy vests, bandannas and bikini tops, berets and flak jackets. The attire was eclectic, disrespectful, exuberant—

And to me, horrifying! I had hatched some ideas for a script while going through the materials at the library yesterday, and the actual parade was not coinciding with them at all. Unfair, I railed to myself. No one needs a complication like this his first day on the job. I tried to adapt my thoughts to the reality, the reality to my thoughts; neither worked.

But before long it occurred to me that this break with tradition, rather than being a curse, was a blessing. No, put it journalistically: it was a peg, a hook, something that would make for a much more interesting story than the one I had so prematurely conceived. My network career was not doomed after all. It might even be off to a memorable start.

I had my crew shoot for an hour and a half, three cans of film, two too many for this kind of story. I ended up with enough notes for a miniseries, not counting what I had memorized. I did a standup marching beside three men and a woman wearing dashikis and sandals and carrying a sign in a language I had never seen before. I even sent the crew into a nearby skyscraper to get a shot from overhead. Then I dashed back to *Nightly*, handed my film over for developing, and planted myself at an unused typewriter. Took deep breath, wiggled fingers. Moment now at hand. Literally.

At first nothing came, but I was not blank so much as distracted. All I could think of was the time I had wasted in research: poring over old newspapers, plowing through reference books, even skimming the Irving Berlin biography, for heaven's sake! How pointless it had all proved to be.

Or had it?

Irving Berlin, I may have said aloud. That's it. And then I rolled a piece of paper into the machine and started typing.

VIDEO	AUDIO
still photos of early Easter Parades	SOUND UP FULL (instrumental version of Berlin's "Easter Parade")
keep photos	(SOUND UNDER) NARR: The traditional view of New York's famed Easter Parade suggests a musical accompaniment by Irving Berlin.
wide shot of today's parade	NARR: But here it is 1976, and the way the parade looked today, musical accompaniment by Galt MacDermot, Gerome Ragni, and James Rado would have been more appropriate.

| various tight shots of | SOUND UP FULL (vocal of |
| bizarrely dressed marchers | "Aquarius" from the musical *Hair*) |

I finished the script in twenty minutes, the rest flowing naturally from my starting point. I showed it, as procedure requires, to the executive producer of weekend *Nightly*. After taking longer than necessary to read it and moving his lips in such a way that I thought he was reading another script altogether, he responded, in full, "Interesting." He handed the script to the domestic news producer: "Different." She passed the script to the news editor, who pronounced, "Unusual." Three people, three words: a perfect economy of reaction, if less than a hearty send-off. The three people agreed that I should get started with the editing so they could pass final judgment on the finished product.

I remember the time to the moment: 4:37, with the second hand on the editing room clock a few notches past the twelve and gaining speed for the downturn. The editor had just laid in a shot of a woman with a garland of flowers in her hair and a baby at her breast, and we were wondering how long to let it run. Three seconds, I thought. Three and a quarter, said he. We went back and forth. Then the phone rang, the direct line from *Nightly*. The editor picked it up and handed it to me.

"You're dead," said the domestic producer.

"Pardon me?"

"We've got to kill you. Fighting in the Middle East."

"There's always fighting in the Middle East."

"I'm shaking my head," the producer said. "They took a few hours off for Easter."

"And they're at it again?"

"'Right-wing Christian militia'"—he was reading wire copy at me—"'have resumed their shelling of the Kantari section of Beirut.'"

"Oh."

"'Left-wing Moslem factions have been targeted with a barrage of hundred-twenty-millimeter mortar shells.'"

"My luck," I said, but so softly that the domestic news producer would not think me parochial.

"Look," he said, "it's really not that big a thing, to tell the truth. But it's the only breaking story we've got today, unless you count the Pope, and he had even less to say than usual. We're light, holiday or no. We've got to go with it."

"But we have to have *something* on the parade, don't we? After all, it's—"

"An American institution. I know. We'll have your editor cut us fifteen or twenty seconds for anchor voice-over."

"You think that's enough?"

"Go out and enjoy the rest of the day."

"You're sure you don't want me to keep at it, just in case maybe the satellite goes down?"

"The video's already in. Early feed."

"I don't mind, really."

"Just tell your editor I'll be back to him when I know how much we want."

"But—"

"Thanks for the effort. We appreciate how hard you tried."

Click.

It was the first time in my career as a television journalist that I had been assigned a piece and then had it dropped. I ran through my options as hastily as possible and decided the most reasonable was to take it personally. Rookie paranoia? More likely truth. They don't like me they never liked me they never *will* like me. I should have stayed in Minneapolis they wish I had stayed in Minneapolis maybe I should go *back* to Minneapolis. This is some of what I said to myself as I returned the phone to the editor and scuffled out of the room to begin wandering alone through the halls of 30 Rockefeller Plaza, one of broadcast journalism's most famous addresses, which I had now defiled. Up one deserted hallway and down another, around corners and past elevator banks—I was as aimless as a pinball whacked once and then left to its random caroms.

The *Nightly* people will all go out for drinks after the show and talk. They will wonder who was responsible for hiring me. They will curse the man's existence, throw darts at his publicity still. They will say, Do you be*lieve* the new guy? We send him out on the Easter Parade and he comes back with "Let the sunshine in." And they'll laugh. *How* they'll laugh! And they'll pass the laughter along: the staff of weekend *Nightly* will tell the staff of weekday *Nightly* and the staff of weekday *Nightly* will tell *Today* and *Today* will tell the executives and the executives will tell the bureaus and the bureaus will tell the bureaus of other networks and the present generation of television reporters will regale the next with the story of the kid from Minneapolis who never should have been hired. I will become a legend, a part of industry lore, the man who was to news what "Wrong-Way" Corrigan was to aviation. My picture will appear in textbooks above the caption "Don't Let This Happen to You."

And the tale, when it is told, will always end the same way, with the teller smirking into his beer and saying, "Goddamn *Nightly* producers, they were just sitting up there in the newsroom *praying* for Beirut. 'C'mon, you Christians, Easter's over, blast those Moslems off the face of the earth, willya!' The fighting hadn't started again, they'd've made it up. Anything to get out of running that wacko spot on the Easter Parade."

Of all of this I am certain. I had tried to be creative, and creativity gone awry smells far worse than failure of the garden variety.

I left 30 Rock late in the afternoon, trudging down Forty-ninth to Sixth and then turning uptown. I passed locked stores and dark office buildings and only a few people on the street: probably Christians still reveling in thoughts of Christ arisen while I silently bewailed Burns interred. I arrived at my hotel, went up to my room, and started drinking. A Dewar's with dinner, a second for dessert, and now, with the day's humiliation still acute, my perceptions of it even more muddled than before, and the faint tinkling of bells audible every few minutes from the elevator shafts, I am finishing the dregs of scotch number three and readying myself for action that can only be described as drastic.

I am seated at the desk across from the foot of the bed. I reach into the top drawer and take out a large manila envelope. I turn it upside down and shake it; dozens of slips of paper fall onto the blotter, a variety of shapes and colors, the official record. I have two or three other slips in the pockets of my pants, and I root them out and place them on the blotter as well. There must be more. I walk over to the closet and search through the pants and shirts and jackets hanging there and turn up another dozen slips. As I prepare to sit at the desk again, I notice the copy of Jacob Bronowski's *The Ascent of Man* on the nightstand. One more slip marks the page. I take it out and substitute a piece of hotel stationery.

I spend the next few minutes sorting through them: cab receipts in one stack, hotel receipts in another, entertainment in a third, miscellaneous in a fourth, and three separate stacks—breakfast, lunch, and dinner—for meals. I pull my briefcase out from under the desk and remove a pocket calculator and a pad of NBC News expense account forms. It's a crazy idea, but the day went from promising to desperate on me, and this is what the three scotches determined.

I rip the top sheet from the expense account pad and pick up a pen. I fill in my name, the name of my Div./Dept., and my Social Security number. I leave the employee identification number blank. I do not have one yet. Probably never will. Where the form asks for the name of the story, I write "orientation." Where it asks for the name of the bureau to which I am assigned, I write "Cleveland,"

and think about adding "maybe." I try to be careful; a note at the bottom of the form cautions that no alterations or erasures are permitted.

I begin with meals. I have twenty receipts for breakfast. I set aside five of them, add their totals, and then throw them away. If anyone asks, I will say I skipped breakfast those days or just grabbed a cup of coffee and some toast on the run and did not get a receipt.

TOTAL SAVINGS TO NBC ON BURNS BREAKFASTS: $39.89.

I go through a similar process with lunch and dinner, making certain not to eliminate more than one meal a day from my tally, lest someone in the accounting department think that NBC News has hired an anorexic as well as an incompetent.

TOTAL SAVINGS TO NBC ON BURNS LUNCHES AND DINNERS: $93.44

TOTAL SAVINGS TO NBC ON BURNS MEALS: $133.33.

I nod. The numbers look good. It just might work. I wish the bar were still open.

Cab fares lend themselves even more readily to cheating; no one knows exactly when I have taken a taxi or what my destination was. I could have walked, could have hopped a bus or subway, could have ridden with the crew. I simply pull out half the receipts and punch the figures into the calculator.

TOTAL SAVINGS TO NBC ON BURNS CABS: $39.00.

Cab receipts join meal receipts in the wastebasket, the bottom of which is now papered over.

The hotel bill, however, is an insurmountable problem. It is a single receipt, a day-by-day listing of costs; there is nothing I can dispose of or omit from the whole. My only recourse is to add incorrectly, which the accountants will surely catch. I give the matter some thought, then decide to let them. Of course! Whereas my cheating on meals and cabs was so deftly accomplished that it will never be noticed, hotel cheating, by being immediately detectable, will redound to my advantage. The accountants are likely to credit the money back to me, but at least they will know that my heart is in the right place. Or will they? Maybe they will just think I am stupid in addition to anorexic and incompetent. But does it matter? Surely the accounting mentality does not hold ignorance in numbers against one who is accounted. I will assume not. I have spent twenty nights in the hotel; I record only eighteen. I also slash my charges for phone and laundry.

TOTAL SAVINGS TO NBC ON BURNS HOTEL: $198.74.

I find one receipt for entertainment. I have been told that when my orientation concludes and I am dispatched to Cleveland, one of my first assignments will be to report on the improved condition of Lake Erie. I called a scientist whose name I was given as a source for the story and told him I would like to schedule a meeting when I get to town. He said he would be in New York in a few days for a convention and suggested we get together there. We met for dinner one night at Gallagher's Steak House. I paid. But no one knows. I throw the receipt away.

TOTAL SAVINGS TO NBC ON BURNS ENTERTAINMENT: $66.71.

Miscellaneous. I halve the amount of money I have dispensed in tips, ignore altogether receipts for two shoeshines.

TOTAL SAVINGS TO NBC ON BURNS MISCELLANEOUS: $11.00.

I stare down at the blotter. No more receipts. I have done all I can except make the final reckoning.

TOTAL SAVINGS TO NBC ON BURNS EXPENSE ACCOUNT: $448.78.

AVERAGE DAILY SAVINGS TO NBC ON BURNS EXPENSE ACCOUNT: $21.37.

SAVINGS TO NBC ON BURNS EXPENSE ACCOUNT PRORATED TO YEARLY BASIS: $7,800.05.

PERCENTAGE OF STARTING SALARY THEREBY KICKED BACK: 22.3.

My title to the contrary, I do not yet deserve to be considered an NBC News correspondent. My fears to the contrary, I may one day make the grade. If I am cheap enough to maintain in the interim, perhaps the company will be patient.

JUNE 1976

CLEVELAND AND
BARNESVILLE, OHIO

IT IS ALREADY DOWN TO A SYSTEM: items on a checklist, the most efficient use of time.

I come home from a trip, hold my suitcase over the hamper, and unfasten the latches. Clothes tumble out; the hamper fills. I spread the suitcase across the bed and pack it again with clean clothes for the next trip, which may be a week from now or a day or a minute, may take me to Nashville or Detroit, North Carolina or South Dakota.

I relatch the suitcase, then position it at the front door of my apartment so that I can grab the handle as I race to my next assignment.

After which I ...

Turn on the faucets in the kitchen and bathroom and leave them on until the pipes stop rattling and the rust is gone and the water runs clear.

Open the refrigerator and throw out all the food that has spoiled in my absence, along with other food that has acquired the scent of the spoiled items or has outlived its usefulness, not to mention the expiration date.

Take my hamper down to the basement and dump it into a washing machine. A packet of detergent from the vending machine, two quarters into the slots.

Retrieve my car from the garage and speed to the local supermarket to buy packaged meals, frozen dinners, and fruits and vegetables, some of which I will throw out at the end of my next trip.

Return to my building and shift the laundry to the dryer. Three more quarters.

Go back upstairs, and as a frozen dinner decomposes in

the oven, pay the bills that have accumulated while I was on the road.

Eat dinner, wash my utensils and glass, then return to the basement, where my clothes have finished drying and a surly neighbor awaits the machine.

Tote the clothes upstairs.

Put some mournful music on the stereo, slow ragtime, a record with a lot of scratches suggesting an earlier era.

Fold the clothes on the kitchen table and stuff them back in drawers while mentally cataloguing the aches: in my calves from sitting in cramped airline seats; in my sinuses from riding in pressurized cabins; in my Achilles tendons from pounding the pavement of faraway cities in leather-soled shoes.

Take as hot a shower as I can stand, adjusting the spray so that the water hits me as a rush of scalding pinpricks.

Get out and dry off and slip into bed.

And then call the woman I left behind in Minneapolis and, on this particular night, say that I have something extraordinary to tell her. A maniac, you see, has begun to play the drums in the background of my life, and I am not sure I can keep the beat. He is relentless, unceasing; his wrists are machines that do not wear down. I have no idea where he comes from; I only know what he wants. He wants me to make my deadlines: get to the airport on time and get to the story on time and get my piece finished and fed on time. Move through the workday at the speed of light, or failing that, at least the speed of Hager. When it seems I might fall behind, the drummer picks up the beat, raps louder—and I talk faster, write faster, edit faster, all the while listening to his *ka-boom-boom-boom-boom, ka-boom-boom-boom-boom.*

I don't know, I say to the woman, maybe he works for NBC and we've just never been formally introduced. Maybe he's in a different union, based in a different bureau. Or maybe he exists only in my brain, which would account for the fact that no one else ever sees him, as well as for the extraordinary degree to which I find him real. I ask the woman whether she can hear him. Listen, I say. You love me, don't you? She says she thinks she can make out the strains of Scott Joplin's "The Chrysanthemum" from my stereo, but nothing more.

A few minutes later, we bid each other good night, hanging up our phones gently, as if that will make the parting less abrupt. I hope to see her again soon but cannot make promises. I look at the clock on my nightstand. It is twenty to twelve when the stereo shuts off automatically and I turn out the lights.

2:26 a.m. Phone rings, one eye opens, new day in fast life begins.

2:26:04 a.m. Voice says, Wayne Hays? Big shot on Hill? Chairman of House Administration Committee? Story broke last week he's boffing this bimbo in his office, Elizabeth Ray?

2:26:16 a.m. Umh?

2:26:18 a.m. Well, looks like the old fart tried to kill himself.

2:26:21 a.m. Other eye opens.

2:26:23 a.m. Voice says he already called cab for me. Says I should get up, get dressed, he'll be back in my ear in five.

2:26:33 a.m. I get up and get dressed.

2:30 a.m. Drink glass of milk and eat half of stale donut.

2:31 a.m. Turn on all-news radio.

2:32 a.m. Hays in critical condition.

2:33 a.m. Voice calls back. Says beat ass to Lakefront, meet producer and crew, charter to Wheeling.

2:33:10 a.m. West Virginia?

2:33:12 a.m. Seven-eighths of an inch from there to Hay's hometown of Barnesville, Ohio, according to Rand McNally.

2:33:17 a.m. Me: We feeding *Nightly?*

2:33:19 a.m. Him: Try *Today.*

2:33:21 a.m. Me: Today's *Today?*

2:33:23 a.m. Him: Roger.

2:33:24 a.m. Me: Impossible. That's four and a half hours from now.

2:33:28 a.m. Voice wishes me well, asks for postcard, claims to have collection from tacky places.

2:33:32 a.m. I hang up.

2:33:33 a.m. Maniac drummer awakens, picks up sticks, starts with licks.

2:34 a.m. Cab toots horn in front of my building. Drums in head, horn on street—sounds like start of own personal jam session.

2:34:20 a.m. I grab suitcase.

2:34:32 a.m. Race down back steps.

2:34:35 a.m. Trip over plastic bucket and mop.

2:34:40 a.m. Ram elbow into railing support.

2:34:42 a.m. Fall on tailbone.

2:34:45 a.m. Get up.

2:34:50 a.m. Stumble through emergency exit door without setting off alarm.

2:34:51 a.m. Spot cab.

2:34:58 a.m. Take seat in back, suitcase on knees, head on suitcase.

2:35 a.m. Cab pulls away from building.

2:35:20 a.m. Reaches speed limit.

2:35:40 a.m. Reaches Mach 1.

2:51 a.m. Arrives at Lakefront.

2:51:30 a.m. I dash through terminal to tarmac and find crew and producer already there. Loading gear, cursing fate. Producer hands me story from bulldog edition of *Cleveland Plain Dealer*. Says Hays may have tried to kill self. Or maybe not.

Since starting at NBC, I have learned that there are times when I am not a journalist at all; I am a translator. Given a newspaper article or a piece of wire copy, I am shipped off to find the appropriate means of telling the story in a different medium. A man may have attempted suicide? I need a picture of the man. He is a member of the United States House of Representatives? I need a shot of the Capitol. He is in a hospital? I need an exterior. A doctor has commented on the man's condition? The doctor has to repeat his statement before a camera and microphone.

I used to think that by combining pictures with words a television reporter conveyed deeper levels of meaning than a print journalist did, that the words brought the pictures into focus and the pictures expounded on the words in such a way that the total was greater than the sum of the parts. Now I am skeptical. Too often the pictures seem to dictate the words, the words to lose themselves in the pictures' masses of fuzzy detail. Words sail through the air, one picture erases the next—the coverage ends up being less than the sum of the parts. I have begun to look for ways around this. I have not found any yet.

So perhaps I am not so much a translator as an illustrator, one who earns his daily bread playing an adult version of show-and-tell. The newspaper article or wire copy tells me; I show the television audience. The printed source is a set of instructions, and in most cases a simpler one than the instructions accompanying a child's toy. No special skills required for assembly, even the kid can do it. I do not dig, deduce, research, analyze, place in context, or view with perspective. I do not comment, elaborate upon, or refute. I simply gather my materials and arrange them in the proper order and adjust the pieces so that the fit is smooth. Hammer a little here, sand a little there. When I am finished, there it is, just like the picture on the box—an honest-to-goodness television news story!

Which might mean that I am neither a translator nor an illustrator. It might mean what I really am is a manual laborer, my white collar a disguise that fools all but me.

*   *   *

2:57 a.m. Pilot and co-pilot show up at Lakefront. One bag of donuts and thermos of coffee for selves, one of each for NBC folks.

3:04 a.m. We pile into plane, fasten seat belts.

3:07 a.m. Plane taxis and takes off.

3:19 a.m. Plane hits turbulence.

3:19:10 a.m. Correspondent's stomach hits knees.

3:24 a.m. Turbulence ends.

3:25 a.m. Questions begin, largely existential in nature, largely unanswerable. I look through window at God's unceasing void.

3:29 a.m. Producer says we should formulate game plan.

3:30 a.m. We try. Fail. Too tired.

3:31 a.m. I say we should get some sleep.

3:32 a.m. We try. Fail. Too awake.

3:33 a.m. Time marches on, *Today* closes in.

3:58 a.m. Plane lands in Wheeling and two cabs await.

4:04 a.m. Equipment goes into second cab, people into first. Drivers have coffee and donuts.

4:05 a.m. We speed west through night. Sky as black as assignment editor's heart.

4:39 a.m. We make wrong turn near Belmont, Ohio.

4:41 a.m. Get back on track.

4:52 a.m. Arrive in Barnesville.

4:53 a.m. Find Barnesville Hospital.

4:54 a.m. Turn into parking lot.

4:55 a.m. And pull into spaces near main entrance as ABC rounds bend and comes up behind us. No sign of CBS or locals.

4:57 a.m. Producer and crew shoot exteriors of hospital as ...

4:57:10 a.m. I go inside to nurses' station, pound on desk, and with best journalist's bluster demand to see Wayne Hays's doctor.

4:58:05 a.m. Nurse looks at me as if to suggest deficiency in manners.

4:58:10 a.m. I explain.

4:58:20 a.m. She resists.

4:58:30 a.m. At least tell me Hays's condition.

4:58:34 a.m. Am I a relative?

4:58:37 a.m. Nephew.

4:58:39 a.m. She laughs.

4:58:42 a.m. I plead.

4:58:50 a.m. She points. To chair. All mine, she says. Sit.

4:59 a.m. Can't. Drummer drumming, deadline nearing. I do laps around chair as nurse disappears.

4:59:30 a.m. Producer comes inside, blusters to different nurse, gets same results, joins me for laps. Three thousand eight hundred and fifty circuits of chair for a mile.

5:05 a.m. Hays's doctor makes appearance, ABC crew hot on heels.

5:06 a.m. We decide to share interview, thrust mikes into doc's face simultaneously.

5:07 a.m. Doc tells us what he can.

5:09 a.m. Isn't much.

5:10 a.m. Suicide? both nets demand to know.

5:10:10 a.m. Doc can't say.

But he can, or can at least *seem* to say. There is a trick a journalist employs in a situation like this, a kind of verbal feint that affects reality not a whit but perception to a significant degree. It is a means of forcing an interviewee to respond in the way that best serves the journalist's purpose, which is, of course, to tell as gripping a story as possible.

Myself, I would prefer to do without the trick. I would ask questions that are guileless and make the best I could of the answers. I would think of this as decency; others, however, would detect a manifestation of the same timidity I exhibited when contemplating Sharon Rainwater.

The problem is competition. If the ABC correspondent finesses the doctor and I do not, her piece will be more gripping than mine and I will have some explaining to do. I am too new to the job to get away with explanations. Besides, even as a twenty-year veteran, I could hardly take the heat off by telling the executive producer of *Today,* "Well, I didn't think it was fair to put the question like that."

As a result, I have had to do some explaining to myself. Or, more accurately, some rationalizing. What I have settled on is to use the trick when circumstances call for it, but not to view it as deception. Instead, I tell myself that what I am really doing is holding the truth up to the light at a different angle.

It works quite nicely for me.

The truth is this case concerns the reason that a powerful member of the United States House of Representatives is seriously ill. If he tried to kill himself in the wake of a sex scandal, the story is gripping. If he took an accidental overdose of sleeping pills, it is not. Thus:

5:10:40 a.m. Me to doctor: Can you honestly say, with complete confidence and without fear of contradiction, that you are absolutely certain Wayne Hays did not try to commit suicide?

5:10:50 a.m. Doctor: Of course not.

5:10:53 a.m. Suicide is a distinct possibility?

5:10:56 a.m. Well, yes.

5:10:59 a.m. Thank you, doctor. No further questions.

And so one of the simpler of journalism's smoke-filled-room rules: If it is not possible to confirm grippingness, make certain that it is brazenly suggested.

5:13 a.m. Doctor departs.

5:14 a.m. Hospital publicist shows up, says Hays staffer in cafeteria, if we are interested.

5:14:10 a.m. Two network camera crews dash wildly and loudly through corridors of small Ohio hospital, perhaps not raising dead but certainly annoying sick.

5:16 a.m. Hays staffer says boss did not try to kill self, not that kind of guy.

5:16:15 a.m. So what happened?

5:16:18 a.m. Took accidental overdose of drugs.

5:16:21 a.m. Why?

5:16:23 a.m. Wanted some rest.

5:16:26 a.m. Why?

5:16:28 a.m. Couldn't get it any other way.

5:16:32 a.m. Why?

5:16:35 a.m. Because press has been hounding poor guy night and day since Ray scandal broke. Press has been savaging him, tormenting him, visiting upon him a thousand plagues. Press has been unfair, vindictive, insensitive, corrupt, inquisitorial, vulgar. Press are vultures, monsters, perverts, liars, crypto-fascist hate-mongering scumbag morons.

5:17:10 a.m. Oh.

5:17:13 a.m. Staffer goes on.

5:22 a.m. Staffer stops.

5:23 a.m. *Today* enters homes of America in one hour and thirty-seven minutes.

5:24 a.m. Producer and I enter alcove off waiting area to hit pay phones but find "Out of Order" stickers on both of them.

5:24:10 a.m. Me: Shit!

5:24:12 a.m. Producer: Relax …

5:24:15 a.m. And he reaches into coat pocket and takes out entire stack of "Out of Order" stickers, flashing them at me and grinning. Explains he always uses them to insure access to outside world in places where phones are few and reporters many.

5:25 a.m. Producer calls *Today*, makes arrangements for feed as ...

5:25:05 a.m. I call New York assignment desk, ask whether anything further has moved on wires.

5:26 a.m. It has.

5:26:15 a.m. I takes notes as copy is read to me, will incorporate info in standup, which I now begin mentally composing.

5:27 a.m. Crew and I go outside. I plant myself before sign that says "Barnesville Hospital."

5:27:40 a.m. Soundman hands me mike, asks for level.

5:27:45 a.m. Testing, one, two. Testing, one, two, three.

5:27:50 a.m. Soundman says fine.

5:27:53 a.m. Cameraman turns on light.

5:27:56 a.m. Adjusts lens.

5:28 a.m. Tells me to go.

5:28:03 a.m. Burns standup, Hays Possible Suicide Attempt. Take one. Five, four, three, two, one. "Adding further to the speculation about suicide is the comment of a longtime friend of the Congressman. He did not wish to be identified but told the Associated Press that Hays had been despondent recently and had even talked of resigning from Congress. The send fred— Dammit!"

5:29 a.m. "... the friend said, and I'm quoting, 'I wasn't surprised to hear what had happened. I wasn't surprised at all.' Eric Burns, NBC News, Barnesville, Ohio."

5:30 a.m. Start take two.

5:30:25 a.m. End take two.

5:30:27 a.m. Cameraman says both takes okay.

5:30:31 a.m. Soundman grabs mike.

5:30:35 a.m. Sky stays black.

5:31 a.m. I go back inside hospital and borrow pen from nurse and scribble down script on sheets of notebook paper. No time to think but no need. Pieces like this are pure mechanics. Utilitarian prose, form follows function, physical dexterity more important than mental acuity.

5:32 a.m. Hour and twenty-eight minutes to *Today*. Maniac's drumbeat now a palpable thing; I feel it on insides of skull, and tempo suggests 33-rpm record being played at 78.

5:36 a.m. I finish script.

5:36:10 a.m. Producer says he has scoured hospital for quiet place to record narration. Can't find one. Too many doctors being paged, other sounds. So ...

5:36:20 a.m. We go outside.

5:36:35 a.m. Rejoin crew.

5:37:20 a.m. Find clump of bushes behind maternity ward.

5:37:25 a.m. Hunker down.

5:37:26 a.m. Listen.

5:37:29 a.m. Nothing.

5:37:35 a.m. Not so much as peep.

5:37:45 a.m. Soundman gives me mike.

5:37:50 a.m. Cameraman says ready.

5:37:55 a.m. I start first take of narration.

5:38:09 a.m. Peep.

5:38:10 a.m. Actually, caw. Crows in distance kick up fuss for reasons known only to them as I am reading aloud from script.

5:38:15 a.m. Cameraman: Second take?

5:38:18 a.m. Producer: No time.

5:38:20 a.m. Crows to make national television debut this morning on NBC's *Today* program.

5:39:07 a.m. I finish narration.

5:39:10 a.m. Cameraman pulls magazine off camera, unloads film into can, stuffs can into shipping bag, gives bag to producer.

5:40:25 a.m. Four grown men on haunches in bushes behind hospital in small Ohio town because congressman may have tried to commit suicide or maybe not.

5:40:30 a.m. Producer holds bag in front of me.

5:40:33 a.m. I toss in script.

5:40:45 a.m. Producer seals bag with gaffer's tape, and four grown men run around to front of hospital, wake up cabbie, and toss bag next to him in front seat.

5:42 a.m. Producer: Get this to NBC affiliate in Wheeling ASAP.

5:42:05 a.m. Me: We'll double meter.

5:42:08 a.m. Producer: Ring buzzer on back door of affiliate and hand over bag to person that answers.

5:42:12 a.m. Me: Triple meter.

5:42:15 a.m. Cabbie burns rubber out of hospital parking lot.

5:42:20 a.m. Me to producer: Think we'll make it?

5:42:22 a.m. Producer: Stranger things have happened.

5:44 a.m. Cameraman and soundman split in other cab for z's in nearby motel.

5:45 a.m. Producer and I go into hospital to monitor developments.

5:47 a.m. Producer: How do you like life at network so far?

5:47:05 a.m. Me: I was in Wisconsin yesterday.

5:47:09 a.m. Producer: Wait till tomorrow.

5:48 a.m. Large block of time begins.

6:19 a.m. Continues.

6:53 a.m. No end in sight.

6:58 a.m. Monitoring developments a lot like sitting on ass doing nothing.

6:59 a.m. Producer and I go to hospital lounge and turn on television.

7:00 a.m. *Today* begins.

7:07 a.m. Piece not on first newscast.

7:36 a.m. Piece not on second newscast.

8:07 a.m. Piece not on third newscast.

8:32 a.m. Piece. Floyd Kalber intros.

8:34 a.m. "... Eric Burns, NBC News, Barnesville, Ohio."

8:35 a.m. Producer and I stagger out to parking lot, forced to squint by cruel daylight.

8:36 a.m. Cabbie takes us to same motel as crew.

8:45 a.m. Producer and I get last two rooms.

8:51 a.m. We write threats on "Do Not Disturb" signs, hang them on our doors.

8:52 a.m. My head hits pillow.

8:52:02 a.m. REM.

I have known a unique kind of tiredness in my two months as an NBC News correspondent, the result of hours that are not merely long but irregular, shift work in which the shift changes not weekly or monthly but daily; the result, as well, of tension, the constant engagement in tasks that must be completed not by a certain day or hour but by a certain minute, tasks that demand perfection because a single mistake is magnified millions of times by the millions of people who see it.

The tiredness is not easy to describe. It seems more like the latter stages of a disease than like mere exhaustion. It makes my palms cold and my fingertips numb and my eyelids leaden. The insides of the lids feel like a medium grade of sandpaper, so that when I blink I am afraid of scraping away layers of conjunctiva. My shoulders constrict into a single knot of muscle; my tongue thickens, making precise enunciation a struggle; my stomach roils as though I have eaten something rotten, although the likelihood is that I have not eaten anything at all for too many hours and that the roiling is a cry of protest.

And so I find a kind of shell developing around me, a layer of insulation between self and surroundings that makes me at once a part of my world and not a part. I hear things late, respond slowly, act with hesitation if at all. I am out of sync, like a character in a film on which the sound is running a fraction of a second behind the picture. I am also surprised; I never would have guessed, nor would I have believed it had someone told me a few months ago, that being a network news correspondent demands far more of one's body than of his mind.

10:06 a.m. I dream I am falling through endless space.

10:07 a.m. I dream I am running from monsters, losing ground.

10:08 a.m. I dream I am having sex with a woman several times my size and she is on top.

10:09 a.m. I dream the phone in my motel room is ringing.

10:09:20 a.m. I answer it.

10:09:24 a.m. Producer says New York wants us to get started right away on *Nightly* piece.

10:10 a.m. I get out of bed, balance on both legs, waver but remain upright. *Ta-da!*

10:10:15 a.m. Drummer welcomes me back with flourish: Where ya been, boy, missed ya! Grabs his sticks and raps out a little something: *Ka-boom-boom-boom-boom! Ka-boom-boom-boom-boom-*boom!

10:18 a.m. Producer and crew and I meet in motel lobby and eat leaning against walls. Donuts have pink glaze and multicolored jimmies, coffee is lukewarm and watery. Producer says best he could do, short notice, better than nothing.

10:22 a.m. Four of us get into cab.

10:32 a.m. Arrive at hospital.

10:33 a.m. Consider checking in.

10:34 a.m. CBS here now, as are locals and newspapers and wires and radio nets and most of rest of free world.

10:35 a.m. Crew shoots exteriors by daylight.

10:37 a.m. Producer and I go inside and ask for Hays's doctor.

10:37:05 a.m. Are told he's home sleeping.

10:37:10 a.m. The congressman?

10:37:13 a.m. Resting comfortably.

10:37:16 a.m. Why aren't we?

10:38 a.m. Producer and I divide duties. I camp out at nurses' station while he places self near front door to survey comings and goings.

10:39 a.m. Crew gets different angles of exteriors by daylight.

10:44 a.m. CBS correspondent joins me at nurses' station, declines donut.

10:46 a.m. He says this is story for supermarket tabloid, not august organization like CBS News. Says good thing Murrow's not around to see this, even so is probably rolling over in grave.

11:01 a.m. Hospital announces press conference to update media on condition of Wayne L. Hays, Democratic congressman from Ohio. Eleven-thirty in auditorium.

11:01:10 a.m. Crews bolt for auditorium like settlers racing to claim land under Homestead Act. They stake out camera positions by setting up tripods in aisles.

11:03 a.m. Producer tries to call New York, finds ABC producer using one phone, AP reporter the other, despite "Out of Order" stickers.

11:03:05 a.m. Producer: What the hell?

11:03:08 a.m. ABC producer: Didn't think we'd fall for *that*, didja?

11:07 a.m. AP reporter hangs up, NBC producer takes phone.

11:07:10 a.m. Dials.

11:07:35 a.m. And is told that as matters now stand, *Nightly* wants a minute and a half, tops. If something big comes out of press conference, we call back and reassess.

11:27 a.m. Producer and I wend way through hospital corridors to auditorium, me making sound that is cross between conventional breathing and full-throated snore, him muttering, All this for a minute-thirty, all this for a minute-thirty ...

11:30 a.m. Press conference due to start.

11:47 a.m. Press conference starts. Doctor introduces other doctors and members of hospital staff, thanks media for cooperation, says Hays has taken overdose of medication, no way of knowing whether or not intentional. Doctor says Hays has made no statement. Mrs. Hays not with him but expected. Condition serious but prognosis good because Hays strong as horse despite age.

11:53 a.m. Doctor yields podium.

11:54 a.m. Hospital spokeswoman takes over, promises further updates, thanks media again for cooperation, says hospital has set up table of coffee and donuts for us.

11:55 a.m. Press conference ends.

11:55:01 a.m. Producer, not normally known for quick acceleration, does hundred-yard dash to pay phones and comes in first.

11:55:50 a.m. Dials *Nightly*, tells domestic producer about all the insights we gleaned from press conference.

11:56:15 a.m. Piece now one-fifteen.

12:06 p.m. Producer and crew and I send cabbie to fast-food joint.

12:07 p.m. Six hours and twenty-three minutes to *Nightly*.

12:08 p.m. Five months to vacation.

12:09 p.m. Thirty years to retirement.

12:10 p.m. Forty-six years to Second Coming of Christ, according to certain vegetarian sects in southwestern United States.

12:14 p.m. I run into ABC correspondent and have conversation with her but not really because I cannot get word in edgewise. She says if I think I've got it bad I can just think again buster because she had even less sleep than I did last night and none at all this morning and to make matters worse this is about the fourth or fifth night in a row she's had hardly any sleep because of one story or another but who's counting and actually it's not *that* bad because she's getting on the air a lot which is really name of game except getting on the air with a story like *this* fiasco is *not* name of game because there isn't any story here or at least there isn't any way to sink your teeth into story which there would be if you could actually get to Hays or Liz Ray or something like that but instead all there are are doctors and flacks and just official bullshit and it really pisses her off in fact nothing makes her crazier than this kind of thing but ABC doesn't have journalistic tradition like CBS and so there's no one there to roll over in grave.

12:41 p.m. Cabbie returns with burgers, fries, onion rings, shakes, Cokes, bags with grease stains the size of softballs. Asks how much longer we'll be needing him. We say several hours at least. He says with fares from NBC he will buy condo in West Palm Beach for sunset years.

12:42 p.m. Lunch begins.

12:45 p.m. Indigestion begins.

12:54 p.m. Lunch ends, indigestion goes on, all this for a minute-fifteen, all this for a minute-fifteen ...

1:16 p.m. Producer and I join other producers and correspondents and cameramen and soundmen and newspaper reporters and radio reporters and stringers of various sorts in hospital lounge for group monitoring of developments.

1:26 p.m. CBS soundman turns on television.

1:27 p.m. ABC cameraman wants *As the World Turns*.

1:27:05 p.m. Local radio reporter goes crazy: You national guys think you own whole goddamn world, just bust into town and figure you'll do anything you want, everyone's supposed to roll over and kiss your almighty butts and just admire you from afar, well, screw yourselves. She wants *Days of Our Lives*.

1:28 p.m. *Cleveland Plain Dealer* political reporter asks for show of hands.

1:28:20 p.m. *Days of Our Lives* it is.

1:30 p.m. Soap starts.

1:31 p.m. Woman tells man she will let his wife know he is adulterer unless he forks over large amount of money. Dissolve to …

1:32 p.m. Doctor cautioning beautiful cancer patient he will do what he can but deck is stacked against her. Dissolve to …

1:33 p.m. Sexy older woman in cocktail dress kissing sexy young man in garage mechanic's overalls. Dissolve to …

NBC affiliate in Wheeling, more than an hour and a half later. I am seated behind a typewriter in the newsroom with my arms held out at the sides, rotating them in small circles forward and then backward. Bones crack, muscles stretch, cartilage whimpers. Next I extend my arms toward the ceiling, flicking the wrists back and forth, and after that I roll my head from side to side, stretching the neck. Exercise for the terminally cramped. But nothing works; I still feel like a candidate for traction, still hear the haunting screech of existential questions.

My producer has remained in Barnesville to continue development monitoring; he will let me know if there is a change in Hays's condition or further reason either to suspect or rule out a suicide attempt, in which case I will make necessary changes in the script. I pick up the phone, dial the familiar New York extension.

3:08 p.m. Piece still one-fifteen? I want to know.

3:08:05 p.m. One-ten.

3:09 p.m. I take out stopwatch, start to work. Time one sound bite from press conference, twenty seconds. Time another and get thirteen. Time standup, twelve. Add up numbers, twenty plus thirteen plus twelve. Forty-five seconds. Most of piece already accounted for and sheet of paper not even in typewriter yet. Twenty-five seconds of script left. Fewer words to write than appear on cover of average matchbook.

3:16 p.m. I write them.

3:17 p.m. Call New York again and dictate script to *Nightly* production assistant, who types it out and passes copies around to various producers. I leave number in Wheeling. They will get back.

3:28 p.m. Nothing left in affiliate vending machine but two bags of pork rinds.

3:34 p.m. *Nightly* gets back. Script fine. Proceed.

3:37 p.m. I begin editing with NBC editor flown in from Cleveland.

3:42 p.m. Finish pork rinds with his help.

3:58 p.m. *Nightly* calls again. Feed window tight, 4:30 to 4:40, no leeway. Will we make it?

3:58:10 p.m. We're pros, I say to New York.

3:58:20 p.m. We're dead, I say to editor.

4:26 p.m. We finish editing.

4:27 p.m. Editor cleans film.

4:28 p.m. Editor and I screen piece, decide there's shot we need to change.

4:28:20 p.m. Decide no time.

4:29 p.m. Editor grabs reels from flatbed and runs down hall to affiliate control room with ...

4:29:01 p.m. Me right behind him and ...

4:29:02 p.m. Maniac drummer bringing up rear. *Ka*-boom-*ba-ba-boom! Ka*-boom-*ba-ba-boom! Ka*-boom-*ba-ba-boom!*

4:29:43 p.m. Editor hands film reels over to technician as ...

4:29:50 p.m. I call *Nightly* control room to say we're loading projector.

4:30 p.m. I stay on line.

4:30:30 p.m. Seconds zoom past.

4:30:35 p.m. Technician tells me we're loaded.

4:30:38 p.m. I tell *Nightly* control we're loaded.

4:30:42 p.m. *Nightly* says stand by to feed bars and tone.

4:30:45 p.m. Wheeling stands by.

4:31 p.m. Keeps standing by.

4:32 p.m. Stands by some more.

4:33 p.m. *Nightly* says feed bars and tone.

4:33:15 p.m. Wheeling feeds bars and tone.

4:33:35 p.m. *Nightly* acknowledges receipt of bars and tone.

4:34 p.m. *Nightly* says stand by to feed piece.

4:34:03 p.m. Wheeling getting good at standing by.

4:34:30 p.m. Editor pops pill that appears blue.

4:35 p.m. *Nightly* control says Wheeling should roll.

4:35:05 p.m. Film starts winding through Wheeling projector.

4:35:06 p.m. Taking sweet old time.

4:35:07 p.m. No hurry, la-di-da.

4:35:09 p.m. Leader appears.

4:35:10 p.m. Clock ticks.

4:35:12 p.m. Feed window closes in less than five minutes. One chance and one chance only. Can't afford rip in film, hair in gate, foul-up in New York.

4:35:13 p.m. Numbers show on leader.

4:35:16 p.m. Five.

4:35:17 p.m. Four.

4:35:18 p.m. Three.

4:35:19 p.m. Two.

4:35:20 p.m. One.

4:35:23 p.m. "Wayne Hays's personal problems began with Elizabeth Ray. Apparently, so did his health problems. ..."

4:36:32 p.m. "Eric Burns, NBC News, Barnesville, Ohio."

4:36:36 p.m. Last frame of film goes through projector.

4:36:37 p.m. Waiting begins.

4:36:38 p.m. *Nightly* evaluates.

4:36:39 p.m. Wheeling frets.

4:38 p.m. *Nightly* gives technical buy.

4:39 p.m. *Nightly* gives editorial buy.

4:39:01 p.m. Wheeling lets out whoop and offers thanks to deities of all shapes, sizes, and denominations.

4:39:15 p.m. Editor pops pill that appears green.

4:39:16 p.m. *Ka*-boom-*ba-ba*-boom-*ba-ba*-boom-boom-BOOM!

Four hours later, the producer and cameraman and soundman and editor and I are being shown to a table in what we have been assured is the finest restaurant in all of Barnesville and environs. There are bowties on the waiters, tassles on the menus, linen cloths on the tables. Specialties of the house include Surf 'n' Turf and flaming desserts with polysyllabic French names, prepared before your eyes. Flame, in fact, seems a motif of the place; candles flicker on tables like the votive offerings in a Catholic church, and an uncommon number of our fellow diners are smoking.

The service is slow, but no one minds. We sit calmly, talk idly, and what we say does not matter; what matters is only that words can be spoken in quiet tones and received without urgency. All five of us take turns speaking and receiving, reassuring ourselves that it can be done, savoring the sensation. Our conversation would probably remind someone at an adjoining table of the talk of the pod creatures in *Invasion of the Body Snatchers;* we are to all appearances alert and functioning, but there is a curious lifelessness at the core.

I take long moments to ignore the conversation altogether and tune in to the gentle ringing in my ears, which begins to sound almost like a mantra as the night wears on. I strain to distinguish individual notes or chords that I can repeat to myself later to achieve an even more reflective state. I am coming down, decompressing.

And in the process, feeling like a fool. I have been hard on myself today, and worse, hard on my profession: regarding as sinister what is more properly viewed as pragmatic, becoming depressed about matters that I should have found at most annoying. The tiredness does not seem like a disease to me now, but the by-product of honest labor; the tricks of the trade no longer seem to have originated in a smoke-filled room. In fact, the mellower I get, the less I think they should be called tricks at all. "Methods" might be more like it, or some other word of equal neutrality.

Why was I so guilty of overreaction? Why did I dwell so much on means and not at all on ends as the day progressed? Ends, of course, being the pieces on this morning's *Today* and tonight's *Nightly*. I was the man with the Wayne Hays story, after all. Mine was the version of events that millions of Americans heard, my voice reading my words expressing my editorial judgments. My face was even visible for a few seconds in each report, all the thousands of dots and hundreds of lines of resolution of it, making the identification complete. And John Chancellor, introducing the *Nightly* piece, told everyone listening that the man on the scene was "our Eric Burns." *Our*. Okay, it's a folksy little rhetorical device, and not much should be made of it. Still, I could not help but feel part of a proud tradition, a descendant of all the notable NBC journalists who had gone before. Our Eric Burns. As if those strangers watching at home could somehow sense my lineage. As if the goddamn Easter Parade had never happened!

It is not until our plates are cleared and the five of us order after-dinner drinks that the producer tells us he has talked to New York again and has further instructions.

10:07 p.m. Cameraman: Aw no!
10:07:01 p.m. Soundman: Son of a bitch!
10:07:02 p.m. Editor: Jesus, Mary, and Joseph!
10:07:03 p.m. Maniac drummer: Do I hear a downbeat?
10:07:04 p.m. No response from our Eric Burns.
10:07:05 p.m. We are to overnight in Barnesville, the producer says, and ...
10:07:10 p.m. Four voices as one: *Monitor developments!*

But this time we will do it by proxy. The producer informs us that he has slipped a crisp new picture of Ulysses S. Grant to one of the hospital's nightside nurses in return for a vow that she will be our eyes and ears in the hours ahead. She will call us if anything newsworthy happens, will let us sleep if the Hays status remains quo. In event of the latter, we will book ourselves back to Cleveland by commercial carrier early tomorrow afternoon. If the former, we will pass the night ahead as we did the one preceding: stalking the hospital corridors, scrounging for information, snarling at the dawn through hooded eyes. That, says the producer to those assembled at the table, is the plan.

Solemn nods all around. The pod creatures get it.

Then the waiter brings our brandies and the producer holds his in the air, candlelight flickering warmly around the curves of the snifter. The rest of us do likewise. A moment of silence as the producer collects his thoughts, emotion showing around the edges of his fatigue. He closes his eyes, then reopens them and says it has been a good day under trying circumstances and he has nothing but the highest regard for each and every one of us on the Hays detail. Including me, the kid. He admires our skills, respects our dedication, applauds our drive. If push came to shove, he would entrust his life to any of us without qualm or hesitation. We are comrades in the foxhole, partakers of the kind of experience that creates a deeper bond among mortals than the average person, trapped in the humdrum of his nine-to-five existence, reporting to the same office on the same street of the same city every day of his life, will ever know. Our bond is sacred, he says, a treasure to him. He will value it all his days. He is honored to share it with the likes of us.

And if he sees so much as *one* of our lousy rotten faces before noon tomorrow, he will take a chainsaw to the offender's neck and then run the blade over his own miserable wrists.

It is a sentiment to which we all drink heartily.

AUGUST 1976

BASSE-TERRE, GUADELOUPE

THE MOON IS IVORY, and the purple clouds that drift across it are blown by breezes so soft they barely ripple the leaves of the palm trees below. But they carry conflicting scents tonight, sweetness and sulfur: sugarcane from the surrounding fields and volcanic emissions from Mount Soufrière, which has been bubbling under the surface for several weeks and threatens to erupt at any moment. As a result, more than twenty thousand people who normally live on the volcano's southern slope have been evacuated to hospitals and churches and schools. Authorities allowed them to return to their homes this afternoon to gather possessions, feed animals, and tend to crops, but the visit was confined to two hours. Then it was back to the safety of the institutions.

Some people did not want to go, claiming they would rather die in their homes than spend another night in a public building "like cattle in a barn," as one man said. These people had to be removed forcibly, with the more violent of them being taken to yet another public building, the jail. One teenage boy threw rocks at policemen as they approached him; an older woman repeatedly spat on a policeman's uniform, ignoring his demands to stop until he bloodied her face with a club. I later learned that the two were distant cousins.

My crew got shots of it all.

I am staying in a hotel on the northern slope of the volcano, and I return to it now after a solitary dinner and stroll through the village. My path is lined with red and yellow hibiscus, fiery colors that seem oversaturated even in moonlight. Iguanas skitter around me, and from a distance comes the howling of an animal I have never heard before. I ask a woman I pass on the path what the animal is, but she does not speak English and my French is of the dime-store guidebook variety.

This is my first time in the West Indies, my first foreign assignment, my first volcano.

I walk through a gate onto the hotel grounds and turn down the sidewalk, passing my producer's room and finding it dark; I assume she is still out drinking with our interpreter and her friends from ABC. I pass my cameraman's room. Also dark. He must still be at the disco with the woman he met at the car rental counter at the airport. Then I pass my soundman's room, and although the curtains are tightly drawn, I can make out a light inside. I step up to the door, put an ear to it, and think I hear classical music, something I should recognize but do not. I knock. The music stops. Overhead the clouds seem to be picking up their pace across the moon, causing eerie movements of shadow on the hotel courtyard.

"Who is it?" The soundman's voice is strangely gruff.

"Me."

"Eric?"

"Yes."

"Oh," he says. "What's up?" Strangely unwelcoming.

"I was in the neighborhood and thought I'd drop by."

The door opens the width of the security chain, and two eyes look out through a pair of wire-rimmed glasses. "Yep," he confirms, "you, all right," and he forces a chuckle.

My soundman on this trip is a veteran of the television news business, and practically a legend for his accomplishments. It is said he can pluck a single voice out of a cheering crowd and make it comprehensible, or disguise a Mafioso stoolie so that even the guy's own mother wouldn't know who was speaking. He can make an orchestra sound almost as resonant on television as it does in the concert hall. The man is to audio what Brooks Robinson is to third base.

"I suppose you'd like to come in," he says.

"Look, if I've caught you in the middle of something, I'm sorry. I was just taking a walk and happened to be going by your room."

He shakes his head and offers a sotto voce apology that might be sincere. "The thing is," he explains, "I wasn't expecting anyone. You caught me off guard, that's all."

"See you in the morning," I say, starting toward my room.

"No, no, come in."

I stop. I have no desire to return to an empty hotel room in a strange land at so early an hour. I have already memorized the furnishings, the number of steps from bed to television, television to phone, phone to bathroom. "Are you sure?"

"You've just got to promise me one thing."

"What?"

"You won't tell anyone what you see in here. Not Linda, not Howie, not anyone back in the bureau or anywhere else."

"Pretty sweeping." I did not expect entrance requirements at the gate of a co-worker on the road.

"I mean it."

"Do you have a woman in there?"

"Promise?"

"A *guy?*"

He chuckles, unlooping the wire-rims from behind his ears and folding them into his hand. "I asked if you promised."

"All right, I promise. Now, what's going on?"

The soundman closes the door, unfastens the chain, then opens up and steps aside to let me enter. He secures the chain behind me the instant my feet come to rest on the carpet. He drops his glasses onto the bed.

The room appears to have been converted into a recording studio. On the dresser built into the side wall are two reel-to-reel audio tape decks, each the size of a large suitcase. Between them is a turntable with a record in the final throes of its recent spin. Next to the turntable are two spare converter plugs and a small tube of some sort that has obviously burned out. In his hand the soundman holds a patch cord, and there is another connecting the turntable to the tape deck closest to me.

"What is all this? Where did you get it?"

"It's mine."

"Yours? You brought it with you?"

He nods.

"All the way from *Cleveland?*"

"Only three extra cases," he says, "and skycaps and bellhops did most of the lugging."

"But what's it for? Are you moonlighting?" I pause, leaning against the door. "I know, a calypso group's coming in later. You're starting your own record label."

He reaches into the breast pocket of his shirt and takes out a small plastic container. "Like some Tic-Tacs?"

"No, thanks."

He holds the container to his mouth, shakes several pieces in, and smashes them to powder with a single bite.

"It's my hobby."

"What is?" Now I notice a stack of records piled alongside one of the tape decks. The album on top is *Mozart Horn Concertos: Herbert von Karajan and the Philadelphia Orchestra.* I also notice a small pouch of extra patch cords and what looks like a partially folded schematic diagram of the tape deck circuitry.

"Wait," I say. "I think I've got it. You're transferring your records to tape."

"Well, you might say that."

"What else might I say?"

"I'm transferring, all right, Eric," the soundman admits, "but there's a lot more to it than that. What I'm actually doing to the music is molding it into shorter units, compressing it."

"Compressing it?"

"Making miniatures, tiny reproductions of the greatest music ever composed and recorded. It's like the audio equivalent of those wonderful little dollhouses you see in museums, with perfectly scaled-down figures and furnishings. Know what I mean?" The soundman is warming to his explanation. "It's my own idea, really. Want me to tell you how it works?"

"Please."

"Okay," and he takes a seat on the dresser next to one of the tape decks, wrapping an arm around it.

I have never worked with the man before. Despite the regard in which he is held, I know that there are whispers about him. It is said that he disappears after the day's shooting is done, keeps to himself, does not emerge until morning. This is meant to sound ominous. What does the fellow do? Why, he *keeps to himself.* Suspicious behavior in a communal vocation like television news, a granting of too much license to colleagues with perverse imaginations.

I step farther into the room and sit down in a captain's chair near the front window.

"The first thing I do," the soundman says, "is take the record and dub it across to audiotape, the simple transfer." He inclines his head toward the turntable. "Panasonic SP-10 Mark II, best piece of equipment on the market. Lowest wow and flutter rate of any turntable ever made."

"Is that right?"

"So I put the record on and then dub it over to tape, but at the slowest speed the machine will go, which is one and seven-eighths." The soundman points to the speed-selector dial on one of the tape decks, a Panasonic RS-1500 UF. "Then the good part." His heel has begun to tap against the bottom dresser drawer, enthusiasm building. "I transfer the tape on the first machine to another reel on the second, except now I have the second machine set at the *fastest* speed it'll go, fifteen inches per second."

"So the music sounds faster." I lean forward in the chair; I am lonely on this smoking island in the Caribbean, willing to be interested in anything tonight.

"Eight times faster, to be exact. Which means it takes only one-eighth as long to play. But I'm not finished yet. Now I change the speeds on the two tape decks, making the *second* one play at one and seven-eighths and the *first* at fifteen. I reverse the patch. Then I take the speeded-up tape and play it back so *that* version is eight times faster than the previous one, or sixty-four times as fast as the original."

I settle back and prop one foot on the other knee. My associate is having me on.

"Then I do it again," he continues, "and I keep doing it until the whole side of the record, the whole concerto or symphony or chorale, which is maybe twenty or twenty-five minutes of music, sometimes even longer, goes by in only a few seconds. Want to hear a few samples?"

"Why not."

"Any particular requests?"

I laugh. "If we're talking about a symphony that lasts two or three seconds, I can't believe it would make much difference."

"Ah," the soundman says, "but that's where you're wrong." He reaches behind the turntable, takes a reel of tape out of a box, and slips it onto the first machine. "The trained ear can tell the pieces apart even if they're a fraction of a second long."

"You can't be serious."

"You bet I can."

"But why bother?"

"I already told you. To train the ear. Identifying the music as it goes zipping by becomes a game, one that requires a great deal of skill. And as I get better at it, it helps me appreciate the music more as it was first conceived. I go back and listen at normal speed, and I hear things I never heard before. And there's something else, too."

I cannot imagine.

"The sheer fun of it." So reticent to share his pastime at first, he is now aflame. I am probably one of the few employees of NBC News ever to have gained the soundman's confidence, and he is carried away with the momentum of opening up. "The dabbling, the tinkering. It's play, pure play, the kind of thing that children are masters at but adults somehow lose the knack of. A shame, really." His hand caresses the turntable. "And then, after I get my entire collection of records transferred to tape, know what I'll do?"

Haven't the foggiest.

"I'll transfer the reels to cassettes so I can play them on my new portable Sony. I bought a set of stereo headphones for it. Amazing, just amazing. I don't have them with me this trip, but take my word for it. They make it sound like the orchestra is right there in your ears. And with headphones on I can listen to the cassettes in a car, on an airplane, or in a motel room without having to haul all this heavy equipment around the world and without bothering anyone even if I have the volume up full blast. Ready?"

"Ready."

The soundman flicks on one of the tape decks and pushes the play button. In less time than it takes the average pianist to skitter his fingers up the keyboard, I hear three separate units of music, the gaps between them longer, it seems to me, than the selections themselves.

"What do you think?" the soundman asks. "Could you tell them apart?"

"Don't be silly."

"The trained ear, Eric, the trained ear," and he grins, his peculiar ability confirmed. He tells me I have just heard Chopin's Etudes in A-flat Major, D-flat Major, and G-flat Major, performed by Ludwig Hoffman; Ravel's *Bolero*, performed by Sir Georg Solti and the Chicago; and Bach's Sonatas for Cello and Harpsichord, performed by Edmund Kurtz and Frank Pelleg.

"No."

"Word of honor."

"I'm astounded."

"You're bored."

"No," I protest.

"It's all right," the soundman says; he seems unperturbed, but a shadow has crossed his face.

"I'm not bored, really I'm not."

"At least now you know why I didn't want to let you in." He squeezes the corners of his eyes with thumb and middle finger. "How long have you been at this?"

"What?"

"Reporting. For the network."

I do a hasty calculation and arrive at five months.

"And you like it?"

"For the most part."

"Why shouldn't you?" he says, looking up at the ceiling, his head angled back severely. I follow his gaze; there is nothing to see. "Pretty exciting stuff, the kinds of things you do. At least, that's the way most people would look at it. But what about the other part? Have you gotten around to asking yourself that yet?"

I am supposed to say, "What other part?"

"Being on the road all the time. How many nights do you think you've spent at home since you started with NBC?"

"I don't know."

"Half?"

"Maybe. A little less."

"Are you married?"

"Not yet."

The soundman shrugs and steps to the window. He pulls aside the curtain and peers into the courtyard as if there is something he wants to see but cannot bring into focus. Then he retreats and takes the chair next to mine. Between us is a flimsy table with an open notebook on it. It seems to be a log of the records he has shrunk and the dates upon which the shrinkage was accomplished.

"Do you have any hobbies?" he says.

"I have things I like to do."

"Because that's what you're going to need on this job."

"A hobby?"

"You think you need to be able to figure out the facts of a story and then put them together so that people will understand them. And keep your cool under fire, that kind of thing. Believe me, Eric, that's the easy part. After a while, if you've got anything on the ball at all, you'll pick that stuff up. Let me tell you, reporting is over-rated. I've been working with television reporters for a lot of years, and I know it for a fact. You do your script, and even if it's a mess, you've got the people back in New York to straighten it out for you, tell you to change one thing or another, make this point this way and that point that way. As for the rest of it, you just have to be curious and stick to your guns, not give up. That's all. Big deal.

"But," he says, reaching for the table and slapping the notebook shut, "those are just the days. After you've been on the job longer than five months you'll realize that the days don't matter nearly as much as you think. The hobby, if you want to call it that, is what keeps you sane the rest of the time. Take it from me, the people who ultimately make it in this business are the ones who figure out the nights. And by 'make it,' I don't mean make it as journalists, because like I say, that part's a breeze. I mean make it as human beings. You take Linda. She's a sweet kid, but she drinks too much, way too much. She's been drinking too much ever since I met her, and she's already having problems with her liver. Did you know that?"

"No."

"I'm not surprised. She won't talk about it. But it's true, and she's only thirty, maybe thirty-one. Think what kind of shape she'll be in after another five or ten years of this life. Then there's Howie, who couldn't keep it in his pants if you put a gun to his head. He'll whip it out for anyone, anytime, and who knows what kind of disease he'll get one of these days. I've worked with hundreds of people like Linda and Howie in my time, hundreds. They burn out so fast you can't even remember their names. They end up living in shabby little apartments, going to outpatient detox, and working as freelance corporate flacks or overnight rewrite men on small-time newspapers—where all good journalists go when they die. And why?" He sits back in his chair, poking a fingernail between two front teeth. "Because they never knew how to handle the nights. Me, I've got something to do that's undemanding enough to be fun and yet involving enough to take my mind off the days. Heck of a combination, Eric, when you think about it. After the day's work is done, I have dinner, call my wife, talk to her and the kids, then work on my music for a while and the night is gone. I'm in the sack after that, and before you know it it's morning. A few more nights and I'm home again. The time goes by, and everything's all right."

"Do you do this at home?"

"Don't need to," the soundman says. "At home I've got a life. But on the road nobody does. All you can do is look for ways to get along."

On this night, the soundman and I get along well enough. He tells me not only about co-workers ruined by the nights, but about the stories he has covered and the places he has been, about working in the old days of television news, which is to say the first days, which is to say the days when every event covered and every story filed was another step in the invention of the process. He tells me about his experiences with the pioneers, Huntley and Brinkley and Scherer and Frederick, about the mistakes they made, the innovations they devised, the business they helped to create. Did I know that Huntley started out as more of an actor than a journalist? Did I know that John Cameron Swayze was more of an actor than Huntley? Did I know that nobody took it seriously at the start, that the best journalists could not be pried loose from newspapers and radio?

But then came Mobile and Montgomery and Oxford, Mississippi: southern whites turning on blacks and beating them and jeering at them and blasting them with hoses that had the force of bazookas; the blacks coming back for more and even more, refusing to give up their seats at lunch counters and stay in their seats in the back of the bus. The civil rights movement of the sixties, and footage of such power and eloquence that newspapers suddenly seemed a relic from the age of Gutenberg and radio a mere talking box. Television was no longer a plaything or an experiment; it was a must, the only medium that seemed up to the demands of the time if you were a serious journalist.

This is the tradition of which I felt myself a part when John Chancellor used his possessive pronoun.

The soundman also tells me what he did at night on the road before the idea of musical miniatures came to him. He drank himself senseless, he says, could have outgulped Linda by a gallon or two at a sitting, narrowly missed a burnout of his own. He dabbled with drugs and sex, foundered hopelessly for longer than he can stand to remember. In similar situations, millions of people over the years have found God; the soundman, already religious, turned to recording technology. Different means, same end: salvation of a sort.

He takes his leave for a few minutes, trundling across the courtyard to the hotel lobby to buy two Cokes and fill an ice bucket. He returns, pours the drinks, and then plays more music for me: some Strauss waltzes, a little Schumann, Wagner's entire *Ring* cycle, every symphony Beethoven and Tchaikovsky ever wrote. That kills a minute or two. After I have heard them all I begin to think I can actually tell them apart.

The soundman yawns and I get up. I thank him for sharing his pastime with me.

"What's the call?" He also rises and unfastens the chain on the door.

"Wheels up at six-thirty," I say. We exchange handshakes and goodnights, and the second I am outside he latches the door again behind me. Security immediately reestablished, privacy assured. I hope he is not cursing himself for being so forthcoming. I stand in front of his room long enough to hear the start of some regular-speed Brahms, then walk away.

The night has turned ominous. There is still a hint of sweetness in the air, but the sulfur overwhelms it, and I think I taste particles of ash on my tongue. I also think I hear a rumbling in the earth and feel a quivering at my feet, as if Soufrière can contain itself no longer. A seismologist I interviewed today told me it is impossible to know when the mountain will finally uncork. Into the camera he said, "Predicting when a volcano will erupt is as imprecise a science as predicting when a recession will bottom out. You just can't do it. Too much guesswork."

Cut to shot of mountaintop and continue with narration.

The unknown animal that was howling from afar before I entered the soundman's room is closer now and seems angry; there is something he wants that he is not getting, and his voice is a wail of complaint and frustration. Maybe he will get something else. Surely he will keep trying.

I look up. A large flock of small birds swoops low across the courtyard. Clouds continue to float across the moon, but they have turned gray, a sickly shade, one that reminds me of winter in the north.

I hurry back to my room.

I wonder how many more days I will be here.

I wonder how many nights.

SEPTEMBER 1977

CHICAGO

"WHAT DO YOU THINK of Charles Kuralt?"

The question surprises me no less than the circumstances. The executive producer of the *Today* show has turned up unannounced in the bureau this morning and taken over the bureau chief's office. He has asked me to come in and closed the door behind me, telling a secretary we are not to be disturbed. She is to hold all calls, deflect all visitors.

The executive producer says it's nice to see me again, I'm looking good, he has enjoyed my recent work. He wonders how I am finding Chicago, to which I was transferred six months ago, and solicits my initial impressions of the Midwest. He asks whether I am a Cubs man or a White Sox man or have retained loyalties to eastern teams. I answer his questions as best I can, but they are so obviously a prelude to something else that the main topic is made to seem mysterious.

He gets to it after I confess a lack of interest in the Cubs *and* the Sox, not to mention the Bears and the Bulls. He lights a cigarette, takes such a long first drag that he might be trying to suck the smoke down to his toes, and then says some changes are being planned for *Today* that might interest me. It is for this reason that he wants to know my opinion of television journalism's premier feature reporter. The executive producer's eyes have narrowed and fixed on mine, and he has stopped his idle rustling of the papers on the bureau chief's desk.

"Charles Kuralt," I say, and remember the first time I ever saw one of his "On the Road" pieces for the *CBS Evening News*. I was a few years out of college, holding down one of those early jobs that did not make the résumé, and when I saw Kuralt's report I was as startled as if I had been walking across a desert and encountered a rose.

It was the tale of a professor at a small college in Ohio who had been forced to retire at the age of seventy. Or was he the president of the college and his age sixty-five? Either way, the man had such a fondness for the school and its people that he could not bear to leave. So he stayed, in the only position open to so senior a citizen: janitor. For the past several years he had mopped the floors and given advice to students, vacuumed rugs and bucked up the faculty, emptied wastebaskets and kibitzed with the administration. As presented by Kuralt, the man was without human imperfection, a cross between a latter-day Socrates and a heartland Albert Schweitzer. I had goosebumps when the report ended. It may have pushed me a little closer to a career in TV news.

Several other Kuralt pieces come to mind. The man in Montana who was trying to save the wild horses of the Pryor Mountains, and the woman in California who had put more than a hundred hummingbird feeders on the roof of her porch. There was the poet who ran a service station, selling gas for thirty-nine cents a gallon and verses he had written for a dime, and the fellow who had such a way with deer that he fed them oatcakes right out of his hand.

I also remember Kuralt's profiles of the collector of the world's largest ball of string and the architect of a house constructed entirely of beer bottles. I recall that I laughed at the foolishness of each man until a point about midway through, when Kuralt performed some verbal legerdemain and convinced me that both the string collector and the bottle architect were noble in their pursuits, heroic in their achievements. As was the subject of the Kuralt piece I remember most vividly, the man who had taken a pick and shovel and started building his own road because the government agency that should have done it did not see the need. What energy the man had, what discipline and commitment.

I can call to mind the smile on Walter Cronkite's face when he introduces one of Kuralt's stories. I can see the merriment in his eyes and hear the relief in his voice and feel, with him, the entire newscast slip into a different, more comfortable gear. Suddenly all is not as grim as it had seemed; the catalogue of woes that precedes Kuralt notwithstanding, the ultimate message of the *CBS Evening News* is that the world will always give shelter to those who dare dream.

I find Kuralt's work exceptional. I am supposed to. I find it uplifting and encouraging, and I am supposed to do that too. As far as I am concerned, "On the Road" is evidence that CBS has a broader view of the planet and its workings than the other net-works. I do not suspect that this kind of reporting will one day pro-liferate to such a degree that it will trivialize the presentation of more serious stories and so contribute to a narrower view of the planet and its workings. Which will not, of course, be Kuralt's fault.

I believe that by telling story after story of people who have beaten the system, Charles Kuralt is demonstrating an admirable persistence of vision, not a limited professional range. I believe that by telling story after story of people who have found happiness through perversely inconsequential activity, Kuralt is being quirky, not tedious. Everybody knows that systems usually beat people and that happiness built on insignificance has quicksand as a foun-dation, but I believe that by ignoring these truths Kuralt shows him-self to be an optimist, not a gentle deceiver. I also believe that the absence of cynicism in his work is refreshing, not unrealistic.

Kuralt's oeuvre is informed by the same throbbingly cheerful sensibility that informed situation comedies in the 1950s—Father always knowing best, Lucy constantly being forgiven her eccentrici-ties, Ozzie and Harriet transforming suburbia into utopia—and I am not troubled by this. In fact, it pleases me, in much the same way that a happy dream brings a smile to my first few waking moments.

I do not think there is anything pernicious about the way Kuralt's tales pander to the classic urbanite fantasy that the real meaning of life lies in small-town America, when what lies in much of small-town America is a suffocating cultural aridity. I do not yet realize that in addition to being the place from which Kuralt reports, the rural hamlet is the shrine at which he worships; nor has it crossed my mind that he is as much missionary as journalist. Unlike the conventional reporter, Kuralt means not to relate the facts but to convert.

At the moment I am only aware of Kuralt's reputation and his image and the fact that he is justly considered a master at the dis-covery and presentation of the little truth. I simply have no idea how little. All that lies before me on the morning when the execu-tive producer of the *Today* show materializes in Chicago and closes the office door as I enter.

"I'm a real fan of Kuralt's," I say. "What makes you ask?"

He rises from the bureau chief's desk and slides over to an east-facing window, staring out toward the Tribune Tower and, beyond, the white-capped gray waters of Lake Michigan. An ore barge rides choppily at the horizon; another, empty, drifts closer to shore. Droopy black clouds hang low in the sky, threatening a downpour later today. The executive producer sits on the sill, shoving a flower-pot out of his way.

"We're pulling you out of general assignment," he says. "That is, if you're game."

"For what?"

"A new segment. I'm not sure about the title yet, but I think we're going to call it 'Cross-Country.' The idea is to do the same kind of pieces Kuralt does but let them breathe more. We'll give them four or five minutes every day and close the first hour of the show with them. They'll make a nice send-off for people heading out to work. That's the idea."

"Sounds great."

He flicks a long ash from his cigarette into the flowerpot. "We want two correspondents assigned strictly to 'Cross-Country.' No other duties. We're thinking about Jack Perkins in Burbank and you in the Midwest." The executive producer folds his arms across his chest, leaning back against the window, giving me a moment to consider the offer.

It really does sound great. It also sounds like remarkable timing. A few weeks ago, I started on the eleven volumes of Will and Ariel Durant's *The Story of Civilization*, and was so struck by a passage that I copied it on an index card and taped it to the wall above my desk at home, the first time I had done something like that since college.

Civilization is a stream with banks. The stream is sometimes filled with blood from people killing, stealing, shouting, and doing the things historians usually record; while on the banks, unnoticed, people build homes, raise children, sing songs, write poetry, and even whittle statues. The story of civilization is the story of what happened on the banks. Historians are pessimists because they ignore the banks for the river.

I have been a river man for a year and a half—three years, actually, counting my time in Minneapolis—and have grown uninspired. Crime and catastrophe, animosity and accident: too many of my days have been devoted to such stories, stories that are topical as opposed to relevant. Topicality, which seems the obsession of *Nightly*, is a virtue without a point, an example of what writer Bill McKibben will one day call television's "relentless dailiness," evidence of what Neil Postman will refer to as the severing of "the tie between information and human purpose." HAYS POSSIBLE SUICIDE was topical but appealed almost entirely to voyeuristic rather than information-seeking impulses. GUADELOUPE VOLCANO was topical but did not in any direct way affect *Nightly* viewers, an eruption so feeble, when it finally came, that it was more like a leak, and of little consequence to either the local populace or the atmosphere.

Hard news, these kinds of stories are called, and they are a freak show of occurrences, carnival booth after carnival booth of aberration. They add up to an unbalanced view of the world, a false sounding of alarms about the dangers of reality, a primer for pessimists. Hard news is, and always has been, a register of benumbingly similar items. "And I am sure that I never read any memorable news in a newspaper," Thoreau wrote in *Walden* more than a century ago. "If we read of one man robbed, or murdered, or killed by accident, or one house burned, or one vessel wrecked or one steamboat blown up, or·one cow run over on the Western Railroad, or one mad dog killed, or one lot of grasshoppers in the winter,—we never need read of another. One is enough. If you are acquainted with the principle, what do you care for a myriad instances and applications?" And yet hard news remains the preoccupation of the entire journalistic field: the reporters, those who assign the reporters, and those who indoctrinate the assigners.

Now, though, it seems that the executive producer of *Today* is offering me a way out, a chance to eschew the topical for the relevant. I will be able to present a more accurate, if less dramatic, portrait of life in America. There is just one thing.

"Any idea what the travel schedule will be like?" I ask.

"No." Clipped, terse, just like that. He is not pleased with the question.

"It's just that I spend so much time away from home now. I'd like to have a more sensible schedule."

"Oh yeah," he says. "You just got married, didn't you?"

"We live together. We're getting married in the spring."

"And you'd like to see her once in a while."

Nod.

"Well, two points." He lifts himself from the windowsill and resumes his position behind the desk. "First, you'll have a hand in choosing your own stories, you and your producer. Chicago's a big place, and I assume you'll be able to find a fair number of pieces you can do right around here. Day trips. And then, when you do go farther afield, you'll almost always know a few days in advance. You can make plans. You won't be getting phone calls in the middle of the night anymore. As far as I know, there's no such thing as a breaking feature."

"But Kuralt," I say, suddenly overwhelmed at the length of the man's shadow, his status as patron saint of soft news.

IT IS THE SMALLEST POST OFFICE I have ever seen. If a dozen people stood in the lobby and inhaled at the same time, they would jostle each other. There is room on the counter for a scale and a postage meter and almost nothing else. On one side of the counter is a narrow wall of mailboxes, four vertical rows with eight boxes in each. Several of the doors are open, a few others missing. A water bug scuttles around one of the boxes, clicking against the metal sides like a loose marble. At the other end of the counter is a bulletin board displaying a single wanted poster, for a relatively minor offense as wanted posters go. At the bottom of the board, centered in the plastic frame, is a bumper sticker: REDNECK POWER!

I am standing in the post office with my producer, cameraman, and soundman, the floorboards creaking beneath us like springs in an old bed. We look around, hear water lap against the pilings that support the building over the bayou, a soft but steady slurping. The air smells used, musty. The blades of a ceiling fan make their appointed rounds, but to little avail: comfort is a wish that never comes true at this time of year in this part of the country.

"Where is everybody?" the soundman says.

The producer steps forward and slaps a bell on the counter.

My glasses have begun to fog in the humidity. I take them off, wipe them on my shirt, and replace them just in time to see a woman of Brobdingnagian proportions heave herself into place behind the counter. She wears a denim shirt that could double as a tent, a bandanna around her forehead, and sweatbands on her wrists. Her smile stretches from one earlobe to the other.

"Howdy," she says.

We ask for Pierre Francis.

"You the television folks?"

"That's right."

"Well, how's about that!" She slaps her hands on the counter so hard that the scale rattles. "Me and Pierre didn't think you'd really show, all the way down here."

"Is he around?"

"Loading up the boat. Almost time for him to start his run. You cut it purty close."

"We got lost."

"Yep," the woman says, "tricky around these parts, ain't it? But you made it, that's what counts. So, let's get a move on." She squeezes herself out of view behind the counter, reappearing a few seconds later to open a door by the mailboxes. "Follow me, boys," she says, leading the way down a corridor so narrow that her hips, as she sways along, brush against the walls. We pass an alcove crammed with empty plastic postal trays and empty canvas bags; a rusty tricycle sits next to the trays, and several lawn chairs are folded in a stack behind it. There is a cobweb over the alcove window, and on the sill is a glass of water holding a set of novelty-store false teeth. I wonder what the postmaster general would say.

The woman opens a door at the end of the corridor, and the five of us pick our way down a rickety set of steps to another door and another REDNECK POWER! bumper sticker. She kicks the door open, and we step outside onto a small dock that hugs the building around two turns. The smell down here is of decaying animal life and primeval vegetation; the sense, despite expanses of land and water so vast that they seem to curve down with the earth, is of things closing in on this bayou morning, escape denied.

Pierre Francis either has not heard our approach or does not care. He stands at the end of the dock, tossing a mailbag into a vessel with the words *Crooked Island Catboat* stenciled in script on the side: an eighteen-footer, it appears, wide of beam, a wooden tiller in the stern. A canvas awning supported by four aluminum poles stretches from stern to bow, a measure of protection from sun shining down white heat. The boat is painted with standard insignias in the standard United States Postal Service colors, stylized eagles port and starboard.

"Pierre," the woman says, and he looks up. "The TV people, hallelujah!"

Nothing moves in the mailman but his eyes, which are gray and hollow and settle on the four of us from NBC in turn, spending no more time than necessary to form an impression. It does not seem positive. We are city boys and he is country; we are high-tech and he is manual.

"Fellas," he finally says, clenching the word and taking a step forward.

The four of us from NBC make up the distance to him and shake hands. Tattoos ripple on his biceps; I think they are something amphibian.

"This all of ya?" he says after hearing and dismissing four names.

"We're it," says the producer.

Pierre sighs. "Was afraid, ya bein' from up north an' all, some of ya'd be niggers."

It is one of those moments when things suddenly hang in the balance. If we react honestly, we run the risk of angering the mailman and imperiling our story; we are journalists, after all, not preachers of brotherhood. But the remark has caught us so totally unawares that there is no time to camouflage disgust. Surely, despite our efforts to the contrary, at least a flicker will be noticeable.

The producer says, "Well."

The cameraman looks away.

The soundman looks down.

I clear my throat; there is nothing in it.

The woman, seeing our unease, says, "Careful, Pierre, could be they got nigger friends," which for some reason strikes these two employees of the United States Postal Service as a statement of incomparable wit. The woman laughs so hard the dock shimmies; I feel as if I'm caught on one of those rope bridges over a South American gorge in an old movie serial. Pierre, for the first time, reveals teeth. Some are yellow, some so pointy they might have been filed, a few others missing. Have I really come all the way from Chicago to make this man a star?

"It happens there aren't any blacks on this particular shoot," the producer says in due time.

Pierre spits into the river. "Oh, right. Blacks," he says.

"Yup," the woman agrees, "blacks is what they are nowadays."

"Like coal, mebbe."

"Or sin."

But the two of them cannot keep the joviality alive; their laughter trickles out, and their smiles fold back into more natural suspicious expressions.

"So," Pierre says, flinging a final bag of mail into the boat and stuffing some nose hairs back inside a nostril with a pinkie, "what ya got in mind?"

The producer tells him. He will make his run as usual this morning. He will be alone in the boat some of the time while we shoot from the shore; we will accompany him the rest of the time to make tighter shots. He will repeat certain actions, perhaps more than once, so we can shoot from different angles and match our cuts in editing. He will wait for us to set up, proceed when we are ready, wait for us to strike and rejoin him. He will act and speak as if we were not around. After he delivers the mail we will do brief interviews with some of the people along his route. But first we will interview Pierre at length.

It is a version of our customary spiel before shooting a story, but I have never heard it rendered so brusquely. The producer is usually warmer in tone, less direct in language, making his statements into questions even though the answers are preordained. But Pierre is not a folk hero, not at all the kind of leading man we had envisioned for this piece, and the producer cannot keep the resentment out of his voice.

"Whooo," the mailman says, "sounds like yer gonna gum up the works purty damn good."

"We'll set you back half an hour or so," I say, knowing it will be closer to two hours, maybe three.

"Oh, well. Special occasion, eh? Ain't every day a mug like me gets his puss on the national TV, now, is it?"

"No," the producer tells him, "it sure isn't."

The Mississippi River is silty and polluted near Pilotville, the color of coffee with light cream. Pickerelweed and cattails grow along the banks amid scrub grass so profuse it seems a cultivable crop. There are a few bald cypresses on shore, but they are listless, bedraggled; they seem to be wilting more than growing in the dank bayou summer, and the scrub grass is a pale, sickly ocher. Dark birds the size of vultures fly low over the water as the *Crooked Island Catboat* sputters away from the dock; insects the size of frogs make rattling noises.

About ten minutes out from the post office, and no more than two miles, the producer tells Pierre to kill the motor.

"What fer?"

"The interview."

"What interview?"

"With you."

"Ya wanna do 'er on the boat?"

"We'd like to."

"Mebbe the first stop up the Landin', eh?"

"We'll be interviewing other people on shore. It would be good to do you in the boat, just to give us a different look."

"Good fer who?"

"Well ..." The producer looks at me for guidance I cannot give.

Pierre shakes his head but reaches behind himself to still the two-cycle, seventy-horsepower Renault diesel engine. It lets out a roar, then winds down quickly, coughing out blue-black clouds of gas and oil that settle on the water in dark rainbow rings.

Later that day, when I get back to our hotel in New Orleans, I will transcribe the interview from a tape I now make with an audio cassette recorder.

EB: So, Pierre, how long have you been on this run?

PF: Oh, 'bout twenny years, I'd say.

EB: Twenty years? That long?

PF: Nah.

EB: No?

PF: Say eighteen. That's closer to 'er, now I think 'bout it.

EB: Tell me what it means to you.

PF: Eh?

EB: The job.

PF: What does the job mean t' me?

EB: That's right. In other words, you're the main link between the people who live in Wilson's Landing and the rest of the world. You keep them in touch, help them break out of their isolation. And you're the only mailman we know of in the entire country who uses a boat for his route because there aren't any roads. That must give you a feeling of doing something that's not only out of the ordinary but really worthwhile.

PF: That's what ya think, eh?

EB: It is.

PF: Well, if ya wanna think it.

EB: You don't agree?

PF: It just ain't somethin' I ever paid no mind to, one way or t'other.

EB: Why not?

PF: Couldn't say.

EB: Say.

PF: Fer what?

EB: Pierre, give me a break. What does your job mean to you?

PF: Means a paycheck, bub. What's *yer* job mean t' *you?*

EB: But apart from—

PF: Means a bottle of Ol' Grand-Dad on the weekend, okay? Mebbe a few extra bucks fer the track, if I can find the time t' get my butt down there. Ya ever see the dogs run? Prob'ly not.

EB: I wonder what it means to them, then.

PF: Who?

EB: The people in Wilson's Landing.

PF: Ya wonder what *what* means to 'em?

EB: Your job.

PF: My job?

EB: Jesus, the mail. Seeing as how that and the phone are the only ways they can reach the outside world, and I understand the phone service out there isn't always so good.

PF: Got a cousin works fer the phone company.

EB: Stay with me, Pierre.

PF: Well, yer askin' these questions, ain't no way t' answer.

EB: Listen to me, just listen to me. The mail is something most people take for granted, people in places like New Orleans or Chicago or New York, let's say. But for people who live in an out-of-the-way spot like Wilson's Landing, it must take on a special significance. Your visit is probably the high point of the day. I imagine people really look forward to seeing you.

PF: Boy oh boy oh boy.

EB: What?

PF: Jus' … aw, I dunno.

EB: What?

PF: Yer really makin' up some kinda story here, is all I can say. Ain't the news supposed t' be true?

EB: Why am I making it up?

PF: Beats the shit outta me.

EB: Let me try it this way. Maybe this will work. How many people live in Wilson's Landing?

PF: Hunnert fifty, mebbe a little more, that lives there year-round.

EB: Tell me in a complete sentence.

PF: Eh?

EB: Say, I deliver the mail to a hundred fifty people a day.

PF: I jus' did.

EB: But not that way.

PF: What way?

EB: I'd like it in a complete sentence, a complete thought. It'll just help us in the editing room.

PF: I don't follow.

EB: Would you just say, quote, I deliver the mail to a hundred and fifty people every day, unquote. Please.

PF: I deliver the mail t' a hunnert fifty people every day. Awright?

EB: Thank you.

PF: I mean, ya don't like the way I talk, ya shouldn'ta come down here.

EB: It's not that.

PF: Nobody invited ya, ya know. Was yer idea.

EB: I remember.

PF: Yessir, yer idea alla way.

EB: And you're the main link between these hundred and fifty people and the rest of the world, aren't you?

PF: Ya keep sayin' that.

EB: I want *you* to say it.

PF: Aw, nuts.

EB: Look, Pierre, the folks in Wilson's Landing have *got* to be glad to see you each day, don't they?

PF: Suppose.

EB: Of course.

PF: Then agin, I bring 'em bills lotsa times, too. Ain't nobody in their right mind gets excited 'bout a bill.

EB: Yes, but—

PF: An' letters from people they'd jus' as soon never hear from at all, like moochin' relatives an' that.

EB: But what you—

PF: An' ya gotta unnerstan' that nobody really says too much round here. Not these kinda people. They jus' 'spect me t' be there an' I'm there, an' what else can ya say.

EB: But I'm wondering—

PF: Been doin' it twenny years now, like I tol' ya.

EB: Eighteen.

PF: Whatever. Either way, it ain't like it's anythin' new er a big deal anymore. Yer comin' in on this thing late, is all.

EB: Time out.

PF: Eh?

EB: Just … time out for a second.

PF: Yer dime, bub.

EB: Here's what's going to happen.

PF: Yeah?

EB: I'm going to ask you a question, and you're going to answer it. Okay?

PF: Gosh.

EB: Okay, Pierre?

PF: Let's hear it.

EB: All right, here's the question. Do you think the people on your route would miss you if you weren't around anymore?

PF: Fuckin' A, Jack!

EB: Jesus Christ, Pierre, this is television! You can't say that.

PF: Ya keep talkin' 'bout editin'. Hell, jus' edit 'er out, ya don't like it.

EB: It's not that easy.

PF: Now, lissen up, jus' lissen up. First ya tell me what t' say, then ya tell me what *not* t' say. This story 'bout me er ain't it?

EB: The story's about—

PF: Ain't nobody says I gotta do this, ya know.

EB: What's that?

PF: This story.

EB: No, not you.

PF: Eh?

EB: Lou, I mean. What's that noise I hear in the recorder? Something grinding?

"I don't hear anything," says the soundman, puzzled not only because he knows his BVU-200 recorder is operating at usual efficiency, but because I am not standing close enough to hear a malfunction if there were one. "Are you sure?"

"Positive," I say. "I think maybe the cassette's not running at speed."

He is watching the cassette spin smoothly, without a hitch, not a care in the world. "Can't be."

"Although now that I think about it, maybe it's more of a whining than a grinding."

He is looking at dials, checking for warning lights, seeing nothing out of the ordinary. "I don't get it, Eric."

Pierre turns away from me to swat at a mosquito, and I wink at the soundman, a signal for him to play along. "Just shut down for a few minutes and look it over, Lou. I'd hate to get back to Chicago and find a tape full of hash. All right?"

"If you say so." He is still stumped as to motive, but relieved that the recorder's condition is no longer in question.

"Guys got a snafu?" Pierre inquires, eyes on the horizon, mosquito in his fist, ambushed by a fast, ugly death.

"Nothing serious," I tell him. "We just need a few minutes."

"Well, I'm already wastin' all kindsa time here."

"Start up the engine, then," the producer says.

"Yeah?"

"Let's keep heading for Wilson's Landing. We'll tell you when to shut down again."

"Boy oh boy," Pierre says, "this is really somethin'." He bends over the old Renault and turns the key, bringing the engine back to life in a burst of more oily clouds. Then he seats himself on the stern railing, tiller in hand, and presides over the lurching boat as it closes the distance to the houses on his route.

The producer does not need a wink or any other signal from me; I make my way to the bow and he follows. There is a pallor to his complexion and a slackness to his jaw, neither apparent before the camera started rolling and Pierre and I redefined the art of conversation.

"We're dead," he says under cover of the engine's roar, "dead and buried and heading to hell."

"Didn't you pre-interview this turkey?"

"I couldn't."

"Why not?"

"He was never in." The producer tugs at a clump of hair. "He's at the post office maybe ten minutes a day before he hits the water. You saw him this morning. He gets the boat ready, then he's off."

"You should've called him during those ten minutes."

"It didn't jive with my schedule. This story wasn't the only thing I had to do last week, you know."

"Why didn't you tell *me* to call him, then?"

"Because it just didn't seem necessary, dammit. The wire story made this bigot sound like some kind of saint. I wasn't worried. I should've been, but I wasn't, okay?"

"But you know how pieces like this work in print. Somebody in the Chicago office of AP sees a local newspaper story about this mailman in a boat and calls down here and gets his home number from the reporter. He talks to Pierre one night and does the whole story long-distance and never has to deal with the kind of guy Pierre really is. He leaves out the worst of it, airbrushes over the rest, and gets a stringer out of New Orleans to come up and make some beauty shots of the boat plowing through the river. Sunday supplement stuff. Then, presto chango—the king of the monosyllabic rednecks turns into a living, breathing piece of Americana."

The producer wipes his forehead, but to no avail; the shade of the awning is intensifying the heat, making us both feel like fast food under the lamps, waiting for customers to order us.

"I don't know," I say, "maybe it's our fault."

"*Our* fault?"

"You heard what he said. It *is* a story about *him*."

"He's a caveman."

"But the way we're treating him."

"We have an alternative?"

"All we're doing is making things worse."

"I repeat."

"Criticizing, carping, and then me with the interview. Do it this way, Pierre, do it that way. Fetch. Roll over and play dead. I know he's first cousin to a tree stump, but I'm practically writing his goddamn lines for him."

"Somebody has to. We can't put the guy into people's living rooms in his natural state. You're just dealing with the fact."

"But we asked for this. We're the ones who picked *him*."

"I know, I know. He said that, too. What're you, his lawyer? All I can tell you is this is the last time we ever do a piece, I mean *ever*, without making the phone calls first."

"Which doesn't help us now."

"Yeah," the producer says. "Yeah." He flaps his elbows a time or two, unsticking his underarms.

I am opening and closing my grip loosely over one of the aluminum poles that support the awning. "But there must be something we can do."

"There is. Take our lumps."

"Meaning?"

"Scrap the story, what do you think? It's the only choice we've got." The producer looks past me to confirm Pierre's continuing lack of interest in us; I turn and see that he has withdrawn a pack of chewing tobacco from his shirt pocket and wedged a plug into his mouth. After a moment he takes it out and examines it quizzically, as if he has tasted something peculiar. Then he jams it back in again, shaking the juice off his fingers and wiping them on his government-issue shorts.

"Look, here's what we'll do," the producer says. "We'll go through the motions a little more—finish the interview, shoot some cover footage at the first stop on Wilson's Landing. Who knows, we might even be able to use it for some other piece sometime. Then we tell Pierre we've got enough. He won't know the difference. We have him take us back to the post office and we're out of here, on our way back to civilization."

"Keep going," I say, knowing where the producer's scenario will end.

He shrugs. "Tomorrow we give Friedman a call and tell him the story didn't pan out. If he doesn't believe us or wants to know what the problem was, we ship him the tape of the interview so far. He'll see what we're dealing with. I don't care what you say, it's Pierre's fault, not ours. We're in the clear."

"No," I say, "we're not."

He takes his sunglasses off and squeezes the bridge of his nose between his thumb and middle finger. His head bobs once, a single sign of acknowledgment.

The soundman has gone along with the subterfuge to the extent of taking a tool kit out of his equipment bag and unscrewing the recorder lid to remove one of the panels of circuitry. He pretends to make adjustments with a pair of tweezers, then taps the panel a few times, as if to verify that the adjustments have held. He shouts over the engine, "I think I see the problem."

Me: "No, you don't. Not yet."

"Oh," he says, "oh yeah."

"I'll bet you find it in another five minutes or so, though."

The soundman looks into the machine and nods. "Seems about right. Yeah, I'd say five should do it."

I turn back to the producer. "If we tell Friedman we don't have a piece and show him the tape to prove it, he says the same thing I just did. 'If the guy is such a slug, why did the *Today* show go down there in the first place?' Then we have to explain to *him* why we didn't do a pre-interview."

The producer replaces his sunglasses, but even though the lenses are black I can see behind them; he has closed his eyes and begun to squint, perhaps seeking a better view of our options.

"But we haven't got anything," he says after a moment. "We're not going to *get* anything. What are we supposed to do?"

"Fake it."

"How?"

"I don't know," I say, but feeling cornered by the circumstances, I find that ideas, at once practical and devious, are beginning to per-colate.

"This should've been such a winner," the producer says, sinking onto the nearest sack of mail. I have read magazine articles about the stages of grieving recognized by psychologists; this, I believe, is the second or third. "A profile of a real, small-town, everyday kind of American hero. Take away Pierre Francis and Wilson's Landing might as well be a village somewhere in the heart of the jungle. Put him back in the picture and it's welcome to the twentieth century. And he's there for them every day. Neither wind nor snow nor gloom of night nor fucking alligators—which would've been a decent line for your script, by the way. It seemed like a natural, perfect 'Cross-Country' material. But it's not there, and I don't see how we can make something up."

I push my own sunglasses onto my forehead. "I do."

"No," the producer says. "I won't be part of anything shady."

"Our asses are on the line here."

"Friedman'll understand."

"Accounting won't. Four first-class plane tickets from Chicago to New Orleans. Four rooms for one night at the Fairmont, and by the time we get back there and check out, we'll owe for a second. Plus meals, cabs to and from O'Hare, car rental. We've spent a lot of money on Pierre already. Do you think Accounting's going to give a damn about our editorial judgment?"

He opens his eyes, beams them at me behind the dark lenses.

I press on. "Only insofar as they wonder why we didn't make the right one before we started."

"But—"

"We'll be like a couple of Mafia bagmen trying to explain to the don why we came back with the bags empty. I'm telling you, it won't play."

"I know it won't," the producer says. "I know it's our asses on the line. Jesus, I know all of it. What I don't know is what choice we have."

"Same choice any writer has when his material doesn't live up to expectations."

"Which is?"

"Get creative."

The producer stands, props a leg between two mail sacks for balance, and waves a finger at Pierre to let him know it will just be another minute. Give or take. Pierre seems oblivious; his head is twitching at a peculiar angle, and his lips are moving. It might be Parkinson's disease; it might be an a capella solo of "Jambalaya."

"What do you mean, 'creative'?"

"Sit down."

"Just for the sake of argument, now. That's all." He sits.

Only some of the scheme has come to me at this point; the rest, I assume, will make itself clear as I speak, each word, like an oxidizing agent, causing a further remnant of integrity to corrode and flake off. I lean back on a sack of small packages. "When we pick up the interview, we change our tack. No more questions about mail."

"Huh?"

"Or public spiritedness or humanitarian impulses or any of that."

"But what's the—"

"Instead, I hit the guy with a barrage of questions about other topics, and I keep going until I find something he'll respond to. And I mean anything at all: politics, the weather, prison reform, astrology, sex education, the cost of living, professional wrestling—"

"Race relations."

"*Anything.* If Pierre Francis shows an interest in it, I push for an explanation, for details. Then I continue until we've got bites on three or four different topics, bites that are tight and coherent and suitable for morning television."

"But what do we do with them?"

"Hear me out."

"This is a piece about a guy who delivers mail to the boonies. What possible good does it do us to have a bunch of sound bites about astrology and sex education?"

"I write a line of narration to the effect that even though Pierre is forced by his job to live an isolated life, he is deeply concerned with the world around him."

"You're kidding."

"His mind reaches out to that world, ranging over the distances. Against the backdrop of the forlorn swamps of rural Louisiana, Pierre conducts interior dialogues with himself on the great issues of the day."

"You wouldn't dare."

"As his sturdy craft slices a path through the muddy waters of America's longest, mightiest river, Pierre invariably finds himself lost in thought. Can the United States and the Soviet Union ever achieve true happiness? Can the world's starving masses ever be adequately fed? Will the homeless find shelter, the disease-ridden a cure, the poverty-stricken a means of supporting themselves?"

"But that's—"

"Possibly even true."

"True?"

"Sure. Pierre spends a couple of hours every day on this boat all by himself. There's no radio on board, nothing of interest to look at on the shore, and besides, he's seen it all before. It's only natural to assume that most of the time he's thinking about things that interest him."

"The fate of the starving masses?"

"Okay, so what he thinks about isn't particularly high-minded."

"Or even mentionable."

"But I'm sure we can come up with a few subjects that will fill the bill while at the same time accurately reflecting Pierre Francis, the inner man."

"Look," the producer says, "call it what you want, rationalize it the best you can, it doesn't matter. It's still bullshit. What you're suggesting is totally, completely, one hundred percent unethical."

"There's that," I concede, and begin to rearrange my body; the mail sack on which I am leaning has caved in slowly, like a beanbag chair, leaving me in a position my spine cannot maintain: shoulders angled clockwise, hips counterclockwise, a painful dip in the small of the back. "On the other hand, where's the harm?"

"What kind of question is that?"

"It's a victimless crime, inventing little virtues for Pierre. It's not as if we went on the air and said John Mitchell escaped from prison the other day when he really got out on parole. Not as if we said there were half a million of those so-called Nazis running around Marquette Park when the real number was closer to two thousand. That's hard news. If you get hard news wrong there can be serious consequences: people being afraid to fly a certain airline even though it's safe, afraid to buy a certain product even though it really doesn't have any harmful additives. But this is a feature story. What we're talking about is the journalistic equivalent of a little white lie."

I try for a moment to put myself in the producer's position, wondering what it is like to listen to all this. Speaking it, I can attest, is grossly disconcerting. Where do the words come from? What's the point? How did a nice fella like me hook up with logic like this?

The answer arrives in an instant. Lack of respect. I no longer feel about the feature story as I did when I started on the beat. I have lost the edge, the drive, the desire to follow in the estimable Kuralt's footsteps. Soft news now seems to me as aberrant, in its own way, as hard news; the latter may be unrealistic because of its pessimism, but the former is unrealistic because of its romanticizing. I want to be a mythmaker no more than I want to tell tales of wrecked cars and robbed stores and mugged pedestrians.

What does it mean, though, that this is now my view? Have I attained maturity or cynicism? Am I wising up or merely curdling? In television news, does the one inevitably lead to the other?

"But these are five-minute pieces," the producer says, a welcome interruption to my musings. "Even if we do it your way—just for the sake of argument—we're still a good four minutes short."

"I know."

"So?"

"We open the piece up for music."

"Of course we do."

"We get extra shots of the boat on the river: long shots, close shots, medium shots; rack focus, tilt from sky to boat and vice versa, pan from shore to boat and vice versa. Engine churning up the water. Star filter off the water. Fisheye, if we have one in the case. Then we cue up a little Fleetwood Mac. Do you know 'Never Goin' Back Again'?"

"I don't think so."

"The *Rumours* album."

"I always thought Fleetwood Mac was overrated."

"'Never Goin' Back Again' is a vocal, but there's a great guitar interlude. It has the perfect feel for a piece like this: almost country, but not quite. Bouncy. It's short, but we can loop it a time or two and it'll give us another thirty seconds without Pierre doing a damn thing."

"How would you set it up?"

"A line about how life in this neck of the woods doesn't only have a rhythm of its own, but a melody."

"My God."

"And we'll get even more ideas when we see what happens on shore."

"I'm afraid to ask."

Somehow I have turned into Fagin, revealing to young Master Twist the byways of deceit. I swear they are as alien to me as they are to him, that I have been cast in this role against type. And yet: "Let's say Pierre goes to a house and the people have a dog, but the dog's old and toothless and mangy, so instead of bugging Pierre, he just looks up at him kind of wistfully. Whines a little, sniffs his leg. But what I say in the script is that Pierre is so important to the community of Wilson's Landing that even the dogs treat him with respect."

"Where do you get these things?"

Good question. "Or maybe what happens is, we get a shot of Pierre handing some mail to a woman, and we keep the camera on her after Pierre walks out of frame and then tell her—off-mike, of course—to look at her watch. Later, when we cut the shot into the piece, I say, 'Pierre Francis's visits mean so much to the people of Wilson's Landing that no sooner does one of them end than they start counting the hours until the next.'"

The producer laughs. At first the sound just escapes from him, something inadvertent; he barely seems aware of it himself and is tentative in letting it go. But the laugh gathers momentum quickly, gains in volume and heartiness, and in a matter of seconds becomes a rollicking expression, not of amusement, but of sheer incredulity.

As for Pierre and the crew, they look at him and cannot understand how someone who seemed so frustrated a few seconds ago—hands flailing the air, head shaking back and forth—could suddenly have been overtaken by hilarity. To them it is not contagious; they only stare and shake their own heads. I, on the other hand, join in the laughter the instant it starts, equally astonished by my proposed machinations. My eyes water; it might be my conscience crying.

At least two minutes pass before the producer can compose himself, and it is several seconds more before he speaks. I follow his eyes, look upriver with him at some tumbledown houses on a slowly approaching shore.

"Wilson's Landing, I guess," he says.

"Must be."

"Doesn't look like there's much to it."

"What did you expect?"

"Maybe twenty minutes before we get there?"

"I don't know."

"Yeah, I'd say twenty. About. Of course, it's hard to tell when you're used to traveling on land." The producer shudders and falls silent again for a moment. Then, abruptly, to the soundman: "Lou, you found the frigging problem yet or what?"

"Got it," Lou says, "just this minute nailed it down."

"About time."

"Yeah, well."

"How long till we're back in business?"

"Minute or two, that's all. Just let me get things together again and we're all set."

And the day, like the river, rolls on.

When the interview resumes, I ask Pierre about attempts to extend the ratification deadline of the Equal Rights Amendment and demonstrations against nuclear power in the Northeast and some recent decisions of the Supreme Court of which he is not aware. I ask him about his favorite baseball players and movie stars. I want to know what he thinks of civil service, campaign financing, restrictions on foreign trade. I wonder about the odds that the New Orleans Saints will finally win more games than they lose this year. Most of the topics he dismisses, but a few register and he is surprisingly forthcoming. He ponders, he reckons, he expresses himself. His answers are … rustic.

When we make our first stop at Wilson's Landing, I talk to several of the residents, discovering that they are kindred spirits of the mailman. One man asks whether I am a Communist like all the other reporters in America. His wife, an elderly woman with a Bible in the pocket of her apron, tells me to beware the harlot at the far end of the island; by her pink halter top shall I know her. About Pierre's daily visits, the woman is without comment. The grandmother next door has one, though: "Oh, he's all right, I guess." A young man at the next stop says, "Hell, he jest delivers the mail, is all."

But I also find a tall, slender woman with children clutching at her legs who answers my prayers as well as my question. She says, "I don't know what we'd do here without Pierre. We didn't have him, we'd just as well be a hundred miles out in the ocean."

Back on the boat, we set Pierre in front of the camera again, and at the soundman's cue I hang some ornaments on the truth. "I talked to a woman back there, Pierre," I tell him, "and here's what she said about you." I flip open my notebook and pretend to read. "She said, 'Pierre Francis is the greatest thing that ever happened to Wilson's Landing. It's not just that he brings the mail, it's that he has this wonderful way about him that makes the day brighter for everyone he meets.'"

"Who said that?"

"The woman at the last stop." I check my notes for real. "Helen Esterhazy."

"Helen said *that?*"

"She sure did."

"Well, I'll be jiggered," Pierre says, and smiles, showing those Halloween teeth of his, a scrap of chewing tobacco pasted onto an incisor.

"What do you think?"

"Well, it's mighty nice of her t' say it. I'm kinda surprised."

"Surprised?"

"Never really had all that much t' do with 'er, is what I mean."

"But it makes you feel good?"

"Ya could say. Yeah, ya sure could."

The piece is coming together.

We shoot Pierre at several other locales on Wilson's Landing: as he ties up his boat, hefts his sacks, trudges along dirt pathways, and exchanges greetings with patrons, greetings that become noticeably warmer on his part after he learns of Helen Esterhazy's latent goodwill.

No one has a dog.

After his last delivery, we send Pierre out on the river by himself and shoot him from shore for a cassette and a half. Thirty minutes. We could play the whole *Rumours* album if we wanted to.

And then, about three in the afternoon, the taping completed and the mail sacks empty, Pierre drops the four of us from NBC back at Pilotville. We tell him he can look for the piece on the air sometime next week. He says, "Whatever," and spits some tobacco juice into the murky Mississippi. He plods down the dock away from us, waving goodbye over his shoulder, and enters the post office through the back door. I look at the producer and the producer looks at me. Pierre Francis, bayou mailman, has passed from our lives forever.

Two hours later I am in my hotel room in New Orleans, the conventions of yet another television feature story having been scrupulously observed: the principal character has been made to seem heroic, the supporting players duly appreciative, the way of life idyllic. Reality in the conventional sense has not been faithfully portrayed, but is of no special importance, for the reality of the feature story is a world unto itself; it need only conform to the collective agreement about which illusions are most acceptable to the viewer.

Pierre did.

I helped.

When the piece airs, I will receive compliments from co-workers and mail from all over the country. In one of the letters a woman will tell me how amazed she is that places like Wilson's Landing still exist in this day and age and how it pleases her to know that there is a Pierre Francis to take care of it. He restored her faith in human nature, did old Pierre. Another letter, from the vice president of an investment banking firm in Boston, will say that he is tired of the rat race and thinks he could do worse in life than settle in a place like Wilson's Landing, where the people seem to know how to appreciate the little things that mean so much. A viewer from Louisiana will send me a clipping from the weekly paper that serves Pilotville; the *Today* show's visit is the front-page headline, and the viewer commends me for my sensitivity, expressing surprise at a certain "backwoods way" about me. Several months from now, during the Christmas season, when *Today* repeats the best "Cross-Country" pieces of the preceding year, BAYOU MAILMAN will be honored with a second airing.

My wife thinks it is one of my better efforts. So does my producer. No one calls it one of my better moments.

And the executive producer of *Today* was wrong. I am not going to make people forget about Charles Kuralt. Nor should I. I do not have the homey charm of the master, nor the ability, or willingness, to see only the best in my fellow man. I do not have Kuralt's patience, do not have his faith. Kuralt has long been, and will continue to be, the television audience's favorite chronicler of life in small-town America.

But Sinclair Lewis remains the most accurate.

DECEMBER 1982

New York

AND THE YEARS, like a river, roll on.

In 1979 I report stories with slugs like CHEWING TOBACCO CLUB, HUNGARIAN DOG, and ICE FISHING.

In 1980 my repertoire includes BEER BOTTLE COLLECTORS, CHOCOLATE NEWSPAPER, and MODEL TRAINS.

Nineteen eighty-one brings CLOWN COP, MAGIC PROFESSOR, FROG RACE, and, direct from Devonshire, England, starring Chef Raymond of the famed Imperial Hotel, DOG RESTAURANT, although the slug in this case is misleading because the canines qualify for room service only.

Forget about jugglers. Forget baggy pants comedians and buck-and-wing hoofers and dime-store divas doing maudlin renditions of the works of Victor Herbert. Forget strippers and their fans and dances. Who needs them anymore? There are characters on television news these days who can jangle your libido or split your sides or tug at your heartstrings with the best of the old performers from the variety hall stages. The Keith-Albee and Orpheum circuits are dead; the feature story is the new American vaudeville.

Early in 1982 I quit the *Today* show and go back to *Nightly*.

In the spring I anchor bulletins on the progress of the Falkland Islands War.

In the summer I track Yasir Arafat and the Palestine Liberation Organization to various stops in the Middle East.

In the fall I interview Henry Kissinger and cover the National Football League strike, which wipes out half of the regular season.

Important events, important people. I am finally meeting the needs of my psyche as I perceived them a long time ago. Hanging out with the right crowd, calming the old insecurities, regaling the strangers. But at the same time, raising doubt as if it were a bed of flowers and I the possessor of the world's greenest thumb. It is possible to become famous covering stories of magnitude; is it possible, as well, to continue to be yourself? To what extent can you be sub-servient to the whims of event and still be captain of your own soul? It will be several years before I understand the implications of the question, and a year or two more before I can answer.

But even putting aside the doubt, as I do for the time being, I realize that stories of magnitude have been the exceptions in my career, a fact that is not likely to change. The same is true for most other journalists. It is a matter of numbers. There are tens of thousands of people in the world reporting the news, only a handful of events with coattails long enough to be ridden to glory. The wise journalist, as well as the stable human being in other professions, is one whose goals at mid-career are different from those at the start.

On this day there is news from South Africa. There is news from Western Europe and the western United States and, as ever, from Washington, D.C., where a spokesman for one party is blaming the other for a legislative impasse and a spokesman for the other is returning the favor. But in the New York bureau, to which I have been assigned for almost two years, all is quiet. It is a day for busy-work, for going through necessary motions.

I answer mail, call sources, screen video for a future piece. I take my stopwatch up to the maintenance shop for repairs. I file some recent scripts: HALLOWEEN CANDY, COLLAPSED CRANE, SOLAR HOUSE. No coattails here.

The scripts go into folders that go into drawers in a metal filing cabinet that was empty when NBC consigned it to me more than six years ago and is now almost full. It was shiny and smooth when I got it and is now dull and scuffed. I am almost up to the second filing cabinet of my life's work.

I leave early for lunch and spend an hour and a half at the restaurant and another hour browsing at bookstores: the lemon chicken at Pearl's and John D. MacDonald's most recent Travis McGee novel at Scribner's. The day is frigid but clear; icicles hang from the awnings of Saks Fifth Avenue, and large granules of salt have turned the snow on the sidewalk to slush. My eyes water, nostrils crackle, but as I look around I see that most people are discharging breath like tiny locomotives, apparently invigorated at being out in the open. Their cheeks are ruddy, and they walk briskly and pump their arms. Or is it just that they are in a hurry to get back inside?

In the bureau this afternoon I continue in the downtime mode: reading a research packet for a story about a slump in the video game industry, writing a memo requesting file tape from another bureau for a piece about a possible strike by professional basketball players, and getting a shoeshine from the old man who comes around with his little wooden box and his tales of the giants whose shoes he shined in the old days. "I remember Mr. Swayze told me once ..." "Mr. Huntley was the kind of man who always ..." "Now, Mr. Garroway, he was a little before your time, but ..." I used to like to listen. Today I just want to get the slush off my shoes.

I look out the window at the usual view: the skating rink at Rockefeller Plaza, circled by the flags of different nations, and across Fifth Avenue, which has seen seven Easter Parades since I joined NBC, the spires of St. Patrick's Cathedral, soaring toward heaven, almost making contact. The clouds today are the same shade of gray as the spires, the sky the same shade of blue as some of the flags around the rink—everything somehow coordinated, a genuine postcard view.

I drift past the newsdesk and watch the wire machines clack out the day's record. When I started in the business they were as loud as the typewriters in old-fashioned newsrooms; now they have been electronically muffled, the sound almost down to a hum. Above them a fluorescent bulb has begun to flicker.

At quarter to three a story seems to break.

At quarter after it proves a false alarm.

At quarter to five I decide to go home early.

I stuff the McGee novel into my briefcase along with the latest issue of the *Columbia Journalism Review* and the foil-wrapped piece of chicken that I did not finish at lunch. I zip up the briefcase, slip on my coat and gloves, turning my back to the office door in the process. Tuck in my scarf, turn up my overcoat collar.

When I face the door again, ready to make my getaway, I find the path blocked. The obstruction is an NBC News vice president. His smile is sheepish, his mission apparent.

"Not again," I say.

"You love it."

"I'm willing to do it from time to time. That's a long way from love."

"Well," the vice president says, shoulder against the doorframe, "I'm afraid tonight needs to be one of the times."

"There've been a lot of them lately."

"I know," he says, shaking his head; he is no more pleased with the purpose of his visit than I am. "I know." It is, we both realize, an extraordinary situation.

I put my briefcase down. Pull off gloves, unwrap scarf, unbutton coat. "So what the hell is it with this woman? What's going on?"

The vice president slumps into the chair behind my desk and

spins around to face me. He takes a thumbtack from a small plastic container and pushes it into the blotter. He says nothing. We are friends, but he is management; there is a limit to how much he can say and how chummy he can be in the telling.

"When did she call?" I ask.

"A few minutes ago."

"Later and later."

He agrees.

"Almost five o'clock and this is the first you know about it."

"It's probably the first *she* knew about it," the vice president says. "She probably didn't get up until late this morning, didn't start snorting until this afternoon, and is just now realizing it's not going to wear off in time for her to go on the air tonight."

"What excuse did she give you?"

"Speaking engagement."

"She's done better."

"When she's in better shape. She didn't even make the call this time."

"Her 'associate'?" I say, referring to a young man whom the lady in question keeps on her payroll more as a social secretary than as an aide in journalistic endeavor.

The vice president chuckles. "He said it was his fault. He forgot to tell her about the speech and just noticed it on the calendar at the last minute, and of course, since she made the commitment a long time ago, there's no way to back out now. And think how bad it would look for NBC if she did."

"Nice of her to worry about appearances. Did he tell you the name of the group she's speaking to?"

"What do you think?"

"Or where?"

"Slipped his mind."

I take off my coat, drape it around a hanger, and put the hanger on a hook on the wall.

We are talking about Jessica Savitch, a wiry blonde of manic disposition who came to work for NBC in the fall of 1977. Trumpets blared her arrival; press releases amplified the sound. Savitch spun through the door at 30 Rock and made an immediate mockery of the timetable John Chancellor had spelled out for me a year and a half earlier. Her first beat should have been a small domestic bureau. It turned out to be the United States Senate. Net gain over timetable: fifteen years. She also started out as the anchor of the weekend editions of *Nightly News*, which Chancellor had figured for the vicinity of year twenty. Jessica Savitch, in other words, was hired for the top. It had never happened before at NBC, and the effects have been devastating, for both the company and the employee.

Many of Savitch's co-workers despise her. They call her bitch, usurper, ice queen, bimbo, loon, madwoman, amateur, incompetent. It is unprecedented vituperation, chilling to hear, shameful to utter, as I sometimes find myself doing. The woman is dismissed as an intruder, vilified as a saboteur, regarded as a virus in the bloodstream of pure journalism—which already seems rife with contagion to me. The reactions may not be defensible, but they are easily explained. Some of Savitch's detractors are people more qualified than she to cover the Senate, others more qualified to anchor weekend *Nightly;* still others belong to a third group who simply resent her on principle. I am among the latter, but unenthusiastically.

For, however daunting Chancellor's schedule seemed, however much an impediment to the itch of youthful ambition, there was something numinous about it. It was a constant in a business of variables. I remember, as Chancellor recited it for me on that day of orientation more than six years past, that I had the sense of being read to from stone tablets, and I have since come to think of the timetable as others do of Calvinism; in some cases, great reward is promised after a long period of trial, and if the latter seems at times to be unending, the former at least gives it a point. The Chancellor timetable has always represented, in other words, hard justice.

Savitch represents smashed tablets. Her hiring was to many NBC journalists a realization of the worst nightmare: that style is not the partner of substance in television news but its foe, and destined in the end to triumph. According to this scenario, Savitch is the sexy young thing whom the patriarch has married in his dotage and with whom he has become so mindlessly infatuated that he makes her the sole beneficiary of his will. The journalists of substance are the dutiful but less glamorous sons, now to be punished after years of ploddingly faithful service. The hussy has come between them and their expectations. Such is the view of so many, sexist as well as cruel.

But not without foundation. As an anchor, Savitch reminds me of the men who call square dances, punching words so hard that delivery overwhelms meaning. And the words are not her own. She is no more capable of writing a script than she is of doing her own makeup, and no more interested in the one than the other. At the end of each *Nightly* she anchors, she looks into the camera and smiles the way I used to smile in Parkersburg when trying to imitate Dan Rather's goofy grin. Then she says, "Thank you, and good night for all of us at NBC News." At which point most of us at NBC News blanch. We do not want this woman speaking for us. Who said she could? She is not our idea. She is the new value system, and the rest of us are the old. Are we not noble in our suffering?

As a reporter, Savitch performs even less credibly. Her grasp of events is tenuous, as is her command of television storytelling techniques, and her commitment to learn, say the producers who work with her, seems nonexistent. Without the producers to tell her what to do and when to do it, and in many cases to do it for her, she would not get facts straight or finish stories in time to air. Producers prime her for interviews, arrange her supporting video, devise her standups, make reservations for dinner. Because of the complexity of events or the vagaries of scheduling, there are times when most correspondents have to work alone. For Savitch this would not be possible. Jessica Savitch without a producer is as inconceivable as Howdy Doody without strings.

Of course, she knows what people think of her. She hears the whispers, hears the shouts; she translates the body language, reads the pained expressions and averted eyes. She knows that it is nothing personal, that such animosity would be directed against anyone in whose favor the sacred tablets were broken. But this is hardly consolation; if anything, it is a source of further angst for her, to realize that so much ill will has so little to do with the human being she really is. She did not force NBC to make her an overnight star. She did not threaten violence if her salary fell short of six figures a year. She simply sent a tape of her work to company executives, who responded to her presentation of the news the way movie critics responded to Meryl Streep's presentation of Sophie's choice. They saw in Savitch a chance for box office gold; that she was without journalistic acumen did not seem important. Others at NBC had it; they could utilize it on her behalf and put it up on prompter for her. After all, Streep didn't really have to decide which of her kids to hand over to the Nazis. That was just acting. Journalism could be, too.

But would any of Savitch's adversaries, if placed in a similar position, have responded differently? Would we have turned down the offer she received simply because it exploded the notion of corporate justice as we had always understood it? In all likelihood, she did not anticipate an the reaction against her. She has probably fooled herself into believing she is a real journalist, worthy of the Senate, anchor desk, and whatever else comes her way. She has done so, perhaps, out of insecurities that are not so different from mine. I wonder whether she imitated the dancers on *American Bandstand* as a teenager. I wonder whether she is more of a victim than the rest of us can comfortably admit.

And possibly that is why she moves among us as she does, with forced smile and rigid posture, radiating tension and frustration. She keeps herself tightly coiled and comes undone with surprising ease. She screams at office mates, throws unsecured objects at members of the technical staff, and cries too easily, like a child whose rage at being unable to tolerate what has befallen her is malevolent in its purity. One of her recourses has been to find a small circle of unlikely friends at NBC—production assistants, secretaries, runners—and coil even more tightly within it.

Another recourse is cocaine. High grade, low yield. She stuffs it up her nose and succumbs to its stupefying spells and coils within those, too. It is for this reason that Savitch often fails to show up to anchor *NBC News Digest,* the minute of headlines that airs at nine and ten o'clock each night between the network's prime-time programs. I am the usual understudy, and am being summoned from the wings again tonight.

"How much longer is this going to go on?" I ask the vice president.

"I don't know." He brings one foot up onto the opposite knee and reties a wingtip shoelace.

"Did it ever occur to you that the papers are bound to get hold of this someday?"

He says it has occurred to him.

I take a seat on the edge of my desk, pushing aside a small stack of cassettes. "Can you imagine? All the stories we do on drug abuse and its costs to society in terms of shattered lives and lost man-hours, how it rips apart families and ruins neighborhoods, how it may be doing to a generation of young Americans what World War I did to a generation of young Europeans. And then it turns out that this person who's in the direct line of succession from Huntley and Brinkley to Chancellor to Brokaw, this person who's got a chance to be the first solo female anchor ever at a major network—this person turns out to be a junkie herself! Maybe even knows some of the people getting busted on *Nightly.* Maybe even *buys* from them. Think of it: She's sitting on the set some Saturday night, looking into the camera and introing a piece on this big drug raid, and then the tape rolls and she watches it on the monitor and sees these pushers go by—and she's waving at them. 'See ya, Bernie. Bye-bye, Cheech. Good luck, guys. Write when you can, huh? Oh, and one favor?

Keep my name out of it, okay?'" I pick up a pen, begin tapping on a cassette box. "It's a precarious position the company is in."

"I know."

"A big lie we're living."

"Matter at hand," the vice president says. "Can I count on you tonight or not?"

I look down at the desk. "It's not the best timing."

"Plans?"

"Plans."

"What?"

"Dinner with my wife."

"Oh, hell," he says, "you've probably missed a hundred of those over the years. What's so special about tonight?"

"Final details of the divorce."

"Oh." Silence hits the room with the impact of a fist. "Gee. I mean ..."

"I'm flying down to Haiti next week for a quickie, and there are some things we have to go over."

"I'm really sorry."

I shrug.

"I had no idea."

Maintain the shrug.

"Can you call her?"

"Call her?"

"Let her know you can't make it."

The television news business is not for those of trusting heart. It promises wealth and fame and power, and because these are significant rewards, it feels justified in making demands that are, if not exactly Faustian, at least more than mortals of normally proportioned ego should be prepared to accept. It demands too many hours, too little sensitivity, too exaggerated a view of the importance of self. It requires that events be analyzed superficially because there is no time for detail, and that facts be expressed simplemindedly because viewers have but one chance to grasp the words that come flying through the air as if being thrown away instead of communicated. It asks that friends be sacrificed or not made at all, that marriages be strained to the breaking point or actually broken, that life be lived in narrow channels. It imperils physical health, challenges emotional health. It calls for the consumption of too much airline food and the tolerance of too many hotel mattresses and the cultivation of a hobby to get through the night in places whose names cannot be remembered a few days later.

Like most of the rest of us, Savitch did not know the terms when she accepted the deal. But she was lucky, or so she must have thought. She was one of the few to whom the gaudy promises of broadcast journalism were actually kept. Her bank account is substantial and her renown great and her power such that she can phone in her regrets four hours before she is scheduled to face the red light, without fear of reprisal. Her picture is on the covers of women's magazines and in the hearts of lonely, longing male viewers from coast to coast.

Yet her success is a fragile thing, and her sometimes ruthless behavior a variety of wolf's clothing on a sheep. Somewhere inside the woman, I believe, is a child perhaps no longer afraid of the dark but terrified by much that lurks in the day. I do not think she wants to be a network journalist so much as a self-respecting human being; her occupation is merely the means by which she hopes either to achieve her end or distract herself once and for all from the inability to do so. The distractions are great. Too great. For Jessica Savitch, television news is hell with a twist. Thanks to NBC, every dream she ever had has come true, an exquisitely subtle form of torture. I wish she were here tonight. I'd like to tell her what I think.

The least I can do is fill in for her at the anchor desk.

I leave the vice president brooding in my office and take the elevator down to Pastrami 'n' Things on the ground floor of 30 Rock. I find a seat against the wall and order an eponymous sandwich, french fries, cole slaw, and a bottle of beer. I bring my book along, a distraction of my own for a few minutes, and renew acquaintances with Trav McGee, Meyer Meyer, the trusty old *Busted Flush*, and the damp, deadly sizzle of a Florida summer. It seems that Meyer's niece and her husband have been blown to bits in a boat explosion off the Keys. McGee vows to help his friend track down the culprits. The plot, according to the jacket copy, takes the two heroes "from Florida to Mexico on an investigation which will alter irrevocably both men's lives."

It is a pleasure to spend time with fictional friends. They show up once every year or so for a few days, long enough to rekindle familiar feelings and soothe nerves worn down by inhabitants of the real world.

I have a second bottle of beer.

I go back upstairs to write two newscasts that are in fact even shorter than the proclaimed minute each. Even though it contains three or sometimes four stories, and even though the stories cover the happenings of the entire world for a period of twelve hours or more, a single *NBC News Digest*, less commercial, is forty-three seconds. Sometimes forty-two. I don't know why NBC bothers: so much time and energy going into so inconsequential a product—the broadcast journalism equivalent of one of those tiny dollhouses you sometimes see in a museum, with its perfectly scaled-down figures and furnishings. Of interest as a curiosity, perhaps, but little else.

APRIL 1983

WESTERN PENNSYLVANIA

I AM LYING IN A HOTEL ROOM in Pittsburgh, watching Willard Scott discuss the weather in Montana. Willard is pretending to be responsible for it. He says he warned everyone yesterday about the effects of that low-pressure system closing in on Butte, and *bam!*—today he delivered the goods. He told the Mid-Atlantic states he'd be giving them unseasonably warm temperatures this morning, and he was as good as his word on that too.

As presented on the *Today* show and other television news programs, weather is no longer a force of nature, majestic and elemental; no longer, as a poet once said, "the display to man of God's mood." It has been anthropomorphized, turned into the capricious child of the TV weatherman, who is sometimes able to control its behavior, sometimes not. Today Willard controls, and he is beaming about it.

Cut to tight shot of map. On it are jagged lines of lightning, smiling sun faces, and scowling clouds. Cartoon-O-Rama.

The phone rings.

I slither out of bed to turn down the volume on the television, then crawl back under the covers and pick up the receiver.

"Mr. Burns?"

"Yes?" I have to strain to hear; the air-conditioner in the room is puttering like a lawn mower.

"Oh, good. I was afraid I'd miss you."

It is the man I am supposed to interview later this morning about the closing of a steel mill in a Pittsburgh suburb. Hundreds will lose their jobs; a community already down on its luck will sink further. But something has come up, the man says, an important meeting that might change the nature of what he has to tell me. It will take all day; he thinks he will be available at five, and if all goes well, he will have a more interesting story for me than the one

I initially intended to report. May we push back the interview?

"Sure."

"I'm sorry," he says.

"It's all right," but in truth it is better than that. Already I have another plan for the day.

I hang up and call my producer in the next room, telling her what has happened. She says she will inform the crew and then phone New York.

"What are you going to do?" she wants to know.

"I'd like the car, if you don't mind."

"No." A large yawn into my ear. "What for?"

"I went to school not far from here. I want to take a ride in that direction."

"What's the school?"

"You never heard of it."

"Try me."

"Westminster. It's a small college about halfway between Pittsburgh and Erie."

"Never heard of it."

"I'll be back in plenty of time for the interview."

"Have fun," she says.

A knock at my door. I admit a room service waiter with the breakfast I ordered by filling out a card and hanging it on my doorknob the night before. He leaves the tray on a small coffee table: scrambled eggs, bacon, toast, orange juice, and tea. I slide a chair over and turn up the volume on *Today*. Bryant Gumbel is interviewing an actress who should have won some sort of award but did not. She is not complaining, though—that's not the kind of person she is—and Bryant seems taken by her graciousness.

I am finished with breakfast at eight-twenty, out of the room half an hour later, and on the road by nine.

A few miles north of Pittsburgh on old Route 19, the sense of a large eastern city disappears and the character of the land begins to change. It becomes less hilly, more gentle; it rolls, like a sheet fluttering down over a bed. The factories give way to shopping centers that give way to industrial parks that give way to trailer parks, ranch houses, and farmhouses. Spaces widen; shadows lengthen. Fences no longer keep people out but animals in. I drive past clusters of cattle socializing at the roadside, nibbling on oats or barley or brome. Flies buzz them energetically; tails swat back. In the distance are fields of corn that will be used for silage, the stalks not yet as high as a cow's knee.

The smells are different too: fresher, less civilized, and powerful enough to seep through the windows of a sealed car hurtling north at sixty-five miles an hour. "Thick, country smells," they have been called, "smells of life." The road unwinds gradually, and ahead of me the sky dips low. It might almost be Kansas or Nebraska here, almost be a thousand miles farther.

I roll down the window, turn up the radio, sing along with a station I am rapidly outdistancing. The song is "Maniac," from the movie *Flashdance,* says the disc jockey. I have heard it only once or twice before and have to fudge most of the lyrics. I cannot remember the last time I sang to myself on a day when I was supposed to be working.

As I approach New Wilmington, home of Westminster, horse-drawn buggies appear on the road. They are made of pine, painted black, and do not pull over as cars roar up behind them, even if horns blare and drivers curse and shake their fists. When the cars pass and the drivers look back, the men at the reins of the buggies look through them, paying no mind, continuing with their private musings. They are Amish, these old-fashioned travelers on the modern highway, a Mennonite sect whose disdain for the twentieth century knows few loopholes.

All Amish, including the children, are farmers. Horses pull their plows as well as their buggies, and the earth to them is a sacred trust. If the Amish dedicate themselves to its care, the Lord will see to their crops and to them. It is He who is responsible for the weather, not Willard. The Amish have never heard of Willard Scott. Nor have they heard of Charles Kuralt, and Pennsylvania Dutch country is no dissatisfied urbanite's notion of Eden. It is a demanding place, long on chores and short on diversions, and does not lend itself to the fictive romanticizing of a television feature reporter. It is also a place where nothing unusual ever happens, so it does not suit the needs of hard news either.

The Amish do not believe in utility-generated electricity. They pump their water by hand or use windmills to draw it into huge storage tanks, from which they later remove it manually. Their woodworking shops are equipped with power tools, like saws and planers and drills, but the power is pneumatic, not electric. Electricity is too up-to-date, too much out of the hands of man.

You will not find an Amish family with a telephone in the house. A telephone would be an intrusion, as would a stereo or radio or television, which are also forbidden. To the Amish, these devices are frivolous, not utilitarian, serving no better purpose than to compete with the lowing of animals, the chirping of birds, the howling of winds, and the splattering of rain. It is these sounds that farm people wish to hear, for reasons practical as well as aesthetic. There are pay phones in booths in Amish towns, but not many. The Amish think nothing of riding over to see a friend, even if the trip is several miles. They are, to put it mildly, in no hurry.

The Amish oppose institutions of any kind. There are no Amish chapters of the Boy Scouts or the Kiwanis or the National Organization for Women. There are no Amish Amway distributorships, no Amish fan clubs for Olivia Newton-John. The Amish limit formal education to eight years, and their schools are relics of another time: one-room clapboard buildings with wood-burning stoves over which hands and lunches are warmed on winter days. The desks are small and uncomfortable, the blackboards actually black instead of green. Coats are hung on wooden pegs in the wall. The curriculum is reading, writing, and 'rithmetic, and nothing else; there is only one extracurricular activity in the Amish community, and that is farming. All the kids participate; all are on the varsity. Amish schools meet state requirements in number and length of days, but in no other category. The teachers care more about the behavior of their students than their achievement. God's work, after all, does not demand genius, only perseverance and faith.

The Amish will not fight wars, will not take oaths, and will not hold public office, the latter an unnecessary element of their creed since their neighbors trust them so little they would not vote for them even for dogcatcher. The Amish would probably let the damn things run loose! They do not hold with Social Security, government-imposed health regulations, or, for the most part, government itself. There are no pictures of FDR or JFK on the walls of Amish living rooms, no U.S. Savings Bonds in lockboxes under the floorboards.

It is precisely the kind of isolation I need this day.

Volume up on the radio, hand keeping the beat on the outside mirror. "Hurts So Good," a song from the old days, a song from the present; twenty years pass and the beat stays the same.

During the late spring and summer, some of the Amish set up small booths along Route 19 and the side roads into New Wilmington to sell homemade baked goods. The booths are larger than the lemonade stands suburban children once erected, but almost as primitive in construction: a counter, sides, and a few boards overhead to keep off the sun. Signs nailed to stakes driven into the ground along the highway a mile or two before the stands advertise the varieties and prices of items: breads, rolls, fruit pies, cobblers. The prices are reasonable, the quality of the food excellent. As far as the world around them is concerned, this is about as participatory as the Amish get.

I see my first stand today a few miles south of New Wilmington, on the road that forks west off Route 19 toward my alma mater. It has been set up at the edge of a large field, unfenced pastureland that seems to stretch as far as the horizon and beyond, dissolving into the sky murkily at the edge of my vision. I pull the car onto the dirt shoulder a few feet past the stand and walk back. It is almost eleven. The sun bakes my forehead and nose, and heat waves ripple off the pavement. Willard was right about the temperatures in the Mid-Atlantic states today. He gave us a scorcher.

I am the only customer at the stand. Two girls who might be twins, no more than twelve years old, are on duty. Each is a scale model of her Amish elders in plainness of attire, reserve, and pallor, although the girls are incongruously rosy-cheeked, an almost tubercular flush. They have straight, matted hair and bony faces, and they smell of the soil: musky, loamy.

I try to talk to them, a few words of no particular significance after my long, solitary drive; I suppose what I want is to hear another human voice. But they will have none of it; they only listen, take my order. The Amish are wary of outsiders, sensitive to their derision, some of which was dispensed by my own younger version on midnight rides through the countryside with drunken fraternity brothers. We would shout obscenities, scare horses, give sophomorism an even worse name.

Yet I was curious about the Amish. I would read about them in the local paper, force exchanges with them at the post office, eavesdrop on their conversations at the grocery store. I would ask questions about them of people who had lived in New Wilmington longer than I; once I even withdrew a book about them from the college library, the only one on the shelves. I learned about the Amish, in other words, unhurriedly, prompted not by professional need but by personal interest. And what I learned took hold slowly, like multiple coats of varnish applied to a piece of wood, each coat sealing in the one that preceded it and preparing the way for the one that would come. As a result, even after all these years, I could do a piece about the Amish for tonight's *Nightly* without so much as a notecard of research.

But what if I had originally learned about them *for* a television news report? How much would I still recall? People think that journalists are a knowledgeable lot, and in most cases we are, but it is not the kind of knowledge that serves constructive purposes. As an educational experience, preparing a story for a TV newscast is like cramming for a test; one becomes an expert at the time, but the information is too hastily acquired to sink in, a cheap varnish on unsanded timber. Some of the information flakes off the next day; more is gone with the next report, after a new and dissimilar set of facts has been ingested and prepared for broadcast. The object in all of this is not retention but a good grade: an A from the executive producer, a "Satisfactory" from the viewer. The reporter will remember his story longer than those who watch it, but soon enough neither will be able to pass a test, calling into question the point of the whole exercise in the first place.

I want to do something different on television, something that will last. I think I know what. I have made some notes for a proposal and will mull it over this afternoon, away from it all.

I give one of the Amish girls a ten-dollar bill. She hands me a loaf of bread and a boysenberry pie. I hope the bread still has the nutty texture I recall, and the pie its tart filling and flaky crust. The girl also hands me change, but her eyes avoid me by so much that some of it drops on the ground inside the stand. She bends over, picks it up, and gives it to me again, still refusing to see me. The other girl has angled her body away and begun to stare at a knot in the planking, working a fingernail into it. My smile is wasted. I don't bother with a thank-you. Neither do they.

I return to my car and toss the bread and pie on the front seat. Then I continue down Route 19 on foot. A semitrailer whizzes by, so close that the hot wind in its wake blows me to the side of the shoulder; other vehicles pass less threateningly. In fifty yards or so I come to a dirt cutoff and decide to follow it east. A few minutes later the sounds of traffic become no more annoying than the murmur of distant insects. The road is lined with elms and maples in full bloom and fencing in good repair; a few horses graze on a nearby hillock, but I can see no other animals and no people or buildings at all. I wonder whether a college escapade ever took me down this road, and if so, what I might have done.

I sit against one of the maple trunks and wish I had brought a pillow for my back. Now there is a murmur of closer insects: crickets, they might be, except it is too early in the day and the sound seems too lacking in purpose. Lazy crickets, maybe, idly practicing a few steps instead of going through the entire dance in the heat.

I know how it is.

I roll up my sleeves. I kick off my shoes and remove my glasses, slipping them into my shirt pocket. I slide my watch over my hand

MAY 1983

NEW YORK

I AM IN MY OFFICE this morning making less important decisions: of degree, not kind. They involve a trip I took recently to Phoenix for a story on certain practices of the banking industry. For instance:

The cab ride from the airport to the hotel cost thirteen dollars. But I wheedled a blank receipt from the driver and now put it to use, filling it in for eighteen. I took one other cab ride in Phoenix, from the hotel to a downtown bank one afternoon to do retakes of a standup; it seems that the first time the cameraman forgot to white-balance and my face came out green. The receipt is for eleven dollars, but I change the second numeral to a four. The new ink is a lighter shade of blue than the old; I cannot make myself care.

I have a dinner receipt for $18.87. I write in the amount under "Entertainment" as drinks for a bank vice president, then fill in a blank receipt I have been given by a producer for $23.68. Fill it in left-handed. I pretend *that* is dinner.

I bought a book to read on the flight home, a biography of Thomas Hardy by a professor at the University of Toronto. Twenty-five dollars plus tax. I enter the figure under "Miscellaneous" and describe the book as a critical history of American banking methods, essential for research.

I triple the amount of my tips, double the cost of a shoeshine, neither of which requires a receipt.

It is not as bad as it seems. This is my last expense account for NBC News. I am simply trying to make up for the first.

1983–1985   Writer/Host, *Old Habits,* PBS
New York, Pittsburgh

THREE WEEKS LATER

NEW YORK

IT IS ALMOST SUMMER, and flowers are blooming. Grass has sprouted, trees have regained their leafy coats. Birds are back from the south, insects up from the ground. New life abounding. Bursting forth, shooting out, spilling over. Symbolically, the time is perfect.

The place is perfect, too: Tavern on the Green in New York's Central Park, with its huge windows admitting the warmth of the sun and a view of the renascent earth.

As far as I know, the lady treating me to lunch is also perfect: a high-ranking executive of the Public Broadcasting Service, which, like me at the beginning of my career, truly does regard television as an appliance of high cultural order. She tells me she has flown up from Washington just for our meal, and her taste in clothes is as expensive as her taste in restaurants. Silk shirt by one designer, silk pants by another, linen jacket by a third—elegantly coordinated, an understated smartness to it all.

But there is nothing understated in the woman's manner. She is all twitches and bobs, her body seeming in motion even as she sits, words tumbling over one another in their eagerness to get out of her mouth and start people reacting.

We are discussing my proposal for a television history of smoking and drinking.

"And I'll tell you something, my dear sir. I'm not the only one who feels this way. See, I've shown your proposal around the office, let a few other people take a peek, and they all think we've got something special here, and I'm talking *extra* special."

"Really?"

"And do you know why?"

"Why?"

"Your sense of humor. That's the thing that makes *Old Habits* such a winner. We run so many programs on the network that're histories of one sort or another, and most of them are as dry as the desert sand. You've seen them, you know what I mean."

"I plead the Fifth."

"Like, we have these announcers with the dullest voices that ever went into a microphone and scripts that don't have the slightest trace of life to them. I swear, you could do an EKG on some of the scripts we produce and they wouldn't register so much as a blip on the old screen. I'm talking straight-line city here. In fact, that's one of our little jokes around the office, the EKG read on our scripts."

"Funny."

"But *Old Habits?*"

"A few blips?"

"A few? A *few?* I mean, it's still only a proposal, for heaven's sake, and already we're off the chart. And I'll tell you another joke around the office, but you've got to promise you won't tell anyone, absolutely not a single soul."

"Promise."

"I'm holding you to this, now."

"You can trust me."

"All right. Guess what we call ourselves sometimes."

"I don't know. What?"

"The network for the humor-impaired. Oh Lord, can you stand it! 'Good evening, ladies and gentlemen, and welcome to PBS, the network for those of you who don't have the slightest idea what's funny and don't even care.'"

"Mum's the word."

"But it's true. I don't know what it is, we just don't seem to have the knack for programs that leap off the screen at people. PBS programs kind of recede, you know? Sink back in. A lot of it's the writing. But *Old Habits?* Now, let me just look through the proposal here a sec. ... There was this one line that really hit me. ... Well, there were a million lines like that, actually, but this one in particular about Carry Nation was so good I just don't want to take a chance paraphrasing it. Oooh, here it is, I knew I'd find it. Okay?"

"Okay."

"What you're doing, see, you're talking about how Carry Nation would go into a saloon with her hatchet and just start smashing the place to bits, turning it into a stack of firewood, and you say ... all right, what you say is, 'No one knows precisely what Mrs. Nation felt the first time she picked up a hatchet, but it must have been similar to what Pete Rose felt the first time he picked up a baseball bat; that is, a perfect union of person and object, of objective and means.' Wonderful writing, just wonderful."

"Thank you."

"But the thing is, it's not just humor. Because humor, you know, humor per se would distract from the real purpose of *Old Habits*. I firmly believe that. What makes your humor so effective is that it sets up the serious points so well."

"You're being very kind."

"Nonsense. And I'll tell you what else. You keep everything objective, impartial. It would've been so easy, when you're talking about things like smoking and drinking, to get up on a soapbox and rant and rave. But you don't do it, and it's great the way you hold back."

"Well, take what happened in Jamestown, for example."

"Jamestown, right. And didn't *that* just about knock me off my chair. Now, refresh my memory."

"About?"

"The whole thing. I remember, I'm just a little hazy."

I refresh.

In the spring of 1607, three boats from England, storm-tossed and creaking, sailed up the James River in what is today the state of Virginia. About sixty miles from Cape Henry, they encountered a small peninsula. Captain Christopher Newport, in charge of the fleet, disembarked. He looked around, considered the options, and as much from fatigue as fondness for the location, pronounced the long journey at an end. The result was the first permanent English colony in the New World.

Its permanence, however, seemed anything but assured at the start. Jamestown was built on a swamp, which meant that insects swarmed through the air so thickly they sometimes clouded the sun. Disease spread through the populace as if borne on the breezes, and drinking water was so impure it could at times be painful to swallow. The summers were hotter than anything the settlers had known in England, and the winters so severe that some of them actually froze to death. Others died of malaria and malnutrition, the latter because they had a hard time raising, or even picking or hunting, enough to eat. There were fires, droughts, attacks by Indians who presciently feared the razing of paradise. Something like two-thirds of the original hundred settlers did not survive the first winter in their new home.

Reinforcements were dispatched from England, but Jamestown

did not need people so much as a way for the people to support themselves. The colonists tried everything: raising corn and grapes, making potash, smelting iron, blowing glass. In desperation, they had a fling with silkworms, whose survival rate was even worse than theirs. Nothing worked. Jamestown simply could not find an economic base for itself.

And then, in 1612, one of the colonists, John Rolfe, returned from a voyage to Trinidad with a bag of tobacco seeds. He also brought back some knowledge: a new method of curing the leaves. Jamestown had already tried and failed with tobacco, but Rolfe persuaded his neighbors that they had nothing to lose by experimenting with the new West Indian strain. Reluctantly, they agreed.

For one reason or another, the first few crops were not very good. The colonists had to force themselves to smoke what they grew, perhaps to warm their insides on bitter days, perhaps to kill a few insects with the stench when the weather turned hot. No foreign country, not even the motherland, would import the stuff. But the quality of the product rapidly improved, and within a few years Jamestown was producing huge amounts of tobacco, in a variety of leaf that people in England found more to their liking than what they had long been getting at home. It smoked more easily, had a sweeter taste. Jamestown had finally come up with a cash crop. The colony survived. Tobacco was its salvation.

"Fascinating," says the high-ranking executive of the Public Broadcasting Service at lunch at Tavern on the Green more than three and a half centuries later. "I mean, that is an absolutely *riveting* piece of history."

"Well, you see the importance of tobacco in the grander scheme of the British colonial experience."

"Yes indeed."

"Actually, the British were on the verge of giving up on Jamestown, abandoning it. It was costing too much, returning too little."

"So if tobacco hadn't come along when it did ..."

"Who knows what might have happened."

"Oh, I love it. I absolutely *love* this kind of thing. It's such, such ... grist, you know? It's the very kind of program television ought to be doing more of. And here again, you're objective, you don't slow things down by being preachy or anything. You don't say, 'Now, ladies and gentlemen, you have to realize that what the colonists were really doing was sowing the seeds of a million cases of lung cancer in the distant future.'"

"They didn't know that."

"Precisely the point."

"In fact, the prevailing view at the time was that tobacco had some medicinal properties, that it cured colds, calmed the nerves, helped you sleep better, even lessened the severity of epileptic attacks."

"No."

"Yes."

"Well, it's just *too* exciting. That's all there is to say."

"I hope that means we can work something out."

"Oh, absolutely. Positively. Just as long as you're aware of the fact that it's always tough to get programs funded on PBS and even tougher when there's a Republican in the White House."

"Why's that?"

"Come on. You know how Republicans are when it comes to PBS."

"No, how?"

"Paranoid, that's how. What they say is that we should have to earn our way in the marketplace like the commercial networks do, like it's immoral or something to give us taxpayer money. 'PBS is nothing but an upper-middle-class entitlement program, and we can't stand for that kind of thing, blah-blah!' But that's just a smoke-screen. The real reason Republicans don't want to fund PBS is they're afraid we'll take their Wall Street money and turn out shows in favor of defense cuts and low-income housing, maybe even do a miniseries on how Teddy Kennedy got framed at Chappaquiddick."

"I see."

"But there are always ways, and for *Old Habits* we'll find some, believe me. Now, how many shows are we talking about here?"

"Two on smoking, two on drinking."

"An hour each?"

"Yes."

"So we're talking four hours of television."

"That's right."

"Okay then, given the amounts of money I'm sure will be involved, I think we're looking at three stages of funding. Shall I break them down for you?"

"Please."

"All right. Stage one covers fleshing out the proposal and turning it into four one-hour scripts. Also making a site survey, zipping around the country and figuring out where we should do our location shooting. Like Carry Nation's birthplace, Jamestown, wherever else makes sense."

"Where does the money come from?"

"As it happens, dear sir, that money resides in the bank account of yours truly."

"It does?"

"My very own little discretionary fund. Mine, mine, mine. So consider stage one yours, yours, yours."

"That easy?"

"Here's what you do. Tomorrow morning, go see a travel agent and book a trip, all the places you think you should check out. You'll have the money early next week."

"How much?"

"Twenty-five thousand. Sound about right?"

"I think so."

"Doesn't compare to what you made at NBC, I know, be*lieve* me, I know, but hey, this is Public Broadcasting. Different ballgame, different rules."

"It's fine. Really it is."

"Okay now, stage two. Here's where things get a little bit sticky. Lord knows I wish they didn't, but they do, so there you are."

"What's stage two?"

"Final polishing of the scripts, assembling the production team, firming up shooting dates and all the logistics that go along with it. I mean, we're talking everything that gets us right smack up to the actual eve of production."

"But you say it's sticky."

"Not really. Just sticky compared to stage one. Other than that, not really sticky at all."

"Where does stage-two money come from?"

"Well, in this case, I think our best bet is something called the Program Development Committee, of which yours truly—ahem, ahem—just happens to be the chair. Now, the committee isn't exactly under my control, not like the discretionary fund, for instance. But I *am* the chair *and* the senior member, both in terms of rank and longevity, so I usually get my way."

"Usually?"

"Most of the time."

"Not always?"

"Almost always."

"I'm just trying to understand."

"Oh my. If you succeed, come on over and explain it to me, will you?"

"Are the other people on the Program Development Committee

the ones who've been reading the proposal and enjoying it so much?"

"No."

"Oh."

"These're people who haven't seen the proposal yet, don't even know there *is* such a thing as *Old Habits*. And you know what? They're not going to."

"They're not?"

"I'm not even going to give them a hint, not even so much as a whisper. See, what I'll do is, I'll wait until you've finished the scripts, and then I'll tell them I've got this absolutely sensational project for them to look at. I'll fill them in in my own words, get them drooling over it. Believe me, I know how to push their buttons. Then I'll just slap the scripts down on the table and say, 'Help yourself, folks.' That way we hit them with our best shot right off the get-go."

"Interesting."

"And then it's stage three. Production costs, the biggie. Four hours of prime-time TV, lots of location shooting, possibly some original music, rights to old stills and movies, newsreel footage— my guess is we're talking a minimum, I mean *bare* minimum, of half a million dollars."

"That much?"

"Probably more."

"I've never really gotten involved in budgeting before."

"That's where the underwriters come in. You know what they are?"

"Sure. The companies that get the plugs at the beginning of the show. 'The following program is made possible by a grant from your friends at Smith, Jones, and Blarney.'"

"'With additional funding provided by Brown, Black, and Green.' Now, have we talked about your production facility?"

"WQED in Pittsburgh."

"Right, that's right. You're moving there, I assume."

"Yes."

"By yourself?"

"I'm getting married in the fall."

"Oh, how nice."

"It'll be my wife and me."

"Well, I'd say that by the time we get to stage three, you should be living in Pittsburgh. You'll be working with the WQED fundraisers then. At that point, it's ball-in-their-court time. But they're good, very good. Pittsburgh's a major corporate headquarters city, so there's a lot of money floating around."

"Especially with a Republican in the White House."

"Pardon?"

"Pro-business, you know."

"Oh yes, yes. Right, exactly. Never thought of it like that before."

"So that's it, then? Three stages of funding and the programs are on the air?"

"One, two, three."

"And it'll happen? You really believe everything will fall into place?"

"I wouldn't be here if I didn't, Eric. In fact, I want to tell you something, if you don't mind."

"Of course not."

"And this isn't something I say to just everyone who comes knocking on the door with an idea for a show, okay?"

"Okay."

"This project is going to be a special cause of mine. People are going to know, and I'm talking people outside PBS as well as inside, that if they say no to you on *Old Habits*, they're also saying no to me. And let them deal with the consequences of *that*, if they're up to it. Count on it, Eric, count on it."

DECEMBER 1983
NEW YORK

THE BRANCHES OF THE TREES are bare, pencil lines across a slate sky. No leaves, no flowers, grass smothered under a four-inch carpet of snow that makes all outside sounds seem muted, almost funereal. The temperature is below freezing, the sun a strain on the memory. Birds all gone south again, bugs buried in terra firma.

Perfect, just perfect.

I am sitting in the living room of my house in Westchester County, about thirty miles north of Manhattan, watching the carpet gradually thicken to five inches. An ash truck slides down the street toward the Hutchinson Parkway, the yellow light atop the cab whirling through the gloom of late afternoon. In my lap is a cup of herbal tea, a sissified flavor, easy on the nerves. In my ear is the voice of the high-ranking executive of the Public Broadcasting Service, coming to me over a strangely crackling telephone line from her office in our nation's capital.

"Oh God, this is terrible, absolutely *terrible!* I'm just, just ... well, that's how terrible it is—I don't know *what* I am."

"Look—"

"You're going to yell at me, I know you're going to yell at me, and you're entitled. Go ahead, Eric, let the decibels fall where they may."

"That's not why I called."

"And as for me, well, what can I say? I've been awful and I totally concede the point. But you can't be*lieve* how crazy things've been around here lately. I swear, I've never been so swamped in all my life! I mean it. I've had people quitting on me, new people coming aboard, PR campaigns to launch and then revamp, shows to edit at the last minute, and an absolute truckload of new proposals to go through. Incredible! Not that that's an excuse."

"Did you get the scripts?"

"Did I what?"

"Get my scripts."

"Of course I got your scripts. Why would—oh no. You don't mean to tell me we haven't spoken since *then?*"

"I've called you a dozen times in the past month."

"You're kidding."

"Maybe more. You haven't returned one of them, not one."

"Now, give me a sec, just give me a second to think how long we've had them in house. I can't even remember. Karen, when did the Eric Burns scripts come in? *Old Habits?* Oh, she can't hear a word I'm saying. She's like me, trying to do four hundred and thirty-six things at once. *Everyone* is swamped around this place. Anyhow, we've had the scripts for … let's call it a while."

"And?"

"I like them."

"You do?"

"Yes indeed, I like them very much, you bet. I'd say they live up to every expectation I had from the proposal."

"So we can move ahead?"

"Definitely. No question about it."

"Good."

"Let me just make sure I understand what you mean by 'move ahead.'"

"Second-stage funding. The grant from your Program Development Committee."

"Yes. Oh yes. That."

"Is there a problem?"

"I can't believe we haven't talked about this. Are you sure? Oh, what am I saying? Of *course* you're sure. Who would be *more* sure than *you,* of all people!"

"What's going on here?"

"Why, nothing. It's just that I've thought about *Old Habits* so much I just assumed you and I had gone through it all."

"Gone through what all?"

"The reaction to the scripts."

"You said you liked them."

"I did."

"So?"

"I mean the reaction from the committee. It's eight people, did I mention that? There's me and seven others. Five men and three women, not that it matters."

"And what did they think?"

"They laughed in all the right places. Sure did, every one."

"So what's the problem?"

"They didn't think they should have."

"Why not?"

"Inappropriate to such serious subject matter. That was the consensus. They thought the humor detracted from the importance of the material."

"You thought it enhanced."

"Well, there you are."

"Where am I?"

"I know, I know. Here I am telling you one thing, and then these people in virtually the same capacity as me come along with the exact opposite reaction."

"Carry Nation."

"What?"

"When we had our lunch we talked about Carry Nation."

"A good example. You shouldn't have made her such a laughingstock."

"*She's* the one who made her a laughingstock, not me."

"Well, that's one way to look at it, I suppose. But you could also say she was someone who genuinely cared about the welfare of others."

"She was a raving maniac! A lawbreaker and a threat to life and limb. Daughter of a woman who thought she was Queen Victoria and walked around her farmhouse in backwoods Kentucky wearing purple robes and a crown. Carry ended up in a carnival sideshow selling pictures of herself and tiny souvenir hatchets."

"All right, her methods might have been a little odd, but she did have a noble end in mind, you can't deny that."

"This is Carry Nation we're talking about. Did your committee want me to pretend it was Clara Barton?"

"Oh, come on now. I mean, really. The committee just thought it might have made a bit more sense to view old Carry from a broader perspective. To see the full human being, not just the lady wielding the hatchet."

I finally lose control of my lap and upset the teacup. I set the cup on a coffee table and stand up, cracking my knee on the table's edge. I tug a damp patch of shirt away from my stomach and a damp patch of pants away from my crotch. I keep the phone to my ear. The chill I feel has nothing to do with the weather.

A friend warned me when I left NBC that casting my lot with PBS was risky. It is a network with a hand-to-mouth existence, he said, always begging for money from government agencies and private corporations. As a result, budgets and staff are small, equipment and bureaucratic procedures antiquated. PBS has an inferiority complex about its circumstances, a superiority complex about its cultural worth—the latter, my friend insisted, undeserved.

PBS does not produce quality television programs, as it enjoys having people believe; it depends upon the kindness of strangers, quality producers who have nowhere else to go in the United States and sell their wares to public television by default. Would NBC have made time on its schedule for *Upstairs, Downstairs?* Would CBS clear an hour of prime time for a detailed look at the workings of the central nervous system? Could Big Bird possibly compete with David Hartman? PBS is a beneficiary, not an initiator, my friend said, the only rug merchant at the bazaar.

He knew me too well to urge me to stay with NBC; he simply said I should escape to a place other than PBS. A consulting firm, academia, a tenant farm. I did not listen, and now, as snow begins to pile up on my windowsill and the northern sky to turn black and blue, I am beginning to realize my mistake.

"What else?" I say to the high-ranking executive, sitting back in my chair. The phone line continues to crackle.

"Pardon?"

"What else did the committee think?"

"Well ... oh my, I ... The thing is, you've caught me right in the middle of a million other things, and well, I just ... All right. Okay. Evasive."

"What?"

"The committee thought the scripts were evasive."

"What did they evade?"

"Responsibility."

"For?"

"The dire consequences of using alcohol and tobacco. You know, all the ramifications—and goodness, no one can deny there's enough of them."

"Let me ask you a question."

"Shoot."

"Maybe later. Right now just tell me whether the people on the committee read the scripts."

"You're not serious."

"I'm very serious. I'm almost morbid."

"Of *course* they read them! I mean, how could they have their opinions if they didn't read the scripts?"

"How could they have their opinions if they *did* read them? That's what I want to know."

"I hate to hear you sounding like this, I really do. If you'd just—"

"Did *you* read the scripts?"

"I told you I did. I can't believe you're asking me this. Since when did you become the Grand Inquisitor, if you don't mind my asking? I mean, all of a sudden there's this ... *quality* to your voice."

"I thought so. You didn't read the scripts. You skimmed them."

"Let's call it a cross between the two. And if you'd been as swamped as I've been the past few weeks, like even *half* as swamped, you'd realize even *that's* a miracle."

"The scripts go into detail about some of the protest movements against smoking and drinking."

"I'm aware of that."

"Reasons are given for the movements."

"I should hope so."

"The medical evidence against smoking as it started to accumulate forty or fifty years ago, the destructive effects of drinking on early nineteenth-century family life, on and on."

"Uh-huh, uh-huh."

"To me those sound like dire consequences. Ramifications, even."

"Oh, right, I see where you're heading. But the committee's point was this, all right? You were very explicit about the opposition to alcohol and tobacco, but what you didn't seem to be doing was making your own position clear."

"My position?"

"What did you, Mr. Eric Burns, the PBS expert on the subject, think about it."

"Which side of the rabbit hole am I on? One of the things you liked so much about *Old Habits* was its objectivity."

"I know that."

"How unpreachy it was."

"Yes, of course. But still, some of the members of the committee—we're not talking everyone now, but some of them, kind of like a cross section—thought that by not taking a stronger editorial position yourself, we might be giving viewers the impression that PBS was somehow condoning the use of alcohol and tobacco."

"Oh. *That* side of the rabbit hole."

"What you have to realize, Eric, is that there are different points of view to take into account here. And I must admit that since I've been exposed to them, I can see where the other members of the committee are coming from, I really can. And it's broadening, you know? I mean, it's tuned me into a whole other perspective on this thing."

"Do you agree with the committee?"

"Oh, it's not a matter of agreeing or disagreeing."

"Of course it is."

"No, no. What it is, really, it's a matter of opening your eyes to other takes on reality. And that's a healthy thing, if you ask me. I mean, where's the harm?"

"But it's your committee."

"Pretty much, uh-huh."

"And you told me that if you wanted something, you usually got it."

"I usually do."

"And you said *Old Habits* was something you wanted very badly."

"It was. Is, I mean. Yes indeed."

"So what are you going to do about it?"

"There's nothing I *can* do, when you get right down to it. See, I have to pick and choose my spots with the committee very carefully. It's kind of political, the whole thing, I mean dicey, dicey, dicey. I can't go riding roughshod over them every time they make a decision I don't like, and unfortunately the timing here is bad."

"Why?"

"Because I've vetoed them a lot lately. I've *had* to. Just between you and me, you wouldn't be*lieve* some of the harebrained projects they've wanted to go ahead with the past month or so. I'm talking three parts on the evolution of Swahili, of all things. With some white guy from Chevy Chase executive-producing! But that's beside the point, it really is. The point is that some of the members of the committee are beginning to lose heart, wondering why there even needs to *be* a committee if I'm going to spend my whole life big-footing everything they do."

"So they get their way on *Old Habits*."

"I feel terrible about this, just terrible. You can't *imagine*."

"No second-stage grant."

"We really should've talked about this a long time ago. It's been so unfair, keeping you in the dark like this, but I haven't just been under the gun. I mean, I've been under the whole damn *arsenal!*"

"*Old Habits* is dead."

"Pardon?"

"You heard me."

"I heard you, but I don't know what you mean. How can you think *Old Habits* is dead?"

"Because your goddamn committee rejected it!"

"My goddamn committee, as you so tactlessly put it, dear sir, does not have the final word."

"You're telling me there's another source for the money?"

"Bingo."

"But I thought—"

"The committee was the *best* source, that's what I felt. Obviously I was wrong. Something didn't quite jell there, and that's the name of that tune. But believe me when I tell you there are other places we can go, and go we will."

"Where?"

"For starters, CPB."

"What's that?"

"The Corporation for Public Broadcasting. It's a funding arm for us. What it does is, it allocates the money we get from the federal government, the various grants and subsidies and things like that. We usually go to CPB for stage three. We'll just make an exception in this case. We'll go early."

"What do I do?"

"Come to Washington in a few weeks. Can you clear your schedule?"

"*Old Habits* is my schedule."

"I'll set up an appointment for you and we'll zip you right in. I mean, head of the line, no waiting."

"Can't we do it sooner?"

"Patience, dear sir, patience. Let me just get this set up the right way. Or actually what I'll do is, I'll get Karen on it. Karen's the one. She's plugged in over at CPB like you wouldn't believe. She'll get you an appointment with someone we're tight with, one of our friends. As a matter of fact, there are a couple of people over there who used to work for me, right here in this office. They'll be as flipped out over *Old Habits* as I am."

"Then what?"

"Then you breeze into town, fill out one of their applications, and wait for the money to come rolling in."

FEBRUARY 1984

WASHINGTON, D.C.

THE YOUNG MAN says all the right things in all the right ways, and my suspicions multiply like rabbits. It is something about the flitting of his eyes, the formality of his manner; something even about the building in which he speaks: CPB headquarters, with its austere lines and witless furnishings.

Yes, the young man says, he used to work for the high-ranking executive of the Public Broadcasting Service, and she was one fine boss and no less outstanding as a human being. Yes, he is well acquainted with Karen, and they have spent uncounted hours discussing the directions they hope television will take. Yes, he thinks a series on the history of smoking and drinking would be an excellent addition to the PBS schedule, but he is not in a position to speak for the board. He is only a gatekeeper, although I will not learn this until later; used to the anxiety of those who seek entrance, he has mastered the art of the polished yet empty response. It is Washington, after all; the workings of one bureaucracy cannot be much different from those of another.

"Shall I take the application for you, Mr. Burns?"

"I suppose."

"And the pen, too, if I may."

"Well, I just … just …"

"Is something bothering you?"

"Yes, actually."

"What is it?"

"The question on page two about the percentage of minority employment in the project."

"Ah, a very important consideration these days, as I'm sure you can appreciate."

"I can't answer it."

"You can't?"

"You see, there really isn't any project yet, not in the sense of an enterprise that employs people. The only thing that exists of *Old Habits* right now is a set of scripts."

"And who wrote them?"

"I did."

"By yourself?"

"Yes."

"No outside help?"

"None."

"A researcher?"

"I did it all myself."

"Have you put together a demo reel for underwriters, any other kind of preproduction like that?"

"I'm afraid not. No tape has been shot, nothing else has been done. You see before you the entire staff of *Old Habits* as it's presently constituted."

"Hmmm."

"So you understand my hesitation."

"Indeed."

"What do I do, then? What should I put down for percentage of minority employment?"

"Zero."

"Zero?"

"I can't think what else."

"But that's misleading."

"How so?"

"Because the percentage won't *be* zero once some money comes in and we start shooting. That's what I need to make clear on the form. Once we start shooting there'll be all kinds of minorities involved—on the production staff, the technical side, promotion, you name it."

"Not yet, though."

"No, not yet."

"Then I don't see what we can do."

"How about this? Give me back the form and I'll put an asterisk in the space for the answer and then write a note at the bottom of the page, explaining the situation."

"There's no room at the bottom of the page."

"On the back, then."

"No room there, either."

"Then give me a blank sheet of paper."

"Mr. Burns."

"I'll write down what I just told you, and you can staple the sheet to the form. Would that be all right?"

"I don't think so."

"Why not?"

"We just don't do that kind of thing around here."

"What kind of thing? Tell the truth?"

"Go into all that detail. Turn out little essay papers."

"Do you think you could make an exception?"

"We don't do that, either."

"Why not?"

"Because people are always wanting to add something to their applications, that's why. They always want to make that one extra pitch to help their projects along, put them in a better light than all the rest. It's an understandable desire, of course, but we discourage it because it wastes our time. That's why we came up with the form in the first place, to streamline the procedure and give everyone the same amount of space to make their appeal."

"But if you let zero stand as the answer to that question, it'll give the wrong impression."

"How can the truth be the wrong impression? I'm sorry, Mr. Burns, but I don't know what else to say. If you'd just let me have the pen …"

"You know what you've done, don't you?"

"What have I done?"

"Not you, CPB. CPB has constructed a perfect catch-22. I can't get the money unless I hire minorities, but I can't hire minorities unless I get some money, because without the money there's nothing to hire them *for*."

"You seem fixated on this."

"Fixated?"

"It's one question among, what, maybe three or four dozen on the application?"

"But you said yourself how important it is."

"All the more reason to answer truthfully. We wouldn't want to be caught fibbing on something like minority employment."

"Let me make another suggestion. Give me back the form and I'll answer the question in the eentsy-weentsiest letters I can manage. That way I can get *my* response into *your* space and everyone will be happy."

"May I give you some advice, Mr. Burns?"

"How about some cooperation?"

"You're just going to have to forget the whole business. Even if there were a place on the form to write your little essay—"

"Stop calling it a little essay."

"—it wouldn't wash. It would be like you were making excuses. People on the board would get the idea you had something to hide."

"I've got something to *reveal*."

"And the board, frankly, would not look kindly on something like that."

"You're the one who's making me hide, you twit!"

"I'll tell you what I'll do—just going ahead and ignoring that remark, assuming you're under a great deal of stress, not thinking clearly, et cetera, et cetera. What I'll do is discuss the matter with a few of the people around here and see what they say. Who knows, some of them might even agree with the point you're making, although I certainly can't promise anything. But I assure you I'll see to it that your views get a hearing, and perhaps someday we'll end up redesigning the application with your particular input in mind. Stranger things have happened, I suppose. How does that sound?"

"Irrelevant."

"I'm sorry you feel that way."

"I'm sorry I called you a twit."

"Well, thank you. I appreciate that."

"I shouldn't have done it."

"Apology accepted."

"You were right—stress, unclear thinking, all that."

"Enough said."

"But isn't there anything I can do about this, anything at all?"

"There really isn't. And now, if you'll excuse me, I have another appointment."

"Maybe I could write a letter."

"I'm sure your proposal will get a fair review, Mr. Burns."

"Do you have a bulletin board? I could post a notice."

"One last thing, if you don't mind?"

"Yes?"

"The pen, please."

APRIL 1984

NEW YORK

I LIKE KAREN. All I know of her is her voice, but there is unmistakable humanity to it; she seems to talk rather than recite, and when she finishes she seems to listen rather than simply remain silent. But since she is an administrative assistant or executive secretary or some other PBS euphemism for vassal, she speaks to me only as an intermediary, a mouthpiece for others. All she can do with her humanity is squeeze a few drops of it between the lines. She is doing her best today, on what is approximately the first anniversary of my lunch with her boss at Tavern on the Green:

"But when I called this morning, you told me to call back at two."

"I know, Mr. Burns."

"It's two now."

"But this meeting just came up."

"When will it be over?"

"That's hard to say. But she left a message for you and told me—"

"I don't want a message. I want her."

"I wish you could talk to her, honest I do, but it's just not possible right now."

"What if I call back in an hour? An hour and a half?"

"As soon as the meeting's over, she has an appointment out of the building."

"What a surprise."

"I'm afraid this is just a really hectic day around here."

"Tomorrow?"

"Hard to say."

"You win. Read the message."

"I have it right here. She said to tell you she heard from CPB the other day and they decided to pass on *Old Habits*."

"Another surprise."

"I'm really sorry."

"The guy you set me up with over there was a personal friend of yours, remember? He was going to love *Old Habits*."

"He did. He told me."

"Then what happened?"

"He doesn't have a vote. He's not on the board."

Silent head-shaking on my end of the phone. A little teeth-gnashing, too—incisors and canines, mostly.

"Speaking of people who love your show and don't have a vote, Mr. Burns."

"Yes?"

"Well, I consider myself at the top of the list. I think *Old Habits* is wonderful."

"You read it?"

"Sure did. I wasn't supposed to. I mean, I didn't have to, but I wanted to know what everybody was talking about, so I took the scripts home one night and went through them, and I really enjoyed them. I learned a lot, too."

"Well, thank you."

"It's just such fascinating material, and the way you presented it was so … so … I hope you find a way to get produced, that's all."

"Apparently CPB doesn't share your feelings."

"She gets into that a little in the message. Let's see here. Her sources on the board told her it was a close vote but ultimately they decided *Old Habits* just wasn't up their alley."

"Nice of them to be so specific."

"They don't usually go into much detail over there. It can be hard to read them."

"What do I do now? Is that in the message?"

"I'm getting to that. She said to tell you there aren't really any more sources of government money. Things are even tighter than usual as far as that's concerned."

"So?"

"So you head for Pittsburgh, and you and the WQED people start working on the private money."

"I thought that was stage three."

"Oh, you should forget all that. I know what she told you, but things hardly ever work out that neatly around here. We take the money wherever we can get it."

"Now they tell me."

"There's one person in particular you need to talk to at WQED, the absolute ace of their fundraising staff. She said she sent him the *Old Habits* scripts a few weeks ago and he likes them so much he already has some ideas. He's waiting to hear from you. I'll give you his name and direct number."

"Okay."

"She said this guy is one of a kind. You're going to love him to pieces."

May 1984

Pittsburgh

SO HERE WE ARE IN THE STEEL CITY, my final wife and me, renting a house that is twenty minutes from my childhood home, where I sat glued to the television and determined the path of my career. I never expected to be back. I wonder what it means, what psychic reverberations I will feel about an unintended homecoming at the midpoint of my life. None, I suspect; I have returned neither to gloat nor to lick wounds, simply to follow the path along a different fork.

And I am fifteen minutes from the gym where I tried out my first dance steps, half an hour from the television station to which I first applied for a job, and almost an hour from WQED, one of the most hideous examples of poured-concrete architecture I have ever seen. It makes CPB headquarters in Washington feel positively welcoming.

From the outside the building resembles a bomb shelter. Inside it appears to shelter the privileged classes only. The walls are hung with expensive art, the floors covered with rich carpeting. The furniture could easily be on loan from the robber baron mansions just up the avenue in the city's Oakland section. Lighting is recessed; voices in the corridors buzz quietly with purpose. The third-floor conference room, in which the station's ace fundraiser and I have our first meeting, is a study in walnut with accents of silver and chrome.

"I don't believe it."

"You're in Pittsburgh now, compadre. We get things done here."

"This is wonderful."

"Par for the course, that's all, par for the course."

"For you, maybe. But I was beginning to lose hope."

"Not gonna get sappy on me, are you?"

"I'll do my best."

"No offense to our friends in Washington, but we're a leaner operation here. Not so many layers. We know how to cut through things."

"I'm a believer."

"Besides, *Old Habits* is a hell of a project. I'd take it as a personal defeat if I couldn't come up with the dough for it."

"Tell me more."

"There's not a whole lot more *to* tell, not yet, anyhow. The figure we kicked around was twenty-five percent, but I know the American Cancer Society. I've dealt with them on other shows. They don't like to admit it, but they've got more money than they know what to do with. I think I can jack them up some."

"How much?"

"Half, maybe."

"Are you serious?"

"That may be a bit much, but I'd like to see them pony up at least a third. I think we're in the ballpark there."

"And the rest of it?"

"Nothing to worry about, believe me. Once the first underwriter signs on, you almost always get a bandwagon effect. You start out and nobody wants to commit themselves. Then somebody does and it's like a seal of approval. The others say, 'If it's good enough for the American Cancer Society, it's good enough for us.' Then stand back, you've got a stampede on your hands."

"I guess the thing that surprises me is—well, when you first mentioned the American Cancer Society, I told you I thought there were parts of the scripts they might have a problem with."

"Who said they don't?"

"What?"

"You were right. Some of the things you wrote drove them straight up the wall."

"I don't understand."

"They want a few changes. Nothing major, really, just a little bit here and a little bit there."

"Wait a minute, wait a minute. Changes?"

"That's right."

"You didn't say anything about changes."

"I'm saying now. It's understood. I mean, it's the way things work. Think of it like submitting a book to a publisher. They don't put it out just as is. They have an editor go over the manuscript and smooth it into tip-top shape. It's the same thing here."

"There's a difference between an editor and a censor."

"Censor? Who the hell said anything about a censor?"

"What are the changes?"

"I told you, it's no big deal. What're you getting so hot and bothered about? Somebody hands over the big bucks for a television show, they want a little input. It's perfectly natural. S.O.P. In fact, as far as these things go sometimes, you're getting off easy."

"I am?"

"There are four scripts altogether, right?"

"Right."

"Only one of them is a deal-breaker, and the truth of the matter is that what they want you to do in that one isn't even really a rewrite. It won't take any time at all."

"What will it take?"

"A few dabs of white-out."

"They want me to omit something?"

"Well, let's say closer to half a bottle."

"Which script?"

"Smoking."

"Which part?"

"Jamestown."

"*Jamestown?*"

"The stuff about how if it hadn't been for tobacco, the Brits might've gotten bored with the New World and pulled up stakes."

"You've got to be kidding."

"Do I look like I'm kidding?"

"I *can't* get rid of Jamestown."

"You want *Old Habits* to go back on the scrap heap?"

"Doing a history of tobacco without mentioning what happened at Jamestown would be like doing a history of the Revolutionary War and not mentioning the Boston Tea Party. It would be like doing the Civil War and not mentioning slavery. You can't tell a story about effects and leave out the causes."

"One cause. All they want you to do is leave out one cause."

"I can't rewrite history."

"They don't want you to rewrite history. Nobody's asking you to write anything that isn't true. They're only saying—"

"They're saying they find the truth inconvenient. I'm sorry that's the way they feel, but there's nothing I can do about it."

"Look, bottom line. The American Cancer Society has no intention of funding a TV show that says tobacco is what made America great."

"That's not what the show says."

"It's what the Society hears."

"If the Public Broadcasting Service aired a program about the history of tobacco and didn't refer to Jamestown, every major reviewer in this country would tear the show apart. When they figured out *why* nothing was said about Jamestown, you'd have a first-class scandal on your hands."

"Oh, bullshit."

"It would be the PBS equivalent of payola."

"It's give-and-take, that's all, just the normal process of negotiation on this kind of thing."

"The reality of Jamestown isn't mine to negotiate. Neither is the importance of it."

"Case closed? That's final?"

"Final."

"Well … I guess it had to happen sooner or later."

"What?"

"Seven years I've been in this business, five of them at WQED. I've put together dozens of projects, worked with hundreds of people, shows that've been seen all over the world. Some award-winners, too. Peabody, Columbia-DuPont, Emmy."

"And?"

"You're my first prima donna."

There is a bar a few blocks from WQED, and I stop in for a drink. A double. Straight up. It works. My frustration deepens and my tongue loosens and the combination works me into a sanctimonious froth. I call my wife and pull the safety. People at PBS are morons, I tell her. They're the biggest collection of hypocrites and frauds ever gathered under the logo of a single American corporation. They raise double-dealing to a craft, incompetence to an art. No wonder the government doesn't give the sons of bitches any money. No wonder most viewers prefer commercial television, where the ruling classes might be schlockmeisters but are at least honest about meistering their schlock. The bozos at PBS are con men and poseurs and worse. They have the manners of linebackers and the trustworthiness of streetwalkers and the perceptiveness of judges for the Miss America Pageant. They have treated me like dirt. They have insulted me and ignored me and lied to me. I am disheartened and dismayed, disgusted and discombobulated, enraged and outraged. I want nothing more to do with such people. Right now all I want is to head to Wisconsin and track down my old news director and learn how to make those goddamn fishing lures, and I don't care how many important people I associate with or how many unimportant people see me or whether I make a penny or a dime or a dollar for my efforts or even go into hock!

At which point I stop long enough to come up for air and ask my wife what *she* did today.

Went to the doctor, she says sweetly. We will have another mouth to feed in seven months.

JUNE 1984–MARCH 1985

PITTSBURGH

THE DAYS SLOG BY. Summer does a slow dissolve through fall and turns gradually to winter. Winter is even more reluctant in yielding to spring.

As the seasons turn, the ace fundraiser and I communicate in person, on the phone, and by answering machine.

BEEP!

"Eric, it's Dan. Just heard from our friends at 3-M and it's a big N-O. The show's a little too anti-tobacco for them. It so happens they make some kind of tiny plastic doodad that's one of the components in cigarette filters, and they don't want to rile their clients. I had no idea. Otherwise, I think they would have jumped right in."

BEEP!

"Dan here, Eric. The American Lung Association says they're not interested. By and large, they seemed to feel like the Cancer Society, that you didn't come down hard enough on tobacco. But it wasn't Jamestown that bugged them so much as that Lucy Page Gaston. The one who taught the kids to run up to adults on the street and snatch the cigarettes right out of their mouths. I got the feeling that old Ms. Gaston is kind of a folk hero at the Lung Association, and they didn't take kindly to the fact that you called her the Carry Nation of the anti-tobacco crowd."

"Psychedelic?"

"That's what the man said."

"I can't remember the last time I even heard the word."

"He said he got the feeling that the person who wrote the scripts was some kind of hippie left over from the sixties."

"I wasn't even a hippie *in* the sixties."

"I tried to explain to him. I said you weren't advocating what the Indians did, you were just telling the story. There used to be all these strange weeds growing in North America, and the Indians would smoke them and get a buzz on and start seeing visions. They thought the visions were their gods. That made locoweed like communion wafers for them. I told him that."

"What did he say?"

"He didn't want to hear it. He said he's got kids in school and wouldn't stand for that kind of thing being taught in the classroom. Therefore, no way in the world was he gonna allow his precious company to kick in the money to say it on the tube."

"How could he miss the point like that?"

"I think he's a Methodist."

BEEP!

"Eric, bad news on Cassady. He's a real teetotaler, like I told you, and what set him off was where you said the Revolutionary War was pretty much mapped out in the taverns of colonial America. You know, you said the Boston Tea Party was planned in a tavern and the minutemen always got together in a tavern and the same with Sam Adams and Hancock and the rest of those guys. Cassady told me he didn't believe any of it, and I had to tell him it sounded pretty farfetched to me, too. Are you sure that's the way things went down? Maybe you should double-check."

BEEP!

"Christ, I'm not having much luck reaching you these days. You out looking for a new job? I gotta tell you, the way things are going around here, I couldn't really blame you. Anyhow, the U.S. Steel position, as near as I can decipher it through the bullshit, is that the tobacco industry's down on its luck these days, so why kick 'em. The steel industry's not exactly breaking records either, as you know, so I think they're just naturally simpatico. A couple of fallen giants, the glory days long behind them. Does that compute?"

"I did not call the founder of the Woman's Christian Temperance Union a dyke!"

"You sure as hell implied it."

"I didn't do that, either."

"Eric, I read the scripts. Don't hand me a line like that."

"I pointed out a few facts about the way the woman lived, that's all."

"Reporters. I love the way you guys talk, I swear."

"What?"

"'I didn't call the man a thief, Your Honor. I only said he took a vast quantity of merchandise that didn't belong to him, that's all.' 'I didn't say he was a drug addict, sir. I just mentioned the fact that he injects illegal substances into his veins four or five times a day.' Reporterspeak. Geez."

"What bothered them? Specifically."

"You said the lady—what's her name?"

"Frances Willard."

"You said Frances Willard had a male nickname."

"She did. Frank."

"You said she wrote mushy letters to women telling them how much she loved them and missed them and longed for their tender touch."

"She did."

"You said she never got married."

"She didn't."

"You said she wore a coat and tie sometimes."

"I had to. Some of the pics we'll be using show her dressed like that."

"You said—"

"Never mind, I get the point."

"But I'll tell you what's ironic. I don't think any of that would bother them under normal circumstances. The problem is they've got a couple lawsuits pending against them these days and they've got to be real careful."

"For what?"

"Sex discrimination."

BEEP!

"Just got word from Gulf, Eric. Department of no surprise, I'm afraid. They didn't really give me a reason, but if I had to guess I'd say what turns them off is how much time you spend on all the weirdos who raised holy hell about smoking and drinking over the years. These corporate types aren't really into that kind of thing. They think what happens is that if you mention the weirdos often enough you give people ideas. Like if the price of gasoline gets too high, maybe the good citizens will dig out their hatchets and start chopping up the pumps. Gulf just likes to keep a low profile about things like that."

"What do you mean, antireligious?"

"I'm just the messenger, remember?"

"What does *he* mean, antireligious?"

"He means that all those groups who objected to booze were fundamentalists of one sort or another, weren't they?"

"I suppose."

"So when you point out how daffy some of their methods were, it plays like you're making fun of the good, God-fearing folk of the world."

"*That's* daffy."

"The point is that Alcoa has no intention of getting involved in anything that might offend pious, churchgoing Americans who wrap their leftovers in aluminum foil."

"What about Atlantic Richfield?"

"I didn't tell you? They're not returning my calls anymore."

"It's just that there's too much anti-booze material to suit them."

"But pro-booze won."

"I know."

"Prohibition was repealed and breweries and distilleries have been thriving ever since. There aren't even any serious threats anymore. The WCTU still exists, but it's a joke."

"They're a liquor industry trade council, Eric. What do you expect? They're thinking, 'Why should we pitch in to remind people of the days when our beloved product was public enemy number one?' I'll be perfectly candid with you, I don't blame them a bit."

BEEP!

"… I mean it, I just about fell off my chair. It totally blew my mind. It's the first time since I started working on *Old Habits* that I've talked to someone who didn't have some kind of complaint about something. In fact, they think the whole series is great. Informative, entertaining, just the kind of thing they'd like to see more of on PBS. Not to mention the kind of series they'd like to put their TV dollars into. If they *had* any TV dollars, that is. Unfortunately, one of their divisions is going broke, and another just reported the worst fourth quarter in its history, and they're planning layoffs at both their plants in Ohio, and …"

BEEP!

"Hey, what the hell's going on? This is getting crazy. It's not just that you're never around, it's that you don't even return my calls when you *do* get home. Are you getting these messages? Do you have any idea what I'm going through on this end, how I'm still giving it the old college try? Do you care? Anyhow, a red-letter day today. Two—count 'em, one, two—rejections. The pharmaceutical folks will really drive you up a wall. Wait till I tell you what they said. They said ..."

BEEP!

"Screw it. I'm not going to put up with this anymore. *Old Habits* is your baby. If you want to know what happened, *you* call *me!*"
    CLICK!

WE ARE PACKING.

My wife wraps cups and saucers in sheets of tissue paper and wedges them gently into a small box. I remove books from their shelves, stack them in a larger box, and throw in crumpled sheets of newspaper to take up the remaining space. We seal the boxes with silver duct tape and label them with Magic Markers. Then we stack them in the dining room, three piles so far, each reaching to within a foot or so of the ceiling.

Our son watches from his stroller. He has tossed one leg over the side and is slapping his belly with a plastic bracelet. He seems mildly annoyed at his parents' strange activity, but it is hard to tell at this age. He might be preparing to relieve himself; he might be wondering why his belly stings.

The phone rings. I have nothing more to say. I let the answering machine pick up and simply listen as I close another box.

BEEP!

"Hi, Eric. This is Karen calling from PBS in Washington. The boss wanted me to get in touch with you and tell you how sorry she is she hasn't gotten back before this, but it's been just one thing after another here and we've barely had a chance to catch our breath. Honest. Anyhow, she wanted you to know how much she thinks of you and how much she still believes in *Old Habits*. But she knows how hard it's been for you, and so she respects your decision and wishes you all the best. She says she's really enjoyed working with you and hopes she'll have the chance to do it again on some other project in the future. I second that, by the way. *Old Habits* deserved a better fate. If I ever find myself with a million bucks or so to spare …

"So, best of luck. Take care, now. Oh, and when you figure out what you're going to do next, please let us know. Bye-bye."

1985–1987 Commentator, Reporter,

Video Reviewer

Entertainment Tonight, Hollywood

JUNE 1985

HOLLYWOOD

"WE'RE A NEWS SHOW," says this man who does not want to be misunderstood, "and it drives me batty that more people don't get it. Gracious." He sits across a small table from me, rips open a packet of artificial sweetener, and shakes it into his iced tea. Then he crumples the packet in his fist and mashes it into an unused ashtray. "*NBC Nightly News* is a news show, the *CBS Evening News* is a news show, *ABC World News Tonight*—is that what they call it now?"

I tell him it is.

"That's a news show, too. And so are we. Period, exclamation point, end of discussion." He stirs his iced tea with a long spoon, banging it against the inside of the glass, and takes his first sip. "The only difference," he says, grimacing, "is that those programs cover the world of politics and disaster. We cover the world of show business and entertainment. Other than that ..." He trails off in such a way that the conclusion is inescapable; no other distinctions are to be made.

We are sitting in the restaurant on the lot of Paramount Studios, surrounded by people who appear on shows that are *not* like the news programs of the three major networks. A few tables ahead of us, for example, is a young woman from the situation comedy *Family Ties*. At the table to her left is one of the habitués of the bar on *Cheers*. Behind him is the woman from the Fifth Dimension who hosts a rock-and-roll dance show called *Solid Gold*. As my lunch partner and I walked by on the way to our table, we heard her and two female companions discussing the chord structure of a song called "Boogie Wonderland."

"Same deadline pressure," my partner continues, "same high standards." He takes another sip of iced tea, grimaces again, and dumps in a second packet of artificial sweetener. Mashes this one too. "But people still get confused about us. Ah me." He clangs the spoon around the glass some more, slaps it down on the table. The incongruity of the man is striking: the perceived misunderstandings about the show he oversees seem to have left him permanently indignant, yet his expletives could not be more genteel. He is an effete firebrand. "We're as hungry for the scoop as they are, we're as careful with the facts. Do you know about our research department?"

"No."

"It's absolutely top-of-the-line. The head of the department's a woman with a masters in library science, and she's got a staff of ten people. Nothing gets on the air until they go over every script and dot every *i* and cross every *t*. They check the facts, the dates, the spellings of names for supers. If there's any doubt about something, we insist on a second source for absolute verification. And then we've got lawyers who look at the more sensitive material to make sure there's no chance anyone can take us to court. I tell you, the network news doesn't have a thing on us." He picks up his spoon, whacks it on the table a few times, and flicks it past the ashtray into a salt shaker; a few drops of iced tea splatter onto a bread plate. "They could learn from what we do." He twists the large ruby ring on his finger.

I take a sip of my own iced tea.

"That's why we're so open to the idea of commentary," he says. "As you're well aware, the other shows have a long tradition of it. Sevareid and Moyers on CBS, Reasoner and Howard K. Smith way back when on ABC, and now Chancellor's started doing it on your old show. And in fact, we've tried it ourselves. It hasn't worked out the way we hoped it would, but we're not discouraged. We want to give it another go."

I ask him why.

"Because when viewers see someone doing commentary, it tells them right up front that the show's serious, a real news program. It's a sign of substance, kind of a badge of honor."

We are interrupted by the young woman from *Family Ties*. My lunch partner introduces us and asks whether she agrees that *Entertainment Tonight* is a news show in the truest sense of the term and would more readily be perceived as such with the addition of someone offering astute observations on the pertinent events of the day. She says, "Yeah, you betcha." She looks about fifteen. She is wearing tight pink shorts and a sequined T-shirt bearing the face of a cartoon rabbit.

Then she and my tablemate talk about a scene in a recent episode of *Family Ties* that both found extraordinarily heart-wrenching for a situation comedy: a death or illness or something.

"We like to do that kind of thing once in a while," the young woman says.

"And you do it so well."

"People always respond."

"Do they?"

"I think the first time that show ran was in—oh, February or March. We got more mail on it than any show the whole year."

"I'm not surprised."

"We've got some other scripts just like it in the works for this season. Same kind of emotional pull."

"Should be great."

"Keep your fingers crossed."

"Well, I know you've got to run."

"Yeah," the young woman says. "Meeting coming up, then a photo shoot, and I think some newspaper interviews after that. Some summer vacation."

She shakes hands with both of us, tells me she enjoyed making my acquaintance, and bounds out of the restaurant, followed by several other boys and girls of the same apparent age and vocation.

"Sweet kid," my lunch companion says, fingering the thick gold chain at his wrist. "*E.T.* did a piece on her a few months ago, pegged to the last new show of the season. It worked out surprisingly well. She's a bright girl, good interview. Where was I?"

"Commentary establishes the fact that a show should be taken seriously."

"That's right," the man says, "it does. But you have to give your fellow some latitude, otherwise there's no point." He has now decided his tea is too sweet; from a saucer in the middle of the table he takes half a lemon in a piece of cheesecloth and wrings its neck over his glass. "I remember a few days ago one of the network commentators criticized the way the press has been handling the hostage situation, the TWA flight in Beirut. Did you happen to see it?"

I do not watch much television news these days, some kind of psychological overreaction to my former career, no doubt; an inability to interest myself as a viewer in what I no longer care for as a participant.

"I forget exactly what he said," the man goes on, "but it was something along the lines that media coverage, including his own network's, was excessive. It was playing into the hands of the hijackers by giving them more time on center stage than they deserved, and thereby prolonging the crisis. Now, interesting situation here, interesting. Some people would say you can't let *your* commentator go on *your* air and criticize *your* operation. It doesn't play, makes you look bad or at least disorganized, like the right hand doesn't know what the left is doing. Me, I say just the opposite. I say it plays superbly for the simple reason that it demonstrates to the people watching that the show is big enough to question itself. And I think that's how everybody reacts at home. They feel like they can trust a show that isn't afraid to admit it might not be perfect. Do you know what it reminds me of?"

"What?"

"You go to a restaurant, right? The waitress tells you what the specials are, then says forget it, most of them are lousy tonight, order off the regular menu. You appreciate that kind of honesty. You think the gal's got your best interests at heart, not her company's. You make up your mind right then and there that you're coming back to this place and next time you're bringing your friends."

I cannot say what makes me so ill at ease; the man's assurances are either too much or too little, and I cannot decide which. I say, "So you've tried commentary before."

"A couple times. But the last person we had was a problem. He didn't have any real experience at that kind of thing. In fact, he was an actor."

"An actor?"

"Great pipes, a distinguished look—he was an older man with a nice touch of gray at the temples. Central casting stuff. He used to do commercials, but I doubt anyone recognized him from those by the time he came to work for us. Gave the impression of being really thoughtful, but it was just smoke and mirrors. All he could do was read the prompter. One of the people on our staff wrote his pieces for him. I always felt that took a little of the edge off."

I express agreement.

"But you," the man says. "You ought to be just the ticket. For one thing—now, I don't want you to take this wrong."

"What?"

"Well, you're not particularly flashy. And I don't just mean the way you dress. It's the feeling I get from the total package—the way you talk, carry yourself, react to things around you. The fact of the matter is, you're a little on the square side."

"I am?"

"By Hollywood standards," the man clarifies, "that's all I'm saying."

Hollywood standards. The phrase catches, sets off an inner alarm, not deafening but certainly insistent. I have lived in the movie capital of the world for four days, long enough to know about its standards that they are different from what I have known before and seem all-encompassing. Hollywood is year-round summer instead of seasons, palm trees instead of low-riding oaks and maples. It is shifting tectonic plates instead of firm ground, vanity license plates instead of random numbers and letters, books on tape instead of books on page. It is the car culture and the celebrity culture and the interweaving of the two, the celebrities gliding about in cars that could serve as luxury accommodations for a small family. The celebrities specialize in the acquisition and display of plenty. Their kids have more nannies than blood relatives, their parties more valet parkers than guests, their cosmetic surgeons a celebrity status of their own, with license plates like FACE DR or I CUT U. Hollywood is experimental cuisine and tried-and-true plots. It is conspicuous consumption and subtle corporate maneuvering. Physical fitness as religion, religion as cult. Open shirts in the workplace and jeweled executives. By these standards I am not a little square. I am an inanimate object.

"But the way I see it, that's a plus. It'll be good for the show. We've already got all the pizzazz we need. What you can do is give us some class. You'll be our version of John Chancellor, sitting up there in your ivory tower and commenting on whatever strikes your fancy on a particular day. You even look the part, you've got the same kind of glasses. Sort of. But let me make a distinction. As good as Chancellor and the rest of them are, you can't really take the same approach for us. *Entertainment Tonight* is a news show, all right, but we deal with different subject matter than the others. That means we need a different style. Same honesty and integrity and smarts, just a lighter touch."

Before I can respond, the restaurant is invaded by *Solid Gold* dancers. They storm the place like a conquering army, prancing down the aisles and circling tables, kicking up their legs and swiveling their hips as if still on stage, still charged with keeping the beat. The restaurant is transformed by them, energized, electricity now in the air. The female dancers wear spangly silver leotards and gold lamé shorts, the men gray sweatpants with shorts on the outside. Most have towels over their shoulders, hair that is perfectly out of place, and smiles as vacant as the Mojave Desert.

The dancers wave to some of the people at the tables, pat others on the back, keep prancing. Their destination may be the few empty tables in the rear, or they may simply be taking a few victory laps. They are humming and whistling, and the diners, eager to be part of the show, join in like a chorus. At the table next to me, a young man starts rapping with his knife and fork, picking up the tempo.

I watch my companion. After several seconds of erratic flitting, his eyes have settled on the derriere of a woman who stopped at our table to kiss his forehead, then sashayed away, her cheeks bobbing and squishing together, straining at the confines of fabric, ripe and ready to burst.

"Ever seen the show? Forget the music," he says, eyes still following the bouncing buttocks. "It's worth tuning in just to see the bodies. Incredible things. There must be some kind of machine shop somewhere that turns them out, this assembly line where the tolerances are so fine you couldn't create a flaw if you wanted to. Merciful heavens." He takes a sip of iced tea and almost bites through the glass. "Now then, where were we?"

In very different places, where we are likely to remain. The man with whom I am having lunch is in a realm of fantasy that passes in Hollywood for the workaday world. I am about to move to a seat in the front row of yet another arena, to take my notebook to yet another kind of show. Professional vaudeville this time, not the amateurs; real singers and dancers and comics.

I should be analytical about it. I know that. A career move of this importance, in so unforeseen a direction, requires careful thought engaged in at an unhurried pace. But I am moving quickly, my mind racing. I try to start an inner dialogue about relevance and topicality and the ultimate goals of electronic communication; no one answers. I try to get Freudian again, theorize about the results of childhood mistreatment on adult choices, but at this stage of my life I find that my primary consideration is change. For its own sake. If it is different it is positive, and I want it. Need it. A cleansing of the system, a purging of the effects of recent experience. *Nightly News* might be a classier show than *Entertainment Tonight*, but NBC never gave me a chance to express an opinion on the air. PBS might be a more august organization than Paramount, but you couldn't prove it by me. Besides, I never shot a reel of tape or made any money, beyond the initial grant. As I close within two months of my fortieth birthday and my son approaches his first, the lure of a regular paycheck is stronger than ever, a banquet to a man who has spent two years on crumbs. It is an understandable impulse, surely, perhaps even a commendable one, but the results are just as surely inevitable.

Land sakes alive.

AUGUST 1985

HOLLYWOOD

THE PARAMOUNT LOT is a small town in large disorder. It grew without design or discipline: bungalows next to office buildings, sound stages next to storage areas, trailers next to tool sheds. Here a wardrobe department, there a company store; here a scene dock, there film junking—but nowhere a clue to the sense of it all. The structures are stucco and steel, brick and wood, concrete and corrugated tin. The largest of them are the size of airplane hangars, the smallest could be housing for Saint Bernards.

The lot covers fifty-five acres, and pavement covers the lot. Streets dart and meander, loop and crisscross. They cut sharp angles around buildings and then make random turns and double back on themselves, searching for a destination rather than leading to one. There are tiny swatches of grass on the lot, but not many, and they appear unexpectedly: around the bend from the Marx Brothers Building, on the west side of the Ernst Lubitsch Building, on the east side of Marlene Dietrich. People call them pocket parks, and they have small benches that no one ever sits on.

Hollywood is supposed to be a laid-back place, but the Paramount lot, like those of the other studios, has an unceasing energy to it. Step inside the Melrose gate and you feel a charge to the air. Look around: someone is running or walking fast or pumping a bicycle in tenth gear. Put your ear to a wall and you will hear something humming within; put it to the ground and you will sense vibration, as if a distant locomotive had begun to rumble your way. The lot never sleeps, never takes stock of itself, never tidies up. The energy is that of a boom town, which is what the Paramount lot is, having been erected three-quarters of a century ago by men who discovered that there was gold in celluloid and the biggest shares would go to those who set up shop, however sloppily, first.

As I pull up to the security gate this morning, I am thinking about the recent wedding of Sean Penn and Madonna. My guess is that in New York, John Chancellor's thoughts are on the recent meeting between Bishop Tutu and P. W. Botha. Just a couple of guys doing our jobs, John and I: considering the data, beginning to shape our responses.

The guard checks the parking sticker on the back of my rearview mirror and waves me onto the lot, where I am immediately stalled behind the day's first tramload of tourists. The guide is pointing to Sound Stage 29, which used to be the property of RKO, and where Fred Astaire and Ginger Rogers made such movies as *Top Hat* and *The Gay Divorcee*. I roll down my window, flick off the air-conditioner, tune in to the spiel. The guide is telling the tourists to imagine what it must have been like in old 29: Astaire's effortless grace and Rogers's whirling beauty, the enchanted melodies of Cole Porter, the whole aura of a bygone time so thoroughly romanticized by now that it has become the perfect symbol of modern longing.

Meanwhile, the tourists are looking at this huge gray wall with the number 29 stenciled on it and water stains running down the side from a rusted gutter that hangs loose at one end. Later on the tour, they will be told about Sound Stage 7 and *Lady Sings the Blues*, Sound Stage 3 and *Marathon Man*, Sound Stage 17 and *Sunset Boulevard*. More walls, more stains. They will hear tales of W. C. Fields and Gary Cooper and Alfred Hitchcock, and will confront piles of scrap lumber and stacks of old flats and rows of Porta-Johns that have an oddly permanent look to them.

There is much to envision on the Paramount lot, but little to see.

I swing my car around the tourists and, a block later, turn down Avenue E toward a large concavity in the pavement known as B-tank. Every so often a movie script calls for a boat to be caught in a storm or an airplane downed at sea, and B-tank literally rises to the occasion. Thousands of gallons of water are pumped into it to simulate an ocean or lake or river. A plywood version of the troubled craft is built in the scene shop, then taken apart and reassembled in the tank, where the water is churned into huge waves by fans placed along the perimeter every ten or fifteen feet. Reduced to the frame of a camera's viewfinder, the tank looks like the Atlantic Ocean at a hurricane's peak of fury.

Behind the tank is a four-story canvas flat on which a sky has been painted. If the script calls for a sunny day, the flat gets an extra coat of blue and a whitening of the clouds; if a grimmer setting is required, the flat is accented in gray and black. Today, though, nothing is being shot. The flat is sunny and the tank dry, and my assigned parking place is a few feet in front of a low-hanging cumulus.

Specifically, what I am thinking is that Madonna seems more of a self-promoter than an accomplished singer and Penn more of an enfant terrible than a gifted actor. But those thoughts alone do not a commentary make; I wonder what conclusions Chancellor is coming to about the bishop's criticism of P.W.'s racial policies.

I get out of my car and start walking in the direction of craft services, where I make a right and fall in behind a second tram of tourists.

"... served as the backdrop for the high school in *The Brady Bunch*."

"... where they made the Red Sea part for *The Ten Commandments*."

"... those fabulous costumes Edith Head designed for ..."

Tourist tram number two turns right at the Mae West Building, and our paths diverge.

I ask myself why it was that when Penn and Madonna got married this weekend, the press paid as much attention to the event as it would have if the couple had been heads of state. What does this say about the influence of celebrity news on regular news? What does it say about broader societal values?

I yank open the back door of West, climb the stairs, and open another door on a small second-floor landing. Passing the tape library, I start down a narrow hallway to the newsroom.

"Hi, Eric."

The voice, warm and throaty, comes from behind. I stop, turn, and see her chugging my way, legs pounding the carpet as if driven by pistons. I cannot help smiling. She is full of high spirits and kind thoughts and purposes that will not be clear to me if I work for this program a hundred years. She is, in a nutshell, the embodiment of *Entertainment Tonight*, the essence of all that the show stands for rendered in a single human form.

The form is not that of the female anchor, Mary Hart, who has been known to express occasional doubts about the tastefulness of some of the show's reports. The form is not the male anchor, Robb Weller, who from time to time expresses doubts about the show's entire reason for being. It is not the star reporter, Leeza Gibbons, whose craving for the company of celebrities will at intervals wane. It is not the movie reviewer, Leonard Maltin, whose adolescent worship of the motion picture takes on an almost professorial tone. It is not the executive producer or the senior producer or the head writer or any of dozens of other members of the staff and crew.

No, the heart and soul of American television's only entertainment news program is the reporter Jeanne Wolf, who insists on being called Jeannie even though she is several decades beyond the age at which a diminutive is appropriate.

"Hi, Jeannie."

Chug-chug-chug, and she pulls up alongside me and cuts her engine, idling. "On your way to the board?"

"Thought I'd have a look."

She says she will accompany me, and we motor the rest of the way in tandem, past the clearance department and the courier desk and into the huge open space that serves as the *Entertainment Tonight* newsroom.

The board is on the wall to our left: a large sheet of plastic, sectioned in squares. Across the top are the days of the week and along the left side are the hours of the day. In the appropriate boxes are each day's assignments, or at least as many of them as are known at a particular time. Today seems especially busy. Ralph Edwards is planning to bring *This Is Your Life* back to television as a series of summer replacement specials. Roddy McDowall is starring in a new vampire movie, *Fright Night*. There is a BTS, or behind-the-scenes shoot, on the TV series *Night Court*, and another on a movie that marks the big-screen debut of a well-known singer. Later today, auditions will be held for minor roles in a medium-budget movie, and tonight there is a movie premiere in Westwood that will attract mostly the kinds of stars who do guest shots on *Love Boat* and *Fantasy Island*. The initials "JW" are wax-penciled into both the Roddy McDowall and movie premiere boxes.

"Oooh," Jeannie says, "a doubleheader." Her smile is so wide I can see molars.

Jeannie Wolf is a true believer. When she is shipped off to the Academy Awards and stuffed into the press pen outside and told to scream, "Who did your hair?" as Elizabeth Taylor walks by, she is not demeaned by the assignment; to the contrary, she is honored. She might be Sam Donaldson screaming, "What do you think of the Walker family spy case?" as Ronald Reagan walks by. Not only does Jeannie want to know who did Elizabeth Taylor's hair, she assumes other people do too. She is delighted to be of service to those people, to hold the proxy that enables her to be inquisitive on their behalf.

And she is delighted to ask other questions of other celebrities.

To a singer: "Do you have to live the lyrics before you can sell the song?"

To a comedian: "Do you hope your humor will make the world a better place to live?"

To an athlete: "Do you believe you have a responsibility to be a role model for young people?"

To a TV actress bringing out her own line of perfume: "Where did you get the idea for the smell?"

There is no malice in this woman, no cynicism. She is without guile or duplicity. She is exactly what she seems, the same person on the job as off, a rare trait for a human being in any line of work. Jeannie Wolf is to celebrity worship what Mister Rogers is to child-rearing.

She opens her purse, extracts a small mirror, and examines herself. It is a pointless exercise; Jeannie last had a hair out of place during the Johnson administration. "Did you happen to catch any of the wedding coverage this weekend?"

"A little."

"Fantastic, don't you think?"

"Were you there?"

"Oh, don't I wish! I tried every way I could think of to wangle an invitation."

"No luck?"

"None. Zip, zilch, and zero. I couldn't even find out where they were holding the damn thing until a couple hours before it started. Unbelievable security."

"Sorry it didn't work out."

"But you know what I heard?"

"What?"

"This is unreal," she says. "Guess how many helicopters were taking aerials of the wedding."

"How many?"

"Six."

"Are you serious?"

"Isn't it amazing?"

"It sounds dangerous, that many choppers hovering over a single house."

"One of the local stations had a shot of them on the news last night. It looked like an air show. Tell you the truth, though, Eric, I'm not sure I understand all the fuss." A strange admission from Jeannie Wolf, for whom fuss creation is the summary of a day's work.

"It does seem a bit much."

"I mean, on the one hand you think it's just these two kids getting married and what's the big deal? Then you find out there were six helicopters buzzing around up there, and suddenly it seems like the Second Coming or something. Cripes sake, I wish I at least could've gone up in one of them."

"Didn't *E.T.* have one?"

"We shared with CNN, but there was only room for the pilot and a cameraman."

Six helicopters, I say to myself, and in that instant it all comes together. "That's it!"

"What?"

"You're sure about this, now? There were definitely six?"

"Positive. I told you, I saw video of them on one of the local newscasts."

"Which one?"

"KNBC, I think."

"Could we get a dub from them?"

"I don't know why not. They're the station that carries us."

"Thank you." I grab Jeannie by the waist and pull her to me and smack my lips on her cheek. "I've been trying to figure this out for a couple hours, and I couldn't get anywhere, and now I run into you and I'm deeply in your debt."

"Good heavens." She pulls back, grinning. "For what?"

"For just being you."

"Whatever are you talking about?"

But I am already gone, dashing through the newsroom to the executive producer's office to tell him what I want to do. He approves, but in retrospect I will see his lack of enthusiasm as my first clue.

"You know one of the choppers was ours," he says.

"You know that as long as I don't say anything slanderous, I'm supposed to have free rein."

"Yeah." Just "yeah" and a single nod of the head, but I can swear he wants to say more. I give him a chance; he settles for telling me to keep the piece to two minutes or less. Then his phone rings and he picks it up and dives into the conversation.

I stride back through the newsroom, down the narrow hallway, and past the tape library to graphics, which, as always, smells faintly of hallucinogenic adhesives. I explain to one of the artists what I need and how soon. He says it is a lot to ask on such short notice.

"Can you manage?"

"I'll try."

I tell him I haven't a doubt in the world.

A minute later I am at my desk in the reporters' room, the door closed behind me. I roll a sheet of paper into an IBM Selectric II and rest my chin on the roller for a few moments. My fingers twitch. I am ready to write.

VIDEO	AUDIO
EB on camera	I can't get it out of my mind. Some time has passed now, but I can still see them in my mind's eye …
shots of choppers shooting wedding	Those six helicopters from various news organizations practically bumping into one another as they tried to get shots of the Sean Penn–Madonna wedding from so far away …
aerial shots from chopper shooting wedding	that the bride and groom might as well have been Tiny Tim and Miss Vicky. Six helicopters!
EB on camera	Well, this has inspired me to come up withwhat I call the Helicopter Index of Relative News Importance, or HIRNI. It's based on the assumption that the Sean Penn–Madonna wedding was actually *worth* six helicopters.
EB moves to easel with letters HIRNI on top, takes pointer and points to card; on it is a picture of a car crash, and next to it are 23 tiny helicopter decals.	If so, an automobile accident in the middle of the night on a lonely road outside of Grand Junction, Nebraska, with no one injured and no disruption to traffic is worth twenty-three helicopters.
EB flips card; next card shows an empty government chamber with 37 helicopter decals.	A city council meeting in late summer in Akron, Ohio, with a small agenda and no quorum is worth thirty-seven helicopters.
EB flips card; next card shows Reagan behind presidential seal at podium with 50 decals.	A presidential news conference is worth the entire output of Sikorsky for a decade.

EB on camera	And so on. You get the idea. The television reports on the Sean Penn–Madonna wedding were not coverage of news but glorification of the trivial, further proof—where none is necessary—that voyeurism has replaced the public interest as a primary journalistic standard. Well, I'll stop now, lest I be as guilty of overkill in this commentary as so many others in the media were in their initial accounts of the wedding.
EB checks watch.	Besides, I'm off work in a few minutes. I'll be going home, changing clothes, watering the lawn.
Full-screen picture of EB watering lawn, 8 helicopter decals to the side	Eight helicopters. Eric Burns, *Entertainment Tonight*.

PENN-MADONNA WEDDING is my fifth commentary since becoming the John Chancellor of *Entertainment Tonight*.

It is also my last.

THE FOLLOWING WEEK

HOLLYWOOD

I HAVE GOTTEN INTO THE HABIT of communicating with my agent by listening. I don't interrupt once he begins to talk, don't occupy his rare pauses with thoughts of my own, and wouldn't even think of answering his questions, as they are rhetorical devices only, introductions to answers that he is about to provide himself. We have tried normal conversation before but found it wanting. His knowledge of the machinations of show business is too great, mine too limited; I end up playing second banana to someone who works better alone. So it is that when he calls today, I allow myself a hello and how-are-you, give him a brief update on the family, and settle back to allow his unfolding monologue to reveal my fate.

"The official story is that they've decided to go a new direction and commentary just doesn't fit in. That's what they'll tell the papers if anyone asks, might even be what they'd tell you if you decided on a confrontation. *Should* you confront them?

"No.

"How come?

"You'll put them on the spot, and employers don't like it when employees make them squirm.

"But it's crapola, plain and simple. You know it, I know it, and they know it. The way I read the situation, they actually thought they had the guts for a commentator with a mind of his own. They thought they were big enough to take it. Then they heard you rip them on the air and realized what jellyfish they really are. Said, 'Oops, who was the asshole got *this* idea?'

"I know, bunky. You don't think you ripped them at all. You poked a little good-natured fun. 'I'm watering the grass, eight helicopters.'

"But these people aren't newsies out here, Eric. They're ass kissers. They kiss other people's asses on their way up, and they expect to have their own asses kissed once they make it to the top. One way or another, there's never a day goes by without somebody bending over and somebody else puckering. You come along, you don't bend *or* pucker, they don't know what to make of it. Their first reaction is to be suspicious, like they're the hoity-toity white folks from Brentwood and you're this smooth from Watts who comes knocking on the door one day. 'Hey, lemme in. I'm cool, dudes, you can trust me.'

"Plus, you want to put it in the most basic terms, you hurt their feelings. Yeah, actually hurt their feelings. You thought they were jerks for leasing a chopper to shoot the wedding, they were all proud of themselves because they figured they were being enterprising journalists. I think, if anything, they probably thought you'd back them. Say, 'Way to go, men.' Surprised the daylights out of them when you went on the attack. They felt betrayed.

"So, does this mean you're fired?

"Only if you want to be. They're willing to let you out of your contract, but they'd rather not. They'd rather keep you. They might not want a commentator anymore, but they've still got pretensions, they'd still like to have themselves a token intellectual. What they want is for you to be a reporter, go out and suck up to the celebs. You'd be their high-end Jeannie Wolf.

"I know what you're thinking. You don't want to do it. You want to tell them to take their offer and shove it where the sun don't shine. The whole celebrity culture's a travesty to you, and the only reason you took a job with *E.T.* in the first place was so you could speak out against those kind of values—which you did with your Madonna piece, and what happens? Wham, you're out flat on the canvas, waiting for the count. And now, to make matters worse, Paramount wants to turn you, make you a double agent against your own beliefs.

"Do I know you or what?

"Question is, though: Should you do it?

"Answer: Damn straight.

"How come?

"Because your only other choice right now is NBC, and we both know that's impossible. They'd probably take you back, but you couldn't handle it. The travel, more than anything. You'd miss your wife, miss your kid, flip right out of your gourd if you had to spend a night away from home. Which, P.S., ain't as admirable as it sounds, you ask me. You ask me—and I know you didn't—you've gotten a little psycho over the years, bunky. I think what happened was, you spent so much time on the road with NBC you got spooked. Tripped out, couldn't handle it. Felt like your life was out of control. Someone mentions an out-of-town gig to you now and you react like one of those Vietnam vets when a car backfires in the night. You break out in a cold sweat. You think they're trying to get you again, whoever *they* are.

"You're asking yourself: Any charge for the psychiatric counseling?

"I'll run a tab.

"But you take the job as an *E.T.* reporter, you're not only home every night, you're home most mornings and afternoons too. Huh? you say. Mornings and afternoons? How does *that* work?

"Tell you how it works. Being an *E.T.* reporter's about the cushiest job in town. People're dying to get on that show. It ain't what the word 'reporter' means at NBC, trust me on that. Not only don't you travel, you don't do busywork. Don't do any work at all, hardly. You don't even have to show up at the office most of the time.

"Here's the drill. Let's say you've got an interview with some celebrity at ten in the morning. What you do is, you breeze into the office about nine and pick up a research packet and spend half an hour going over it. There's a bio of the celeb in it, a few articles about what a magnificent human being he is, nothing that'll strain your brain. You even get a sheet from the segment producer with suggested questions on it, in case you just had a lobotomy. Then you drive to the interview site—maybe it's a hotel suite, maybe a room at one of the studios, maybe it's on location somewhere. You get there a few minutes before ten, start rolling, you're done by ten-thirty or eleven at the latest, and that's it—you're wrapped for the day. The crew sticks around, gets the B-roll, but no reason you have to be there for that. So you meet me at Morton's for a high-visibility lunch and then head home. A matinee with the wife, some play time with the kid, after that you ease out to poolside to write the great American novel. And the sun hasn't even started to sink into the Pacific yet.

"Okay, so once in a while there's a second shoot, maybe you have to go out after dinner. Big deal. Another hour or two and you're home again. You'll get by, you'll get by.

"But the piece, what about the piece? How's it get written, how's it get edited?

"Simple. Somebody else does it. Your director. You'll work with a director every time you do a story in L.A. They're the equivalent of the field producers you had in news, except these people are DGA—Directors Guild?—and under the terms of their deal with the studios, they're the ones who write and cut the tape, not you. So they do all that and then you stop by the office the next day, like you're some kind of celebrity yourself doing a guest shot, and you lay down a voice track and the piece is done. *Finito.*

"Of course, you *could* do some writing and editing if you really wanted to, but what's the point? *E.T.* stories are all alike, strictly cookie-cutter jobs. Sound bite/movie clip/sound bite/movie clip/sound bite/movie clip/signoff. And then back to the set and the Hart dolly crosses those legs of hers and America starts drooling. Why waste your time?

"Money. You're saying to yourself: If I'm going to sell out, the price better be good. If there's one thing nobody wants to think of himself as, it's a bargain. Right, bunky? Well, no sweat on that score. I'll have to go a few rounds with the Paramount brass about precise figures, but based on how eager they are to co-opt someone with your credentials, I can promise you you'll pull in a minimum of twice what you made at NBC. Twice. Maybe even more. Let me just take a minute here to let the dollar signs sink into that thick cranium of yours. Two times as much of the long, sweet green …

"Delicious, no?

"Think you can live with it?

"Think you can live *without* it? L.A. ain't cheap, you know?

"So you'll have this job that you'll be so embarrassed about you won't even want to discuss it with the wife. 'Have a nice day today, sweetie?' 'Bug off, woman.' What can I say? But every Friday you'll cash a paycheck, and a Hollywood paycheck is a piece of paper with magical powers. It'll get you out of that tacky little Laurel Canyon rental in no time. It'll buy you all the romantic dinners at L'Orangerie the wife could ever want and all the Lego sets or trips to Disneyland the kid sets his heart on. All the books and clothes and jewelry and furniture. New car, cure for cancer, world peace— you name it. You trade your professional life for a personal life, and before you get all uppity about it, let me tell you it's what everyone with any class in this town has to do to get by. Why should you be any different?

"You're breathing heavy, lad, breathing heavy.

"Look, think of it like this. You're a man with limited options, you and almost everyone else on the face of the earth. All you can do is play the cards that were dealt you, and no one gets the whole deck. Like I said, NBC would probably take you back, that's one option. Maybe you've got a shot at an anchor job in some local market somewhere. Of course, your co-anchor'll be this twenty-year-old bimbo who was fourth runner-up in the Turnip Queen beauty contest at the shopping mall and thinks guerrilla warfare is when big monkeys fight with each other. But what the hey!

"Or you could be a reporter for *E.T.* Believe me, *E.T.*'s the best card on the table right now. Play it.

"Downside?

"No question. The work'll bore you to smithereens, but remember what I said: there ain't much of it. And if you want to look at it on a higher plane, which I'm sure you do, there's the fact that you'll be glorifying singers and actors and jocks, contributing further to the horribly distorted values of a society that pays a movie star more money for one picture than a schoolteacher gets his entire life, despite the fact that the schoolteacher provides a much more valuable service to the world at large—or whatever the hell it was you said to me that day at Chasen's. Remember? Man, you sure run off at the mouth sometimes.

"Anyhow, so what if you're a shill for the celebs? Some people are transcendentalists, some are nihilists, some are objectivists—you're a hypocrite. This is Hollywood, bunky. Hypocrisy's a recognized school of philosophy out here. They've got their own club-houses, ID cards, decoder rings, the whole schmear.

"But tell you what. You're the only one who'll *know* you're a hypocrite. That's the key. Because the rest of America eats this stuff up—all the celebrity news, who's sleeping with who, who's about to break up, who's going to star in Spielberg's next flick. You give America the skinny and they'll think you're one of them. And they think you're one of them, you know what happens? They reward you. They give you those paychecks, the magic pieces of paper. That's why I say take the job, do it for a while, save up some money. Then you sit back one day and see where you go from there.

"You don't do it, remember, someone else will. It's the old drug dealer's rationale. You don't move the product, someone else does it. You can't stop the flow, you might as well make the bucks off it. Better you than some asshole.

"Now, the nitty-gritty. *E.T.* wants a decision, and they want it fast. I told them I'd get back to them by four o'clock tomorrow. That means you've got ... twenty-seven hours, about. So think it over, talk to the wife, whoever else, and give me a call in the a.m.

"Any questions?

"Good man.

"Tomorrow, bunky.

"*Ciao.*"

SEPTEMBER 1987

WEST LOS ANGELES

I AWAKEN THIS MORNING with senses unusually alert. My alarm clock, a feeble instrument most other days, is as shrill as a siren, and the songs of the bluejays in the backyard seem not only amplified but more melodic than I have heard before. I think I recognize one of the tunes; I try to sing along.

I fix myself breakfast, and the orange juice tastes especially sweet and the eggs as fresh as if they had just been laid. I brush my teeth; never have I known toothpaste to be so minty, bracing—I could do a commercial. As I dress I am aware of the feel of fabric on every square inch of my body: linen shirt and chino slacks and thick cotton socks tucked into Cole-Haan moccasins. Each provides a distinct sensation. I am a mass of nerve endings, prickly all over.

Not all of what I detect so acutely is pleasant. I walk out of the house and over to the garage through what might be fumes from a steel mill. The tops of the Hollywood Hills are cut off by turgid gray clouds, and to the south a curtain appears to have been drawn over downtown. There is no quality to the air quality index. Sometimes I can tolerate the smog, sometimes I can't; today my eyes water and begin to itch.

I hurry into my car and back out of the driveway, and a wondrous melding takes place; the car and I become a single piece of machinery. It is as one that we change gears, take bends, and accelerate through intersections where the traffic lights are a redder red, yellower yellow, and greener green than ever before.

It is, I suppose, as Samuel Johnson might have said: When a man knows he is about to interview Molly Ringwald, it concentrates his mind wonderfully.

My route takes me south on Vermont to Hollywood Boulevard and west toward Beverly Hills. I pull up for the light at Gower and note two Japanese tourists staring at the sidewalk while a third takes a picture of them. A few paces away, an American teenager is pointing down excitedly, saying something to a friend who is also looking down. It is the beginning of the most puzzlingly popular tourist attraction in all of southern California: the Hollywood Walk of Fame.

In the late fifties, the cement slabs that made up the sidewalks of central Hollywood were chiseled away and replaced with three-foot squares of black terrazzo. Stars of coral terrazzo outlined in bronze were set inside the blocks, and inside the stars went the names of the anointed, those celebrities judged by a special committee of the Hollywood Chamber of Commerce to be most worthy of pedestrian recognition. The committee's membership has always been a secret, as have its standards. As of this day, there is a star for Edward Sedgwick but not for Paul Newman, for Billy Vera but not for Jane Fonda, for Chuck "The Rifleman" Connors but not for Clint Eastwood, for several Los Angeles disc jockeys but not for Dustin Hoffman or Robert Redford. Rin Tin Tin has a star, but King Kong does not. Fame along the movie capital footpaths is a quixotic thing.

According to a popular southern California guidebook, the Hollywood Walk of Fame functions "both as a tribute to past and present stars of the entertainment industry and as a method of injecting some permanent glamour into the area." But the glamour has not taken; as a result, the Walk's primary function is the more modest one of directing the eyes to ground level. It is no small service. Look up from W. C. Fields's star, for example, and you find a small store that sells porn magazines and dildoes to a clientele only a bail bondsman could love. Look up from Will Rogers's star and there is the garish purple facade of Frederick's of Hollywood, purveying panties both edible and crotchless. Look up from Marjorie Lord, who played the wife on *The Danny Thomas Show,* and you see a tattoo shop, floral and nautical motifs a specialty. Look up from Phil Spitalny, the leader of the all-girl orchestra, and you confront a window full of purple and gold wigs, with as many drag queens considering the merchandise as women of the anatomically correct variety.

The theaters along the Walk feature action-adventure movies. At the restaurants the utensils are plastic and the salt and pepper come in paper packets. Fast-food cups and wrappers litter the sidewalks; graffiti defaces the walls, some of it sexual in nature, the rest pertaining to Central American politics. Street people sleep on the bus benches, their earthly possessions stuffed into Thrifty Drug Store shopping bags that lean in doorways and against garbage bins. Drive past the Walk early enough in the morning and you will see one of the street people peeing on a star; by noon the urine will have caked into a meandering trail of dirty brown granules, to be scuffed away by the footsteps of passersby, scattered to the wind like the ashes of the departed. Ignoble as well as quixotic, fame along the footpaths seems a fate that a person with any sense would want to avoid.

I keep heading west, past Mann's Chinese, where more tourists are bent to the ground, trying to fit their hands and feet into the prints of Clark Gable and Marilyn Monroe and Rock Hudson and Doris Day, and speculating on the significance of near-fits. Some people kick their toes against the pavement as if to compress their feet; some pull at fingers as if to stretch their hands.

A few yards away, a vendor sells copies of Hollywood's most enduring work of fiction: maps to the stars' homes. One of the maps, I am told, reverses the positions of Melrose and Santa Monica Boulevard; another supposedly shows Carol Burnett living at a taco stand on Franklin.

I turn south on La Brea and west again on Sunset and am soon cruising down the Sunset Strip, with its elegant boutiques, fancy hotels, and restaurants known for small helpings, large prices, and discriminatory seating policies. Overlooking it are billboards for current and soon-to-be-released movies: *The Princess Bride*, a fantasy directed by Rob Reiner and written by William Goldman; *Surrender*, a romantic comedy starring Sally Field and Michael Caine; *Barfly*, a drama with Mickey Rourke and Faye Dunaway. And *The Pick-Up Artist*, a comedy featuring Molly Ringwald and Robert Downey, Jr., which I saw two nights ago at a screening for the Hollywood press.

Downey plays a girl-crazy gym teacher in a New York grade school. As the movie opens, he is practicing his come-ons in the bathroom mirror. Example: "Did anyone ever tell you that you have the face of a Botticelli and the body of a Degas?" Later, running into Ringwald on the street and giving the line a try, he gets an unexpected response. "Yeah," she says, "my tenth-grade art teacher," and then Ringwald shows Downey the Botticelli catalogue she just happens to be carrying in her arms. It is too much for both of them; they sense a higher power at work here and within a few minutes are acceding to its will in the back seat of Downey's car, pounding the shocks in a fury of copulative zeal.

But Ringwald, playing against female type, does not want a tomorrow. She refuses Downey's request for her phone number, telling him she likes her sex casual, her involvements uninvolving. She walks out of his car and, she assumes, out of his life. It is the first time the pick-up artist has ever been rejected, and his reaction is a typical scriptwriter's contrivance: Downey decides he is in love with Ringwald and vows he will track her down, phone number or not. The conquest of the fair lady's other parts having already been achieved, the man now sets his sights on her heart.

The way to win it, he soon discovers, is to help Ringwald with her scheme to amass enough money to pay off her father's gambling debts. At first she rebuffs Downey's overtures; she has bought several books on casino games and is confident she can win the money herself. But in time she changes her mind; Downey is persuasive and Ringwald reluctantly smitten, and the two of them join forces and ride off to Atlantic City, at which point a movie that has been only inept becomes preposterous. I will later read a critic who states that Ringwald bent over a blackjack table "looks about as natural as Bela Lugosi supervising a day care center." Another review will dismiss the movie as "an absolute mess," giving it one and a half stars out of a possible five. My own review allots one.

Fifteen minutes after I pass the billboard for *The Pick-Up Artist* on the Sunset Strip, I am knocking at the door of Molly Ringwald's penthouse suite in a swank hotel in West Los Angeles. A bolt slides, the knob turns. The door opens a sliver. I am carefully once-overed. The door opens wider. The eyes belong to a young woman who neither introduces herself nor makes a sign of acknowledgment; after recognizing me, she merely backs out of the way and allows me to walk past her. It is not shyness; there is, in fact, a budding vanity here, apparent in the peculiar angling of her head and a pursing of the corners of her lips. But at the present stage of her career she knows her place, and as soon as I am inside the suite she takes a chair at the dining room table, giving me a quarter-profile and remaining mute.

In the living room a warmer greeting awaits. My cameraman, soundman, and director have arrived before me. The cameraman has just finished fastening his Sony TK-76 to its tripod and is now peering through the viewfinder, mentally composing his shot. The soundman is unrolling the cords of two lavaliere microphones, one of which he places on the corner of the sofa where Molly will sit, the other on the arm of the facing wingback chair that will be my position. He plugs the cords into jacks in his recorder. The director has assigned herself to props; she removes the lamp from the end table at Molly's side of the sofa, sets it on the floor, and replaces it with a bowl of artificial flowers from the dining room table.

"Perfect," I say.

She turns to me and blows a kiss in my direction. The cameraman and soundman also note my arrival, and after saying hello, we devote a minute or two to a recent installment of company gossip: a small ritual of bonding before the rigors of another movie star interview.

But the director, preoccupied, quickly returns her attention to the bowl of flowers. She begins to spin it slowly, unable to decide whether it looks better with the fake reds in front or the fake yellows. She asks the cameraman.

He says it depends on Molly's coloring.

"Hmmm."

"Have you seen the clip reel?" I ask.

Fake reds, she decides for now, then steps back to size up her choice. "I zipped through it." She reaches into an oversized pocket in her skirt, taking out a notebook and thumbing through the pages. "Clip number one, the scene where Downey is hustling different girls on the street. Remember?"

"Too well."

"Next there's the scene where he first sees Molly in a bar, when she's being hassled by the creep her dad owes money to. Let's see, there's the first time Downey and Molly actually meet, so you could ask her about her character's first impression of him. Then there's a clip of the two of them together in her apartment, and her dad's there and he's drunk. You could ask how her character feels about her father. And the only other scene is Molly and Downey and Dad at the casino in Atlantic City."

"I could ask whether she thinks life's a gamble."

At which point, because I have not happened to look there on my own, the director nods toward the bar against the wall behind me. Leaning over it is a public relations woman of obviously superior rank to the one who answered the door, the latter perhaps an intern and the former a vice president, the gulf that great. On the bar next to her are an ice bucket, an assortment of soft drinks and waters, two wedges of cheese, and several bunches of grapes that have been too long off the vine. The woman nods at me. I walk toward her. She offers a hand, and her grip is too firm, one of those handshakes that are supposed to make a point rather than express a greeting. In addition, she holds my hand too long; she is obviously someone who has read the paperback literature on how women should comport themselves in a man's world. She wears no perfume, too little makeup, and so much jewelry that her arms rattle when they move. I do not understand the combination of moderation and excess.

"Cute bit you did the other day with Rickles," she says.

"Thanks."

"Oh yeah," says the soundman, tapping the mikes with his fingertips. "I heard about that. What exactly was it?"

The director says, "Rickles is playing a stain-resistant carpet in a new commercial, and Eric asked him how he prepared for the role."

"Did you really?" says the cameraman.

"Affirmative."

"Really clever," says the flack veep. "What'll you have to drink?"

I tell her a Perrier.

"Coming up."

As she drops ice cubes into a glass with a set of gold-plated tongs, she says that Molly will be along in a jiff. She has just finished an interview in the adjoining suite with the Hollywood correspondent of *Good Morning America* and is taking a few minutes to freshen up and recompose herself. The public relations woman also says she and I have to talk. I am not surprised. She hands me my drink and strides out from behind the bar: an assertive gait, a show of control. I follow her into the bedroom, where I sit on a chair at the foot of the bed and she shimmies onto the desk in the far corner. Her skirt rides up to mid-thigh, and she tugs it down brusquely, as if she were swatting a fly. There is no flirtation here, only business, and with that in mind she fastens her eyes on me, tightens the screws, and bores in. Eye contact does not get any more serious than this.

"Now then," she says, in a voice edged with metal, "here's what Molly doesn't want to talk about."

To a public relations person, an interview is not, as a dictionary might have it, a conversation in which one person asks questions of another for the purpose of eliciting information. It is a video press release, the form far less improvisational than the uninitiated might think. The interviewer has rules to follow and little in the way of latitude. He is not to seek unpleasant truths, bring up embarrassing incidents, or raise thorny topics. The questions should be obvious, phrased to accommodate the answers the interviewee wants to give. Upon hearing the answers, the interviewer should nod his head eagerly, not only to demonstrate agreement but to reveal his pleasure at having been granted the interview in the first place. Puppy-dog gratitude.

There is, in other words, a protocol of banality to be observed. The interviewer is less properly thought of as a journalist than as a batting practice pitcher, someone who tosses up lines for the celebrity to whack out of the park. Which means that the task of the public relations person is to explain how her client likes 'em. "About yay high for Molly, right around here on the outside part of the plate, see? No curves now, nothin' fancy. And make 'em nice and slow, too. Juicy. Then you give 'er a minute between pitches so she can get 'er wind back and be ready for the next one, awright? Okay then, chuck it in there, kid. Hum, babe, hum!"

Molly Ringwald, it seems, does not want to talk about rumors that she is romantically involved with a rock musician of dubious morality and scruffy appearance; this would alienate those in the moviegoing audience who perceive her as wholesome. She does not want to talk about her association with the Brat Pack or with movies of hers that were not commercially successful, lest she be regarded as callow or insufficiently magnetic. Neither does she care to discuss what the public relations woman dismissively refers to as "issues": drug abuse in the movie industry, celebrities and the political process, homelessness, unemployment, the greenhouse effect, Chernobyl, man's inhumanity to man, the possibility of life on other planets—any of it. She does not want to get into her upcoming projects or the work of other actors of her generation or the work of other actors of other generations or her favorite pastimes off the set.

But I should not worry. Molly will speak volumes about *The Pick-Up Artist*. She will talk about the part she plays and how she plays it and why she plays it that way and why she took it to begin with and what she'd like it to lead to in her career and what she hopes the audience will get out of the movie and the feeling of family that developed on the set among stars and crew and production people and even though that sounds like a cliché it was really true in this case because they all cried at the wrap party and vowed to keep in touch and Molly is sure they will. She will be forthcoming, in other words, about anything that accomplishes the goal of luring the unwary to her latest motion picture.

Have I got all that?

I take a sip of my Perrier. The lime-tinged bubbles explode through my sinuses. The public relations woman has broken eye contact now and is staring into her own drink. I look on peaceably.

I am not a batting practice pitcher at heart. No one who has worked at a network news division as long as I did comes away in the habit of grooving his pitches for the glory of an interviewee. But some of the topics Molly Ringwald wants to avoid, notably the issues, are topics she is not qualified to address in the first place. These constitute bona fide major league pitching, and even if she did want to step into the box and take a swing, there is no way she could make contact. This is not an insult. The actress is nineteen years old. At that age even the most promising of prospects are still in the minors.

As for Molly Ringwald's lovers and friends and hobbies, I am no more willing to take part in a public discussion of these matters than she is. She has privacy to maintain, I vestiges of dignity, a semblance of standards. The topics may be too personal for her; for me they are too inconsequential. And so the irony: between Molly's reticence and my apathy, the goals of the public relations woman will be met; my apathy bears such a striking similarity to deference that only I can tell them apart. It is in fact upon this misunderstanding that I have built my working relationship with the entire Hollywood PR community, and although the flacks are not terribly comfortable with me, sensing something uncongenial beneath the surface, there is nothing for them to put a finger on. Besides, this is show business; surfaces are all.

I tell the public relations woman I am looking forward to meeting someone as talented and gracious as her client. I made Pierre Francis look good—how hard could Molly Ringwald be? Taking my leave of the bedroom briefing, I return to the living room.

Where preparations continue, the pace picking up. There is no maniac drummer in the world of show biz reporting; deadlines are looser, pieces easier to construct, and with the exception of Jeannie Wolf, no one is spurred by a sense of higher purpose. Still, there are times when one has to move quickly; a star does not expect to wait and usually does not take waiting well.

The cameraman unfolds a light stand and puts it against the wall behind the sofa. He fastens a set of barn doors to the top and narrows the opening for a stronger beam. The soundman turns an equipment case on end to use as a stand for a monitor, which he plugs into the back of the camera, flicking it on and adjusting the color bars. The director, tapping her pen against her front teeth, says to no one, "Another five minutes, max, and we're ready ready ready to rock 'n' roll."

I step to the window, separate the heavy velour curtains, and look out to the east. The smog has grown thicker since I left home this morning and has taken on a fouler aspect; a purple-gray ring encircles the entire L.A. basin, and downtown, even from this closer vantage point, remains hidden. I can see the Twin Towers of Century City, but they seem to be wiggling a little, as if part of a mirage. That is the Century Plaza Hotel in front of them, but I can make out only the lower floors; the rest seem to have melted away, like the tip of a metal rod dipped into a vat of acid. Across the street, walking toward the hotel from Wilshire Boulevard, is a small group of people who look fuzzy around the edges, like movie extras in a dream sequence. I have always found it eerily appropriate, in a city whose primary industry is illusion, that it is often impossible to get a clear look at anything.

Suddenly the door to the suite opens. The room snaps to attention as if an alarm has sounded. The cameraman turns around; the soundman smoothes his cowlick; the director drops her pen. The public relations intern bounces off her chair, and the vice president streaks from the bedroom.

First to enter is a woman in a pinstriped suit and oversized tortoiseshell glasses, with false eyelashes so thick that when she blinks I feel a breeze. She is of even higher rank than the pitching coach; senior vice president is my guess. Behind her is the young celebrity, followed by two ladies-in-waiting, one carrying a makeup kit, the other a hairbrush and a jar of styling gel. Everyone bobs for position next to the star, eddying around her like a flotilla of tugs and nudging her toward me. Introductions are made. The star's smile is forced.

Molly Ringwald has more freckles in real life than she does on screen, but they serve her well, adding sparkle to a complexion otherwise too pallid. Her auburn hair hangs in bangs on her forehead and in loose curls behind her ears. At the moment she is pulling nervously at one of the curls, wrapping it around a finger. Her eyelids flutter rapidly, shuttering eyes that are a surprisingly deep brown. Her lips, coated with a barely discernible gloss, have already yielded the smile.

"Busy day?" I ask.

"God," she says.

As for her attire, it seems to have been chosen expressly to refute the notion that she dates, or even suffers the acquaintance of, a lowlife musician. Her dress hangs limply on her slender body, accentuating no curves, revealing little flesh; it is a print that seems busy in an old-fashioned way, full of whorls and gyres and curlicues. The collar and cuffs could be doilies. Unassuming pearl necklace, inconspicuous bracelet, no watch. She has dusted herself with powder, leaving a faint scent of lavender.

"Well," snaps the senior vice president, and somehow the word is a complete thought.

The director sweeps her arm toward the sofa, and the tugs pilot Molly in that direction. Alone, I shuffle over to the wingback chair. The cameraman flips on his backlight, looks at Molly through one eye, and decides there is too much glare on her head; he opens the barn doors a little and attaches a scrim with wooden clothespins.

The soundman clips the waiting mikes to Molly and me, hiding the cords under folds of fabric; he slips on his headset and tells us to say a few words. Molly utters several hellos. I count to five. The soundman snaps his fingers in approval.

"I guess the movie opens tomorrow," I say.

"Keep your fingers crossed," Molly replies.

The director, standing behind the cameraman, tells him to zoom in on the star. Slowly her face fills the monitor atop the equipment case. Then the director invites Molly's entourage to have a look, and five heads almost collide as they stare into an eleven-inch television screen as earnestly as jewelry appraisers.

The hair stylist sees a few strands gone astray and repositions them.

The makeup person notices some shine and applies powder to Molly's nose and forehead.

The senior vice president takes the larger view. "She looks tired, don't you think? Like she's really been through it?"

The director says, "No, not really."

"It's just that she's done so many interviews the past few days. She's been going like crazy. She really believes in this movie, though, so ultimately that makes it all worthwhile."

"She looks fine."

"Have you seen it?"

"I had to work last night."

"The screening was Tuesday."

"Then, too."

"How about Eric?"

"He was there."

"What did he think? Did he just love it?"

"Everybody ready?" says the cameraman.

Hair says yes.

Makeup says yes.

Senior vice president says, "You really think she looks okay?"

Director answers in the unqualified affirmative.

Senior veep: "You're not just saying that because you're in a hurry?"

Director: "We want a good picture as much as you do. Trust me, she's great."

Senior vice president takes a sip from a glass of Sprite poured by intern, handed to her by regular vice president.

"Molly," the cameraman says, "if you'll sit up for me just a little."

She does.

"Excellent," the cameraman says, looking through the viewfinder and adjusting his focus. "Just terrific. Couldn't be better."

Director: "Quiet on the set, everyone."

Molly looks at me, makes the slightest of mandibular adjustments, and is smiling again.

"Okay then," from the cameraman. "We … are … rolling."

The soundman is kneeling next to him, watching the cassette, which has just begun to spin. He hears a sound like a shifting of gears. "Gimme five," he says.

I wait five seconds.

Molly coughs.

Hair whispers, "Good luck."

Intern sneezes.

Soundman says, "Speed."

And Molly sits up even straighter.

Leaning slightly to the right so my head will not pop into the frame in a moment of rapture at one of the star's answers, I ask her to what extent Randy Jensen, the character she plays in *The Pick-Up Artist*, is based on her very own self.

Well, she says, crossing her legs and quickly uncrossing them, there's a lot of similarities, actually. Randy is sensitive, and Molly likes to think she is too. Randy is loyal to her friends and family, yet pretty self-reliant, and Molly thinks that's also true of her. And then there are other qualities, like stubbornness and determination, she guesses. So, yeah, you could say there's lots of stuff in common. But when you get right down to it, it was the differences that really inspired her to do the movie.

How so?

Because if she just went on camera and played Molly Ringwald, what kind of challenge would there be to that? It would only be showing up and going through the motions. Do I know?

Oh yes.

The thing that's really neat is to get hold of someone like Randy Jensen, someone with the layers and textures that Randy has because the script is just so good, and then get inside her head, find the key that unlocks the person she really is, because when you do, that's when you really hone your craft, really stretch and grow, not only as an actor, but even more important as a human being. It maybe sounds kind of … well, she doesn't know, hokey or something …

The answers are predictable, but Molly is awkward delivering them, off her game. Her voice is brittle, and the smile, to be convincing, needs a bit more adjusting. It is often like this at the beginning of an interview, this groping on the part of the celebrity. Call it the *60 Minutes* syndrome, the interviewee's fear that the interviewer has suddenly had a change of heart, deciding to make his reputation at the star's expense, and possessed by the spirit of Mike Wallace, wants to nail her not only for being a lousy actress in a crummy movie, but for failing to file federal tax returns on income from a boiler-room scam that fleeced thousands of crippled pensioners out of every last penny they had. The celebrity, timid without the protection of a script, needs to satisfy herself anew with each interview that this is not so. Once she does, she can assume a manner more in keeping with her status. My job is to get Molly over the hump, remind her that I am there to fawn, not expose. Let her know the spirit possessing me is Army Archerd.

So I ask her how she found the key that unlocked Randy Jensen's personality. What was the process?

Nice one, Eric.

Molly loosens visibly. She looks at me for a moment and then lets out a breath and nods so slightly that only she and I can see it, a gesture of reassurance to herself. She is approaching the point of trust in the benign intent of my questions, faith that there will be no curves. She is not only getting onto my delivery, she is starting to see the stitches on the ball as it comes floating up to the plate, soft and inviting.

She tells me how she found the key.

I do not hear. I am not listening. I am not psychologically equipped for such an ordeal. My mind has skittered away from this hotel suite in which yet another person of limited accomplishment is made to seem a major contributor to the common weal. I have found, for the moment, a place where I can pull covers over my head and wrap pillows around my ears. Hypocrisy is not only a recognized school of philosophy in Hollywood; it is a survival kit for coping with one's duplicity.

I snuggle into my fluffy shelter. Aaaah …

But I cannot relax completely. I have to register the silence at the end of Molly's answer so I can lean forward in my chair and exude sincerity and ask whether there might just be a little bit of Randy Jensen in every woman.

That does it. Big smile from the sofa, contented, anticipatory. Molly cocks the bat and raises her elbows. Front shoulder dips, hips square to the plate. Then she opens up: a step forward with the front foot, an uncurling of the arms. Textbook form, textbook

EARLY OCTOBER 1987

HOLLYWOOD

I HAVE BEEN TOLD TO GET WHACKY. My manner is too formal, diction too precise, carriage too erect. I wear socks too often, pastel T-shirts under double-breasted suit coats not enough. No rake worth his salt would wear my kind of hat, no aviator my style of sunglasses. Clunky shoes are in, and mine are streamlined; baggy pants are in, and mine are tailored. After years of reticence, I have begun to leave the first two buttons of my shirt undone, and now the fashion is to secure even the top one. I am not sufficiently receptive to the rollicking humor of sitcoms or the crackling suspense of cop shows like *Miami Vice*. I am square by Hollywood standards, and more than two years after the judgment was pronounced, it is deemed no longer desirable.

I have been told to lighten up, chill out, go with the flow. Rap more, converse less; kick back more, be purposeful less. Trade my glasses for contacts and my barber for a stylist and my Volvo for a ragtop Jag in a sunburst shade. True, these are cosmetic changes, but if the outer man is a reflection of the inner, perhaps I can somehow reverse the process, the inner remaking itself in the image of a newly refurbished outer. The inner getting whacky.

"It's worth a try, at least," says the executive producer of *Entertainment Tonight*, who seems to have been watching me as closely as I used to watch myself in Parkersburg, and to have found even more to criticize. He goes on to explain that he does not expect miracles, just a slightly funkier spirit.

What brought all this on is a segment of the show called "Video Preview," in which I offer my opinions of each week's new video releases. I have been presenting the segment for more than a year, but the executive producer now tells me that although it was fine when it started, it has since gotten too far out of step with the rest of the program. "Everything else is snap-snap-snap," he says. "'Video

Preview' is slog-slog," and he stretches out the words, lowers his voice to a muddy depth. "It just drags everything else down, and we can't have that anymore."

The executive producer is leaning against a wall in his office, posing next to pictures that show him in the company of celebrities and certificates that attest to his achievement in past journalistic endeavors: atypical moments of his life, captured in frames and hung for display in the hope that others will view them as the norm. His feet are crossed at the ankles, thumbs hooked in the belt loops of his dry-cleaned jeans.

"To start with," he says, "you don't review any more foreign movies. People get headaches trying to read subtitles, and they laugh at the ones that are dubbed because they're always so far out of sync. Not to mention the fact that no one can figure out the plots of foreign films. They don't make any sense. Also, you don't review any more ballets or operas or documentaries about great sculptors."

"Why not?"

"You're skewing elite."

I gasp. "Had I but known."

"You think it's funny?"

"That's not the word I'd use."

"The people who watch this show don't give a damn about where Henry Moore got his inspiration, and I have no intention of letting you force-feed them."

"I never use more than one foreign film or doc in any piece I do, maybe twenty seconds out of the whole two minutes, just for a little variety."

"That's twenty seconds too much." The executive producer straightens one of the pictures on the wall, then slides his hands into the pockets of his rumpled linen jacket. "From now on, you just confine yourself to good old mainstream American motion pictures. That's it. And forget about who directed them. Don't mention directors unless the guy's a star in his own right—Spielberg, Lucas, that crowd. And screenwriters? Nobody's ever heard of the writer, nobody *wants* to hear. Who wrote *Casablanca*, you happen to know?"

I shake my head.

"There you go."

"Is that all?"

"No. The next time you figure out that the plot of some movie is borrowed from a work of literature, something by Balzac or Flaubert or Stendhal or whoever else, keep it to yourself. 'Video

Preview' has turned into this collection of facts no one in their right mind has any interest in. You see where I'm coming from?"

I do not answer.

"Now," he says, "that's what you leave out. As far as what you put in—" He interrupts himself to cross the room and jiggle the office doorknob. Locked. We are not to be disturbed. He returns and seats himself on the edge of his desk. "From here on out, I want some sillies in 'Video Preview.'"

"Sillies?"

"Kookies and zanies."

"Just what the hell do you want the segment to be, Dave?"

"Interesting."

"To whom?"

"The kind of people who like the rest of the show."

I look away, but to no avail; I cannot escape an unimpeded view of the truth.

Although this man is new to the job, having been executive producer of *Entertainment Tonight* for less than half a year, we have developed an enmity that suggests not only a longer relationship but a history of feuding between the families. I can barely speak to him civilly; he cannot look at me without disdain. We have only to be in the same room for the air to crackle with tension and third parties to plot their exits. Yet his feelings toward me make far more sense than mine toward him. I am being cantankerous. Foreign films and sculptor docs have no place in "Video Preview," and I am well aware of it. They are my way of persuading myself that although I have sold out, I have not passed the point of redemption. My way of trying to believe that I am fighting the good fight, reforming the system from within, an agent of culture plying his trade behind Philistine lines.

Which is, of course, flapdoodle. Resentful of my circumstances, I am behaving like a child toward a perfectly reasonable teacher whose subject I detest. Release through obnoxiousness.

He, on the other hand, is being nothing more than consistent. He simply wants this program of his to be of a single piece: entertainment news that is frothy and diverting, snacks for the eye and candy for the brain, and why not? That is how *Entertainment Tonight* was conceived, and that is how it has become successful, and that is what it has every right to remain. Meaning that it is up to me to adjust to the show, not the other way around. Adjust, that is, or quit. And though I think about quitting almost daily, I have taken no steps in that direction. Call it prudence; I have a family to support.

Call it self-deception; what I am really trying to support is a lifestyle that seems to mean more to me than my convictions.

Is this, after all these years, where my fear of going unnoticed has brought me?

I am sitting on the arm of a small sofa against the back wall of the executive producer's office, angled away from him so severely that he is almost at my back. Before me is a window giving on Avenue C of the Paramount lot, across which is a sound stage. Twenty-seven. Interiors for the first *Godfather* and the Robert Redford version of *The Great Gatsby*.

If a person chooses a career to satisfy a psychological need and then finds the career unrewarding, what does that say about the psychological need? That it has been ill served? That it was not so great a need after all? Or that however great it was at one time, it has finally been outgrown, replaced by needs of a different nature to which attention must now be paid? The latter sounds right, yet I remain in television. The behavior continues after the reason is gone, and my life's work is becoming a mystery to me.

As is the reason for my getting metaphysical when the topic is silly videos. I ask the executive producer how I am supposed to find them.

"I found them for you."

"Oh?"

"See Carole," he says. "I had her order some tapes from a special catalogue. There's a whole box of them under her desk. I'm sure they're not all going to be suitable, you'll have to use your own judgment. But from now on you're using a different kind of judgment than you did before." He picks up a paperweight in the shape of an apple and rolls it a time or two in his hand. Stage business. "You get the box, you go home, you spend the rest of the day screening the tapes. Tomorrow you come in with a script for next week's piece that's got at least two sillies in it. And you don't just include them, you say something nice about them, something upbeat. That's another thing about you. I know there've been times in the past when you've mentioned an offbeat video in the segment, but you always bad-mouth it. No more. Your new motto is: 'Don't Slam the Sillies.'"

A knock on the door and urgency in the voice on the other side. "Got to see you, Dave."

"What for?"

"Trouble."

"Talk to me."

"The Genesis piece just came in on the bird from London, and it's twenty over. The recut on Valerie Harper's gonna be another twenty over, maybe more. And we still haven't found the Stallone bite."

"Be right out," the executive producer says to the door, and then, turning back to me, repeats that he will see me, script in hand, tomorrow.

That was this morning.

This afternoon I am watching *Mounting a Mallard Duck*, one of ten entries in the series Taxidermy by Video. I have pulled an easy chair up to the television in my living room, dropped the box of sillies within arm's reach. The air-conditioner is roaring. Outside the temperature is in the eighties and the sun a milky yellow.

Mounting a Mallard Duck features a man named Connie Mack Moran, who, as the tape begins, is standing behind a large butcher block table with a knife in one hand and a dead duck in the other. He smiles at me, as if in complicity, and then begins to cut. What follows is an hour and a half of gradually exposed duck innards: membranes, tendons, ligaments, bones, organs—all become increasingly visible as Connie Mack describes with relish the actions of his blade. He cuts, dices, slices, minces, pulls things out and throws things away. *Mounting a Mallard Duck* is as gruesome as anything directed by George Romero and as tedious as anything directed by Andy Warhol. But to less squeamish souls of nontaxidermic bent, it is, I suppose, silly, and therefore not to be slammed.

I stop the VCR, think of a possible opening line for my script.

> Are you a do-it-yourselfer? Do you think you already know
> how to do everything in the world *worth* doing? Have I
> got a video for you.

Next I look at *Bizarre Sports and Incredible Feats*, a collection of scenes from events so extraordinary that ABC's *Wide World of Sports* seems positively narrow by comparison. There is, for instance, cockroach racing.

The segment begins with the owners of the roaches painting them different colors so they can be distinguished from one another once the race begins. There is a red roach and a green roach and a yellow roach and a blue roach and even a roach with a stripe and another with polka dots. The owners use narrow artists' brushes and apply the paint lightly so as not to burden their charges with extra weight; most need only one coat. Then the roaches are stuffed under a cup in the middle of a large circle that has been drawn on a smooth surface of some sort. At the starting whistle, the cup is lifted and the bugs bolt for the circumference. First roach to reach it wins. The owners wager their hard-earned money and cheer the competitors on, clapping and whistling. Afterward they slap one another on the back, offer words of commiseration and encouragement. Maybe go out for a few beers, share their dreams of glory next time around.

The sporting life.

> If you're one of those people who has always thought of a cockroach as a creature with no redeeming social value, well, think again.

I dip into the box and pull out two cassettes held together by a rubber band. *How to Read a Woman Like a Book* states that if a female leans toward me during a conversation at a bar and then holds my gaze for several seconds, she probably finds me attractive, or at least interesting. Conversely, if she refuses to talk, backs off, and stares at the Schlitz clock on the wall even though wearing a watch of her own, she is unlikely to welcome my advances. *The Art and Science of Flirting*, which is billed as the work of "nationally known flirting expert Kathryn Brown," recommends smiling as a good way to begin a relationship. A frown, the tape implies, might be construed as off-putting.

> If you're so hopelessly, blitheringly stupid that you can't even—

Whoops. Take two.

> Having trouble finding that special someone in your life? Think a little well-meaning advice might be just what you need to turn things around?

Also in the box are two so-called environmental tapes, technology's answer to the pet rock. They are *Video Fireplace* and *Video Aquarium*, and the names say it all. The camera that shot *Video Fireplace* did not move—no pans or zooms or tilts—and there is neither background music nor narration. There are only, as the notes on the box put it, "60 Flame-Filled Minutes," with the gentle sounds of monaural crackling as the logs reduce to ashes. *Video Aquarium* is an hour of slowly drifting porkfish, foxfaces, and clown anemones, among other forms of aquatic life. The box says, "No Tank to Clean, No Fish to Feed."

> Do you live in a house or an apartment that doesn't have a fireplace? Would you like an aquarium, but think they're too expensive? Well, whether your game is fish or flame, I've got just what you're looking for this week on home video.

Before I look at *Rent-a-Friend*, I pour a large amount of vodka over a small amount of orange juice and keep the ice cubes to a minimum. The sun, as it streams through the living room windows, has gotten even milkier; only the white light is visible in the sky, not its source. I gulp my drink; small depth charges go off in my stomach.

The title character of *Rent-a-Friend* tells me his name is Sam, and what he does on the tape is sit in his Chicago apartment and talk into the camera, pretending it is I. He asks me questions, then waits for me to respond. As I do, he nods. Rapport.

"What's your name?" Sam says.

Pause.

"Is that right? Gee, I went to school with someone who had that name. Good person, really was. Wish we hadn't grown apart like we did. Anyhow, what do you do for a living, if you don't mind me asking?"

Pause.

"Hey, no kidding? That's always struck me as a fascinating way to earn a buck. Tell me more about it."

Pause.

Nod, nod, nod.

Later in the video, as our relationship ripens and Sam and I begin to feel more comfortable with each other, he pulls out some snapshots of his family and makes quips about individual members. One of the pictures is his older sister, and he tells me that when he was a kid and guys came to the house to pick her up for a date, he made noises to disgust them. He still remembers how they went. Gives me a few samples. Something like an oink, something like a Bronx cheer, an approximation of flatulence. Still disgusting. Then he confesses that one of his favorite adolescent pranks was wiping nose grease on glass; furthermore, he says, the act still gives him perverse pleasure. It is not an idle boast. Sam rubs his finger against his nose and then wipes the finger on the lens of the camera, making a huge smear in the middle of my television screen.

> Are you lonely? Desperately lonely? Will you do *anything* for a friend?

I look at my drink. Almost gone. I look at the box of tapes. Several remain. Among the titles I can make out are *Gore-Met: Zombie Chef from Hell* and *Best Buns on the Beach*.

Unbeknownst to me, I am about to be ordered to get even whackier.

LATE OCTOBER 1987

HOLLYWOOD

THE FLOOR MANAGER STARTS with one stick of gum, his jaws working it like a jackhammer shredding an old highway. Then he jams a second piece into his mouth and chews even harder. It is what he always does when he is worried, and what he is worried about now is what he is always worried about, what he is paid to worry about: time.

"You're gonna have maybe four seconds," he says, chomp-chomping. "Can you do it that fast?"

"Sure."

"Positive?"

"Word of honor." I am poised atop a wobbly stool in the teleprompter room of Paramount Sound Stage 28, interiors for *The Godfather II* and the television series *Mannix*. Behind me is a large soundproof window through which the control room is visible. The director, associate director, technical director, and associate producer sit at a panel staring into a wall of monitors about six feet in front of them. The monitors are like a dozen unblinking eyes, constantly staring back. Most are blank; the taped portion of this week's installment of "Video Preview" appears on a few, and two others show the anchors in the studio. Mary Hart is adjusting a few strands of hair, John Tesh fiddling with the knot of his tie and asking for a mirror.

"It might even be three seconds," the floor manager says.

"No problem."

"Glad *you're* cool about it, man," and he grins at his own nervousness. Chomp-chomp.

We are recording today's edition of *Entertainment Tonight*, and although we started a few minutes later than usual, all has gone smoothly so far. Two segments are in the can; we are halfway through the third; the fourth awaits. The time is 12:32. Twenty-seven minutes remain until 12:59, by which instant the show must be completed and the tape rewound and then cued to the top for transmission. At precisely 1:00 p.m., Pacific Daylight Time, *Entertainment Tonight* will be fed via satellite to affiliates all over the country. There is no margin for error.

"How about I explain it again?" the floor manager says, shifting the wad of gum from one side of his mouth to the other.

"All right," I say, smiling, needing the instruction less than he needs the outlet.

"Just to play it safe, know what I'm sayin'?"

"Go."

He looks at his watch. "We're about thirty into tape as of right now. Say we've got maybe forty more. Then we come outta tape to you for the live tag. You say your thing, whatever, then toss to Mary on set. That's Mary, not John. Yeah?"

"The woman."

"Mary says, 'Thanks, Eric. We'll be right back.' That's all, those exact words, six of 'em. What?" The floor manager presses one side of his headset against his ear; the associate producer has given him a time cue, and he did not hear it. "Gotcha," he says as the associate producer repeats herself. To me: "Twenty seconds left on tape. I'll count you from five. Where'd we leave off?"

"Six words from Mary, not John."

"Yeah. So Mary thanks you. By the time she finishes, you've leaned completely over to the left so the camera can make a bumper shot of the folks in the control room without you in it. It goes like this, then: You throw to Mary, you're upright on the stool. Six words later, you're history. With me, man?"

"All the way."

He reaches over and pats me on the knee. The associate producer barks through the headset again, and the floor manager tells me there are ten seconds left on tape, chomp-chomp. "Ready?"

"Ready."

"Five seconds," from the floor manager, who raises his arm. "Four, three, two, one," and he swoops the arm down to his side in a single flash of motion.

"And that's it for this week," I say to the camera, reading the teleprompter's words as they roll across my field of vision. "Next week's releases include two of special note. One got some pretty shabby treatment earlier in the year when the Oscar nominations came out; the other is called *Video Psychiatrist*, and it answers the question: What should you do if you're feeling a little unhinged but can't afford seventy-five bucks an hour? Mary?"

In the studio, which is on the other side of the prompter room door, Mary smiles and makes her brief expression of gratitude. The floor manager, like a soldier signaling his comrades to sprint from the path of incoming mortar, waves me frantically to my left, mouthing, "Get over, get over, out of the shot." I lean, vanish to the side. The prompter room camera zooms past my vacated space into the control room. Theme music up full. The words *Entertainment Tonight* unfold across the bottom of the screen. Cue commercial. My guess is that it took a second and a half at the most.

But two problems. The first is that the director called the camera switch too late, so that while Mary was thanking me, it was my image that occupied the screen, tumbling out of frame, not hers. The second is that in making so sudden a move on so unsteady a perch I lost my balance; the stool tipped over and I crashed to the floor, cracking my head on the leg of a small table and bouncing the stool back into the camera pedestal.

"Oh no!" yells the floor manager.

"Dammit!" yell I.

"Cut!" says the director, so loudly I can hear him through the prompter room window without benefit of amplification.

The associate director, next to him, hollers, "Stop tape!"

And the laughter begins. The anchors erupt on the set, Mary putting her hands to her cheeks and vibrating on her chair while John slaps his palms on the desk. In the control room, the director throws back his head and clutches his stomach, his mates at the panel responding with similar exuberance. Back in the prompter room, the floor manager takes a quick glance at his watch to determine that there is time for a few chuckles. The prompter operator and the cameraman join in. So does the whacky star of "Video Preview," who, after discovering that the bump on his head is not serious and the wound to his pride even less so, picks himself up and resumes his position.

But as I am moments away from learning, the person most amused by my inadvertent display of slapstick has not yet been heard from. I am also about to find that he is more than merely amused; he is inspired. A vision has come to him, and as visions do, it has taken him over completely. An odd enough fellow *without* a vision, he is in the studio right now, off camera, and was so capitivated by my performance that he is enraged at the control room for not continuing to record it.

The director flicks on the intercom and lowers his voice. "I didn't know you had such a gift for physical humor, Eric."

I smile, reattaching the microphone that fell off my tie in the descent.

"Let's get back to business, everyone," the director says.

In the background, the associate producer calls out, "Recue tape." The intercom snaps off.

The prompter operator rolls back the script to the proper line; the cameraman resets his shot; the floor manager tells me to stand by while tape is whirling backward to the exact spot, chomp-chomp.

And then the door opens and into the room toddles the senior producer of *Entertainment Tonight,* small of stature but large of ego, light of step but ponderous of mien, the twinkle in his eyes making him look ominous, not amused.

"That was great," he says, chortling, "just great. And so unexpected coming from you. That was part of the charm."

Does he think I fell off the stool on purpose? "It was an accident, Jim."

"No matter," he pronounces, "so is life."

The senior producer of *Entertainment Tonight* is a lot like his pal the executive producer: determined to make the show a glittery treat for viewers, impatient with what he perceives as my subversiveness. He is hardworking and imperious, dedicated and ill-mannered. He also wears plaid pants more often than any other human being in the Western Hemisphere. Blue and red on a field of green, green and yellow on a field of blue, black and orange on a field of gray: his stumpy little legs, at one time or another since he became my immediate superior, have represented every clan in the Highlands. He is an avid golfer, but his attire is more a reflection of taste than of sporting passion.

"I have this theory," he says, clasping his hands behind his back and beginning to make small circles around me on the stool.

"Jim," the floor manager says, tapping the crystal of his watch. "Twenty-two minutes till we ride the bird."

The senior producer has a habit of inappropriate action at inconvenient times and is now indulging it, pretending not to hear the floor manager's warning. Without looking at either the floor manager or me, he says, "Do you have any idea what made the Golden Age of television golden?"

As it happens, I do not.

"I'll tell you." He stops pacing and plants himself directly in front of me. "Refrigerator doors that didn't open during commercials. Flats that fell over during *Playhouse 90* or *Studio One.* Actors who blew their lines, singers who forgot the lyrics, comedians who got the jokes wrong and broke themselves up. And all of it going out there live, right into the living rooms of America. *That* is what made the Golden Age of television golden."

Floor manager: "Jim."

"Mistakes. Mistakes were the key. Because mistakes are human, mistakes are real." Jim slaps one hand into the other and wrings his fingers; his face is flushed and his eyes damp. This vision of his is coming into sharper focus. "People could relate to TV in the early days because it was live and things went wrong, just like things went wrong in their own lives."

"Twenty minutes," says the floor manager, who reaches into his pocket for a third stick of gum and goes right back for a fourth. Now I am beginning to fret; I have never known him to surpass three, even on the one day we *did* miss the bird. He packs the two new sticks into the available space in his mouth, and his jaw muscles begin to ripple like a weightlifter's pecs. Probably nineteen minutes now, and a segment and a half to go.

"Which is exactly why people are tuning out today," the senior producer goes on. "Forget all that crap about VCRs and video games and other diversions, the excuses you hear all the time—the real reason people don't watch TV as much as they used to is that they never see anything genuine on it. They see all this packaged stuff, preprogrammed and rehearsed until the blood is sucked right out of it. Do you know what television has become in this country in 1987? Do you?"

I refuse to answer. I will not play. The senior producer looks at the floor manager.

"What, Jim?" he says. "What's it become, huh?"

"Dry fucking marrow."

The words just lie there in the closeness of the prompter room air. No one understands, and so there is no response and no attempt to direct the conversation elsewhere. There is no laughter, no sound. The prompter operator looks down, and the cameraman fiddles with his zoom handle.

The floor manager makes a discovery. Four sticks of chewing gum may be good for his nerves, but they are hell on his diction. "Apepeen," is his next time cue.

"That's why your fall was so special." The senior producer is on fire, a lunatic intensity to his voice. "It gave us something authentic, a moment of truth. And then that, that ... *cheeseburger* who calls himself a director yells cut and we blow the whole damn thing."

"Sebenpeen," the floor manager announces.

"Jim," I say, "let me put this as respectfully as I can. You have the intelligence of a crustacean and the judgment of a slug. Get the hell out of here, back in the studio so we can do the tag again."

His head snaps to the side; whether he is reacting to the harshness of my words or the realization that time is wasting, I am not sure. But he steps away from me and tugs open the prompter room door with both hands, wedging himself between it and the frame. He looks back. "Eric, you hit the nail right on the head. We're going to do it again."

It does not quite register.

"We blew it the first time, but I'm sure we can get it the second. I know that's not quite up to the standards of the Golden Age, but in this business you have to take what you can get. You nail something the second time you shoot it, you're doing pretty doggone good. And if you want to compare it to the movies, it's not even close. Those people, they'll do forty or fifty takes for something that's supposed to play as spontaneous. So we're doing all right, doing okay here."

It has registered. Softly: "Get out of this room and don't come back."

"Let me spell it out for you, Mister Talent. We're going to do the tag again and you're going to fall on your ass again. Do you understand?"

"Fibpeen."

"But with a little change. Because when you did it before, the fall came late. The only reason we saw it at all was that the cheeseburger stayed on your shot too long." The senior producer reaches over to the prompter table and grabs a copy of the script. He skims it, eyes zipping over the page like laser beams; the man makes quick decisions for a living. "Here's what we do this time. This time you start to lean at 'if you're feeling a little unhinged.' Then you fall just as you say, 'Mary.' That ought to work. It'll take a second or so for you to hit the ground, then we'll cut to the studio. And I've got a great idea. I won't tell John and Mary what we're cooking up, so at least their reactions will be fresh, maybe even better when they see the same thing happening again. They'll just be amazed."

"Fourpeen."

"Except there's another point to consider, now that I think about it. Should you fall out of frame like you did last time, or should the camera follow you down?"

"If you want a stunt man, call the union."

"Out of frame, I think."

"We about ready in there, men?" It is the director over the intercom.

"Otherwise," the senior producer says, "the camera might not be able to get back up in time for the bumper shot."

"Thirpeen," from the floor manager, who then pulls the cud out of his mouth and says, "Sweet Jesus, everybody, thirteen minutes until rerack and about eight minutes of show to go!"

"Get out of here, Jim."

"Do it."

"Out of here."

"Trust me."

"Out."

"When you see it later, you'll love it. People will remember this."

"You're a moron."

"You're a coward."

"A coward can always get braver. A moron's doomed for life."

And so the argument goes—mature passions, puerile expression, nyah nyah-nyah *nyah*-nyah—until the floor manager stuffs the gum back into his mouth and sings out, "Elebben!" and the director says, "Come on, come on," and the prompter operator says, "I'm gonna roll this mother whether anyone's ready or not," and the senior producer calls me another name from the handbook of grade school pique and storms back into the studio.

For a moment, no one in the prompter room moves, but it is a moment only; there is no time now to be dumbfounded.

The floor manager reaches over and pats me on the back. "You all right?"

I return a tight-lipped smile.

He tells me to stand by.

The director utters a few calming words via intercom.

The tape machines start rolling again; the associate producer prepares to flick her stopwatch.

I have won the battle but lost the war. It is not the first time something like this has happened to me at *Entertainment Tonight*; it may, however, be the last. Never has it been more apparent that my days on the show are numbered, and that the countdown, like the minutes until feed time today, is picking up momentum like a brakeless freight running express to oblivion.

I HAVE NOT BEEN FIRED. The option period of my contract has passed and Paramount has decided not to exercise its right to renew, but I have not been fired. Terminated by default, let us say, which is not the same as termination by overt act. Not the same, strictly speaking, as being fired.

But there is a ritual of departure to be performed today, nonetheless. I clean out my desk and gather the tapes worth saving and slip them into a shoulder bag. The others go into a box for degaussing. I keep John Cougar Mellencamp, discard Rob Lowe; keep Alan Alda, discard the Gorgeous Ladies of Wrestling; keep Henry Winkler, discard the guy from Brooklyn who won the Joan Rivers look-alike contest. Never had a dub of Molly Ringwald to begin with.

I throw away enough old scripts and press kits to fill a second box. I remove the papers from my bulletin board and the picture of my wife and son from the desk. I say goodbye to people in the immediate vicinity, one of whom is Jeannie Wolf. She is writing a script for a piece on Bruno Kirby, who plays Robin Williams's nemesis, Lieutenant Hauk, in *Good Morning, Vietnam*, but she eagerly puts her work aside for the moment. She tells me she has not been concentrating on Bruno anyhow. She has tried, because it is too sad to keep peeking over her shoulder and see me clearing space for a successor, but she has found her mind wandering. She says she has enjoyed our conversations and admired my work.

"You're different, Eric."

I concede the point.

We exchange pecks on the cheek. She says she will miss my spirit, and the truth is that I will miss hers as well.

And then, wanting to attract no further attention and elicit no further condolences, I sneak out of the reporters' room and down the back steps of the Mae West Building. I cross Avenue E to B-tank, where I pull my car away from the low-hanging cumulus, and for the final time drive off the lot where once John Wayne revived the memory of the Old West and Diana Ross the spirit of Billie Holiday and John Travolta the pulse of the disco era.

Left on Melrose, left on Western, north to Los Feliz Boulevard. Then around the bend to the right, past the entrance to Griffith Park and the narrow road that leads back to the old Cecil B. De Mille house, which has more rooms than I have lines on my resume. So far.

Yes, another departure, but this one is different from the others. This one is attended by the embarrassment of not having made the decision myself. It reminds me of the time during my junior year of college when I was involved in so hapless a relationship with a young woman that we both knew it could not last. We joked about the end, wondered when it would happen. I was not what she wanted, and she was not what I wanted, and yet, for a while, each seemed the best the other could do. We held on. Too long. In the meantime, on our cheerless dates, we behaved with increasing hostility toward one another. Finally unable to stand it any longer, the young woman made the formal announcement of dissolution. I remember how I felt: relieved at the breakup, humiliated that it had not come about more honorably, that I had taken so passive a role. We were so obviously wrong for each other. I also worried about the future, wondering what this experience might portend for relationships still to come.

I am worried about the future today, too. This is the first time I have left a job without believing that the next would be an improvement of one sort or another; without, in fact, even knowing what the next would be. I am now of mixed caste: too much *Entertainment Tonight* in my bloodstream to be taken seriously again as a network journalist, too much NBC News for further employment on the Hollywood beat.

Left on Vermont, right on Gainsborough, right into the driveway at the corner of Hillhurst.

Is there a place for me at all in television? Should there be? Maybe from here it will all be downhill. To a degree I would not have imagined possible a few years ago, I welcome the direction.

1988–1989   Media Commentator

Fox Television, Los Angeles

THE PARKING GARAGE IS COOL even on the most humid nights, eerie even on the most tranquil. Breezes blow in distant corners but are heard more than felt, a series of whistling echoes whose precise location is never easy to detect. Footsteps and conversations also echo; the garage is a chamber with long open spaces, concrete floors and concrete walls. The lighting is dim: recessed fluorescents in the ceiling, caged yellow bulbs over the doors and on the stairwells. Shadows are everywhere—some stationary, some flickering as if in response to the unfelt breezes.

It is 10:34 when I enter the garage tonight, and nothing seems out of the ordinary. Or does it? Is there an extra patch of darkness between me and my car, one or more of the fluorescents having burned out? I walk at my normal pace, but what is it about my footsteps? Does the sound echo more loudly than usual? Does my shadow fall at a different angle? My car is a hundred feet away, but it looks farther. I am, it seems, already aware that something is not quite right.

I close the distance to my car by a quarter, then stop and take a deep breath. I am not sure what I smell, only that it is out of place in a parking garage. I start walking again and realize that the scent is perfume. A few more steps: cheap perfume. A few more: something more likely to repel advances than encourage them.

I look around. No one. But there is a wall to my right, and there are pillars in front of me and to the left; an olfactorily retarded woman could be lurking anywhere, ready to pounce, to chloroform me with her redolence, lift my cash and credit cards, and vanish into the night.

I am still walking, but cautiously: head sweeping from side to side like a radar dish, an arc of a hundred eighty degrees. The scent is getting stronger. Now there is one pillar between me and my car.

Suddenly I hear breathing. Fabric rustles, and the heel of a shoe clicks on the floor. From behind the pillar a woman steps into my path, the movement so quick that she almost falls over. She reaches back to the pillar to steady herself, barely managing because her heels are as high as scaffolding. First one hand against the pillar, now both. There. Balance regained. The woman is upright but ready to teeter.

"Mr. Burns," she says, and the voice is like the chirping of a small bird. "Thank God it's you."

She appears to be in her mid to late fifties, although there is something about her that hints at a younger person who has aged poorly. Her face is narrow and deeply lined along the nose and across the chin. Her eyes are round but as tiny as buttons, and her lips, barely as wide as the swath of a lipstick tube, are a translucent blue, though this may be a trick of the garage lighting. She wears a brown wig in a modified pageboy, the style reminiscent of June Allyson in her commercials for adult diapers.

But except for her shoes, apparently meant to add an air of sultriness, the woman's attire calls to mind Allyson in her heyday, that unremitting innocence: blue pleated skirt slightly below the knees, white blouse with tatted Peter Pan collar, light blue sweater with circle pin. Her stockings are of the support variety, thick seams running crookedly up the backs of calves as spindly as broomsticks; they do not look as if they could prop up even so slight a frame as hers. Curiously, the odor of her perfume is subtler now that I have closed in on the source. Perhaps I'm getting used to it. Perhaps the unfelt breezes have shifted.

"Who are you?"

"Esther," she says, "I'm Esther. Oh, Mr. Burns, it feels like I've been here all night."

"How did you get onto the lot?"

"Does it matter?"

"How did you know where my car was?"

"Just a detail, just a detail." She smiles as if in amusement at the persistent but irrelevant questions of a child.

"What do you want?"

"Just let me catch my breath a minute, do you mind? Now that you're finally here, I guess I'm a little excited. I don't want to blow it now."

And so it dawns on me. The fawning expression, the tremulous voice—the woman is star-struck. I am the star! She wants an autograph or a picture or a sexual experience to remember for the rest of her days on earth. The first two I can easily provide.

"Well, I'm flattered, but—"

"Oh no." She takes a step toward me, maneuvering on her heels like a novice stiltwalker in a high wind. "I'm the one who's flattered, just to have a chance to meet you. I'll prove it."

She claws into the purse she has been holding in the prim way of certain middle-aged women—strap in crook of elbow, forearm parallel to ground, palm upturned with fingers curled together at the tips—and takes out a small notepad. She flips back the cover and reads.

"Listen to this, Mr. Burns. Friday, April 8, 1988." She clears her throat. "The setup is that Richard Nixon is going to be a guest on *Meet the Press* in two days. You say people ought to tune in and pay attention, because whatever the man's failings, he's still a very substantial human being. Something like that—I didn't get it exactly, I think my mother was probably gabbing at the time. But I took down the next part word for word. You said, and I quote, 'Like Nathaniel Hawthorne's Hester Prynne, Richard Nixon wears his scarlet letter—a W for Watergate—everywhere he goes. The rest of us should not be so puritanical that we refuse to acknowledge the rest of the man's garb.'"

I glide a little closer to my car and flip my jacket over my shoulders. "Esther, what is this?"

"I won't read every word, Mr. Burns, don't worry." She waves the notepad at me; the fluttering pages are full of writing. "I just want to give you an idea. Here, listen," and she begins riffling and reciting "Wednesday, May 18, 1988: the Ku Klux Klan wants their own TV show in Kansas City. You say no. Friday, June 3, 1988: Dukakis campaign ads. You say some of them are very effective, the ones where they use clips from all the Republicans criticizing Bush during the primaries. Wednesday, July 6, 1988: Sidney Biddle Barrows, the Mayflower Madam, emcees a cabaret show in New York. You let her have it with both barrels. Wednesday, July 18—"

"I think I get the idea."

She slaps the notepad shut, holds it with both hands, a secure grip. "I've never missed one of your commentaries, Mr. Burns, not even tonight's. I've missed it so far, of course, but I had my mom tape it. I'll watch it later, when I get home. I'll bet you don't even know how many commentaries you've done since you started on Fox, do you?"

"No."

"Ninety-seven, counting tonight. I watched you the first night, which was really just kind of an accident because I didn't know you'd be on, and I haven't missed since. Imagine, ninety-seven commentaries. So you've got an anniversary coming up next week.

Do you think they'll do anything special for you, like wheel a cake onto the set, maybe? I've seen things like that on TV before."

I wish she would get to the autograph. I am tired, eager to go home, but do not want to be brusque with so devoted a fan. A delicate problem, and in the process of considering it I give myself away.

"Oh my," she says, "is that a little yawn I see?"

"I'm sorry."

"Has it been a long day?"

I say it has.

"Well, I guess I better get to the point."

I reach into my pocket and take out a pen.

"Don't you just love *America's Most Wanted?*"

Push the button on top of the pen and pop out the point. "Pardon me?"

"*America's Most Wanted.*"

"I've never seen it."

"Never?"

"Maybe a minute or two in passing, but I've never sat down and watched a whole episode."

"You at least know what it's about, don't you?"

Why is she making small talk? I've got the pen ready; my other hand is prepared to take her notepad—why doesn't she just ask for the damn autograph? "It tries to track down criminals who are still on the loose," I say indulgently; perhaps she is suddenly shy.

She clicks her tongue in disappointment. "I thought, you being a media critic and all, you'd be a little more up-to-date."

If she does not ask me to sign her journal of my thoughts in the next minute, I will have to force the issue. In fact, I will steer her in that direction now. "Esther, what exactly is it you want?"

"A favor."

"Of course." Finally. "If you'll just—"

"I want you to help me get an audition."

"Sorry?"

"For *America's Most Wanted,*" she chirps. "I want to be the co-host."

I retract the pen point and slip the instrument into my pocket in a single fluid motion, unobtrusive, no dashed hopes apparent in either the movement or the accompanying facial expression. An internal sigh, but not terribly deep. It was not an unreasonable assumption: seldom does a year go by without my being asked once or twice for an autograph; this could have been the time. Being under no illusions about the extent of my fame, I anticipate a quick recovery.

But *America's Most Wanted?*

The Hollywood Freeway is within a few hundred yards of the garage, and an ambulance speeds northward on it, siren shrieking in the night. When it passes, there is a faint hum of tires whirring on pavement. Esther and I tune into it for a few moments.

"Is something wrong?" she says. Honest puzzlement, or so it seems. "It's just that *America's Most Wanted* is a Fox show and you work for Fox News. You're my friend in the company. So I naturally thought ..."

"It's a big company, Esther."

"Oh yes, I'm sure."

"Thousands of people work for Fox in different divisions, and most of them aren't even on this lot. The main lot is in Century City."

"I know that. I've lived in Los Angeles all my life."

"Then what makes you think I could get you an audition to—wait a minute."

"You thought of something?" she says hopefully.

"The host of *America's Most Wanted* is a man whose child was kidnapped and murdered a few years ago, right?"

"John Walsh. A very distinguished gentleman."

"The show doesn't *have* a co-host."

"Of course not," Esther says, as if she has just won, not conceded, the point. "That's the beauty of my plan, don't you see?" She slides the strap of her purse down one arm and then up into the elbow crook of the other. "What I mean is, if my goal in life was to get, say, Vanna White's job, I probably wouldn't have much of a chance because Vanna White's already got it, and if she was quitting or getting fired, then everyone in the world would know about it and there'd be a million other girls standing in line to audition. I know, I've tried out for things like that before, and you always get your hopes up and nothing ever happens. In fact, that's how I got the idea for *America's Most Wanted.* I said to myself, I said, Esther, instead of going up for a job where there's all kinds of competition, why not create your own job? It still might not be a sure thing, but at least you're the only one applying."

I feel my head nodding slightly, involuntarily; it cannot be agreement. Perhaps a sort of dazed appreciation for Esther's originality.

She digs into her purse again and brings out a small perfumed envelope. My name is written on the front in a tiny script. She hands it to me and says, "Open it."

"What is it?"

"Please."

I remove some papers.

"It's my résumé," she tells me. "Go ahead."

I unfold the papers and wonder where to begin. Do I tell Esther that a résumé is not supposed to smell like a bordello? Do I tell her that it should not be written on fuchsia stationery, that it should not be handwritten at all, and that even if handwriting *were* acceptable, red ink is not. Do I tell her a résumé should not be folded over several times like an adolescent love note? Or do I just go along, surrender to this puzzling night?

"Don't laugh," she says. "There's a reason I did it that way."

"I imagine so."

"My thought process was that it's more personal like this."

I glance down at some of the entries. There are not many, and they are even less impressive than I would have guessed. Esther seems never to have worked professionally in show business; she has listed only failed auditions and roles in amateur theatricals, most of them more than two decades ago. Nellie Forbush in *South Pacific* at the Winston Heights Community Center, no address given. The headmaster's wife (she has forgotten her name) in *Tea and Sympathy* at the First United Presbyterian Church, no address given. Her most recent entry is employment in the women's clothing department of Bullock's Wilshire last Christmas, where she waited on the weekend anchorwoman of the local CBS station and an actress with a recurring role in the cop show *Hunter*. Dealing with people like this, she writes, helped her "develop poise and self-confidence and an ability to communicate on a more professional level."

I fold up the résumé along the original lines and stuff it back into the envelope.

"It's not much, is it?" she says.

"No, it's not."

"But you know what my thought process is about that?"

"Esther, it's really getting late."

"I think I can turn it to my advantage. Please hear me out. I'm not fooling myself, Mr. Burns, I know I don't have the track record a lot of girls do. But the very fact that my résumé looks like it does proves one thing. I'm honest. Don't you agree?"

I hand the envelope back to her, and she replaces it carefully in her purse.

"No one makes up bad references, do they?"

I shake my head. No one does.

"I think—and I know this is a best-case scenario—but I think my résumé will make me stand out. You get all these girls bragging about these jobs that seem like a lot bigger deal than they really were, and then there's me, telling it like it is and not putting on any airs. Plus, after I get hired, it'll make a great story for the producers to tell the people from newspapers and magazines when they come around to interview me, about how this girl insisted on telling the truth even though it made her look bad, and she got the part anyway. Maybe then I could be an inspiration to others who haven't done so well in the past. I could show them, just by my example, that they've still got a chance to make it in the world."

I take off my glasses, rub the heels of my hands into my eyes, and put the glasses back on. I look past Esther into the night sky, where neither moon nor stars are visible. A red light blinks at the top of a tower several miles away; other lights, even farther in the distance, seem to belong to planes in the LAX flight pattern. Across the lot a car turns a corner, its high beams shining my way for a moment, then angling off and disappearing. Other than that, the night, like the conversation, is black and deepening.

I ask Esther why she chose *America's Most Wanted.*

"Well, it's just that on most shows today you see a man and a woman, and on that show there's only a man, and so I thought they might be in the market. Look, Mr. Burns, I don't think we should be nitpicking here."

"Nitpicking?"

"I do the best I can, but I have to try to figure things out from my living room, just watching the TV. I don't have any input from professionals. Maybe if I applied to *America's Most Wanted* they'd turn me down, but somebody there might like me and see some potential and then put in a good word for me to someone else at another show. One thing could lead to another. According to the stories I've read, that's the way it goes a lot of times in show business. Vanna White didn't start out wanting to be Vanna White, you know. It just happened. What I'm saying is, it doesn't *have* to be *America's Most Wanted,* but at least that could be the place where I get my foot in the door. And that's something I have to do pretty quick, Mr. Burns."

"Why do you say that?"

"Well, look at me." She brings her hands to her face and fans her fingers across her cheeks. "Honesty, remember?" A pout. "I'm no spring chicken, and if I don't get myself a TV job pretty soon, it might never happen."

I slide over to my car and take a seat on the trunk, resting my feet on the bumper. I lean back, bracing myself with my arms. "Why me, Esther?"

"Because you're connected. What do they say, plugged in?"

"I told you I'm not."

"Well, I thought you were," she says, "since you work at Fox. I thought you'd be able to do something. Plus I feel like I know you."

"That's the main thing, isn't it?"

"What?"

"The real reason you're here. You said I was your friend in the company."

"Oh. Yes. I did. You are."

"Esther," I inform her, "I'm not your friend. Friends know each other. You don't know me at all."

"I think we need to talk about this," she says, and gives up on her balancing act, stepping out of her grossly elevated shoes and kicking them at the pillar. "Oh, I feel so much better." She bends down to rub her toes and continues talking. "You think we're strangers, you and I, and from your point of view it's true." She straightens up. "But there are two people here, two points of view. I'm the other half of this relationship and—"

"There's no relationship."

"I'll go on, Mr. Burns, if you please. I'm the other half of this relationship, and what I feel matters as much as what you feel. And I say I *do* know you. So what makes you right and me wrong?"

"Esther, I've never seen you before in my life. I've never heard of you and don't know a single thing about you except for your résumé and the fact that you want to be the co-host of a television show that doesn't have one and probably never will. If I saw you sometime again in the future, I might not even recognize you. Put all of that together and the conclusion is inescapable. I don't know you."

"Yes, exactly, *you* don't know *me*, I've already admitted that. What I'm saying is that *I* know *you*."

"That kind of 'relationship' isn't possible."

"Yes, it is, Mr. Burns. Television makes it possible."

"Television creates an illusion."

"No," she says, "now, you stop right there." Her eyes narrow, her nostrils flare. "You don't know how I'm feeling while I watch you on the TV, and so you're in no position to dismiss it as an illusion. It's not fair."

"Look, I understand how you could get confused, I really do, but—"

"It's not confusion."

"Esther, I—"

"Do you know what I'm asking myself now, Mr. Burns? I'm asking myself why people like you go on television if you don't want this to happen."

"Want what to happen?"

"A relationship, like with you and me. Who do you think you're talking to when you're in front of the camera? What do you think is going on?"

And suddenly the wind is out of my sails. Suddenly, on this curious night in this place of echoes and shadows, it strikes me that Esther the uninvited fan is raising the most reasonable of questions.

I do not recall, in all my years in television, a single conversation among people on the air about the effect we have on people at home, except in the aggregate, and then only because their number is important to us: if it is high, we are successful; if low, we are not. We comb our hair for them; we dress well, speak clearly, try to act as important as we can without crossing over into insufferablility. We hope that our electronic images satisfy the whimsical standards by which viewers judge such things. We may even fancy ourselves, as I once did, parents and doctors and soloists. That is what we do.

But what do we think?

Do we think?

Do we assume that the folks at home want us only for our information, so that the one-way nature of the process frustrates them because they are denied the chance to talk back to us, to clear up their misunderstandings and expand on their points of interest? I suppose we do. But can we admit that some people may want us for other reasons, for our mere presence, such as it is, so that the one-way street is a blessing because it enables them to fantasize about us without contradiction? We speak, they listen; we project, they create. They are like children again in front of the television, and we are their make-believe friends, their secret companions, the ones they talk to who do not talk back.

I look at Esther. How many others like her are out there? What do they want? What responsibilities do I have toward them? To what extent do those of us who were attracted to television because of our own psychological needs draw our strength not from the facts we impart or the events we witness, but from the extent to which we exploit the psychological needs of others? Is this as parasitic as it sounds? As cruel?

The attention of strangers. It can be earned but not controlled.

"Look," I say to Esther, but the heart has gone out of my defense and I am simply filling the silence, distracting myself from my thoughts, "we want the people who watch us to respond, to listen to what we have to say, but as far as, well ..."

"As far as nothing, Mr. Burns. You just think this through. Excuse me for putting it so bluntly—I don't mean to sound rude, not to you, of all people—but have you really thought about what happens when a person at home listens to someone on TV? Like when I listen to you? What happens is, I get to know you. It's the same as what happens when I listen to someone who's *not* on TV, someone I meet in real life. Exactly the same. I develop a—"

"Relationship."

She smiles.

A horn bleats somewhere in the distance.

I plot a getaway. All I have to do is slide off the trunk and get in the car. Open the door and ease behind the wheel and insert the key in the ignition. Turn it clockwise ninety degrees. Jerk gearshift, tramp accelerator. Zoom, goodbye. Nothing complicated, nothing I have not done thousands of times before, and if I do it again in the next minute or so, I will be free of this starlet *manqué* and the annoying issues she brings to the table.

It is, of course, my very discomfort that keeps me in place. And Esther senses it. She knows she has the advantage. She decides to press it. She takes two quick steps away from me, slipping into a pool of darkness and turning her back. She bows her head, then rounds her shoulders and wiggles them. I assume she is removing another item from her purse, but what she reminds me of is one of those impersonators on a TV show who turns from the audience to change appearance for the next character.

Sure enough, when Esther faces me again, it is in a different guise. She has sucked in her cheeks and steeled her jaw. Her teeth are bared, but not in a smile. Her breath is audible. Her right hand is on her hip. Her left hand is shaking. In it is a knife. The blade is out and waving at me. She takes one step forward.

"Time to get down to brass tacks now," she says. "I was hoping it wouldn't come to this."

It is as if Betty Boop were doing an unbilled cameo in a film noir. I can neither take Esther seriously nor afford not to. Some time passes, I am not sure how much; it is probably not as long as it feels.

"What's that for?" I say when I am able to speak.

"I sharpened it tonight before I left home. Can you tell?"

"I don't understand."

"Why not, Mr. Burns? It makes perfect sense to me."

"To stab me because I can't help you get on television?"

"Stab *you?*" She frowns, then looks down at her weapon. "Oh," she says, embarrassed, and flicks her wrist, turning the blade around. "That's more like it."

"You'd stab your*self*?"

"Oh, don't go acting like you care."

"Of course I care."

She raises the knife and touches the tip to her neck; I think I see a bulge in the carotid artery. "I wouldn't be so selfish as to deprive the viewing public of you, Mr. Burns. You're too important. But me—well, that's a different matter. One less fan in the world won't make any difference to anyone, will it? One less person with stars in her eyes who never made it to the top?"

"You can't do this, Esther. Please, put the knife away. This is crazy." It is a plea born of competing emotions: compassion for a fellow human being in trouble, self-interest for another mortal who desperately wishes he were elsewhere. I close my eyes. I envision the tabloid headline that puts the final nails into the coffin of my career.

HARDHEARTED TV PERSONALITY
DRIVES FAN TO SUICIDE

HE DENIES KNOWING HER
SO SHE SLASHES THROAT

I extend my hand to her. "Come on, Esther. I want the knife."

"No," she says, and backs up. "Don't be a hero, Mr. Burns. I just wanted you to make a few calls for me, that's all."

"All right," and I drop my hand. "If it means that much to you, I'll get in touch with *America's Most Wanted*."

"Really?"

"Just put down the knife."

"Oh, Mr. Burns, thank you very much." Her sigh is so deep that it makes her rib cage expand and contract like a bellows. Then it occurs to her. "Except why should I believe you?" Her lips purse crookedly. "You just got done telling me there's nothing you can do, and now you say—"

"I've reconsidered."

"How do I know you're not just humoring me?"

"You pulled the knife to make me change my mind, and it worked, Esther. I changed my mind. Don't talk yourself out of it."

"I just want to be sure."

"Here's what I'll do," I tell her. "Will you please put that thing down?"

"Not yet." The artery still bulges. "Go on."

"When I get to work tomorrow, I'll ask around the newsroom

about *America's Most Wanted.* Someone's bound to know something. I'll figure out a way to get in touch with the show, and then I'll tell them about you."

"You're not just saying that?"

"No."

"You honestly mean it?"

"I give you my word."

"Cross your heart and—"

"Jesus Christ, Esther, will you please get rid of the knife!"

"My résumé."

"What?"

Hand that does not hold knife goes to clasp of purse. "I should give you back my résumé."

"Oh, I think we can hold off on that for now. Let me get the groundwork laid first." Hot bubbles of sweat are popping onto my forehead and remaining; they do not run down my face.

"Oooh," she says, "guess what I just thought of. I'll bet the person you talk to, the one from *America's Most Wanted,* will be a big fan of yours, just like me. So when they get a phone call from Mr. Eric Burns, the Fox commentator, they'll be totally impressed. They'll think this Esther LaRue must really be someone special. That's my last name, in case I didn't tell you. Well, it's the one I use professionally. LaRue. I won't tell you the one I was born with. Oh, Mr. Burns, thank you so very, very much."

I can finally see some distance between the knife and her neck.

"Just leave me your number. Give it to me right now. Put the knife back in your purse and write your number on a sheet of paper and let me have it. I'll start checking around first thing tomorrow morning, and as soon as I find out something, I'll call you."

"Oh, I don't think so."

"What?"

"I think it would be better if I called you instead. That way there's no chance I'll get left high and dry."

"Fine, if that's what you want. You call me."

"What time do you get in tomorrow?"

"Not tomorrow. Give me a few days."

"Why?"

"In case people are on vacation or out sick or I end up playing phone tag with someone."

"You're stalling."

"I'm being practical."

"Well, I can give you until Friday, but that's about it. I'm too excited to let another weekend go by."

"Do you think that's a good idea?"

"What?"

"Being so excited."

"I can't help it."

"I think you'd better try."

"Why should I?"

"Because even if I do get through to someone at *America's Most Wanted*, the odds are they won't be interested in a co-host."

"That's all right," she says. "If you can just get me an audition."

"You can't count on that, either."

"Well, you know what will happen then."

"What?"

"I'll kill myself."

"Don't talk that way."

"Like this, watch," and as her little button eyes pop open to the size of silver dollars, Esther LaRue jams the blade into her neck. I lunge at her, then stop short. She is breathing even more heavily than before but is not out of control. She has stumbled backward a step or two but has not fallen over. And she is not gagging, not wailing, not making any other kind of sound associated with severe physical trauma. There is no sound from her at all. There is no trauma. There is no blood. The knife, as I am now able to tell, is a toy; instead of a steel blade piercing her skin, a plastic one has receded into the handle.

Esther giggles.

I fall back against my car.

"Oh, Mr. Burns," she says, and the giggle turns into a full-throated laugh, a sound deep and hearty and totally incongruous. "You didn't really think I'd do something like that, did you? Oh my," and she pulls a handkerchief from her skirt pocket and dabs at the corners of her eyes, shaking now from the exertions of her merriment.

I am livid. It passes. I am relieved. It stays. The woman is not really going to do away with herself; the tabloids will have to remain content with tales of sexual encounters between humans and aliens. With remarkable calm, or a remarkable facsimile thereof, I shake my head at Esther and get into my car. I close the door and turn on the engine, which kicks in immediately, reverberating through the huge, hollow spaces of the garage. I roll down the window.

"Call me in the newsroom Friday," I say. Remarkable restraint.

"You'll still do it?"

"I'll give you the name and number of someone who works

for *America's Most Wanted*. That's all. Then you're on your own."

"It's not crazy to try to make your dreams come true, Mr. Burns."

"But after you call Friday, don't call again. Ever. Understand?"

"If you say so."

I start to roll up the window.

"I'll keep watching, though," Esther says. "I still respect you for the work you do on the air."

"Good night, Esther."

"Good night, Mr. Burns. Thanks again. But one thing. About what happens if I can't even get an audition? Don't you want to know what I'll do, what I'll *really* do?"

"No."

"Oh, you can be such a stick-in-the-mud sometimes. Let me tell you."

I close the window and back the car out of its space, swinging it around to face the exit ramp. Then I start forward slowly, inching past Esther, ready to swerve if she dives under my wheels or leaps onto the roof or swallows a homemade incendiary device and blows herself up in front of me. But she holds her position at the pillar, shoeless and forlorn, and her hand disappears into her purse one more time.

At the stop sign at the top of the ramp I glance into the rearview mirror. Esther has begun to follow me, but slowly, making no real attempt to catch up. She just wants to get back into the light, allow me to see her more clearly. See, in particular, what she is now holding in her hand. See her bring the object out of her purse and up to her head and push the barrel against her ear. See her finger curl around the trigger. I think her lips are moving; she might be saying, "Bang." Which is the same word, I suspect, that would appear on the red flag that pops out of the gun when the trigger is squeezed.

Or maybe not.

I know now that I am done with Esther; I will not make any calls for her, will not look back on this night in any detail. I will not muse on its significance or consider future implications. What I do not know, and will be surprised to discover, is that she will not call me Friday. She will not call me ever. Her encounter with me has apparently extinguished her flame.

I roll down my window again and wave. With her free hand Esther waves back. Then I snap on the radio and lay rubber down the ramp and speed through the night for the sanctuary of home.

1989–1990   Host, *By the Year 2000*
                 KCET-TV, Los Angeles

THINGS ARE DIFFERENT NOW, winding down, coming to some kind of conclusion. I am restless, edgy, uncertain. I do not talk television with my friends, nor do I skim the ads in *Broadcasting,* hoping to find that one special job. I do not read the trades, do not take steps to keep my name out there. It has been several months since I put in an appearance or circulated or schmoozed.

And I hardly ever call my agent, who returns my calls even less frequently. No matter, though; I know what he would say if he did. He would begin with a deliberately theatrical sigh. Eric, Eric, Eric, he would say. Then the sigh again and the names again, like the verse leading into the chorus of an old familiar song. Just to set the mood. Give me a hint, bunky—it would be something close to a plea—what're we gonna do with you?

I would appreciate the gravity of the question.

My agent would then ask me to put myself in his shoes. Here he was laying himself on the line for me, telling every executive producer and production company head who would listen that I was a man of undeniable talent: good writer, natural performer, quick on the uptake, smarts up the wazoo, versatile—I can do news or fluff, class or schlock.

And then what would happen?

He would set up an audition for me and I would refuse to go. He would arrange a meeting and I would sit there in judgment of my prospective employers rather than the other way around. The word was starting to spread. I was getting a reputation. Not exactly as difficult, but not exactly as one of the guys, either. Which would be okay if my name were Ted Koppel or Geraldo Rivera or something like that. But my name is *not* Ted Koppel or Geraldo Rivera, and I should get it into my head that a name like Eric Burns entitles a person to just so much independence of spirit.

Capisce?

He would tell me how my résumé was shaping up these days. He would say that if the damn thing were a graph it would look like the stock market after the crash of '29. When I started with him I was a commentator for *Entertainment Tonight*. Powerful position, powerful show. All right. Then I was demoted to reporter. Graph line goes down. I got a chance to redeem myself with "Video Previews" but blew it by acting like Pauline Kael or John Simon or one of those other snobs, and then I ended up getting fired altogether. No show, no position. Graph line goes *way* down.

My next job gave me another chance at commentary. Graph line up—any employment is better than being out on the street—but only a little because it was a local station, not a national show. *Local station*—he would practically spit the words into the phone, show biz agents feeling about clients in local TV the way sports agents feel about minor league ballplayers. And the station wasn't even a network affiliate! It was one of those new Fox outlets, and then *they* fired me because I refused to go to the Emmy ceremony and suck up to the talk show hosts and sitcom actresses, and when they asked me why I was being such a pain in the ass I got up on my high horse and said I was afraid of looking like an industry shill and compromising my integrity as a commentator!

And now where am I? Hosting this rinky-dink public affairs show on a station that doesn't even have as many viewers as Fox did. And *what* a show! Topics like Latino political power and multilingualism in the L.A. school system and judicial reform and euthanasia and the dangerous overcrowding in air traffic control patterns. Where's the sex appeal? he would say. Where's the razzmatazz?

He would say: Are you embarrassed to have this crapola on your résumé?

He would say: *I'm* embarrassed to have this crapola on your résumé.

He would say: It's like you're hiding out, the way those creeps do when they go into the Federal Witness Protection Program. You're out there in public, going through all the motions of having a normal life, but you're in this godforsaken hole so far off the beaten path that nobody could find you if they wanted to. You're safe, but what's the point?

I would say: The irony, don't you see it? The subjects on *By the Year 2000* are important, and there is time to discuss them at some length. What kind of business is it when you fail because you're doing something worthwhile? When you lose your audience because there's something to say? I understand the importance of circuses, but does bread have to be an object of indifference? Of scorn?

No. I would not say it. It would sound too defensive. Too self-serving. Besides, my agent would not understand. Or would understand, but would accuse me of going off on a tangent. Would remind me that television is a business, bunky, a business, and in the world of dollars and cents the trapeze artists make a whole lot more money than the bakers. He would sigh. Eric, Eric, Eric. Would say: Line of graph off bottom of bleeping page.

And then, finally, on one of those rare occasions when I call him and he does call back, the conversation is not at all what I imagined.

"I can't believe it," he starts in, "cannot believe it for a second. Just when I thought it was all over for you, that there was nobody left in the business who wanted to hear your name, much less take a flier on you, you get one more shot at the brass ring. And if I read the situation correctly—which I usually do, as you well know—this could be your last shot? Interested?

"Damn straight you are.

"Surely even someone as out of it as you has heard of the King brothers, right? Only the most successful packagers of TV shows in the history of the entire world. *Wheel of Fortune, Jeopardy, Oprah, Inside Edition*—four of the top seven syndies in the country, all King World. That's the company name. Michael and Roger, the guys are unbeatable. They've got the Midas touch even more than Midas had it. But something else about them. The way I hear it—and this is the kind of thing you only pick up in whispers—the King boys are feeling a little guilty these days. They've made all this money on shows that're basically doo-doo, and now they're thinking maybe they ought to give a little something back to society. It's like the robber barons, remember those guys? Just before they died they got these attacks of conscience and started endowing every institution they could put their names on. Gave unto the masses for all the masses gave unto them. So think of this show as the King brothers' version of the Frick Museum or the Carnegie Library or Rockefeller University.

"Think of *what* show, you say?

"Da-da-da-*da*-da-*dah! Arts and Entertainment Revue* on the A and E cable network. It's a firm go for the spring of '90, and it's your baby if you want it. Believe that? What it is, it's this really classy arts magazine, like *Entertainment Tonight* for people who can read without moving their lips. That means it'll never have a huge audience. It could be a real showcase for you, though, give you some real cachet.

"What do you do on the show?

"Well, for one thing, in-depth interviews with real artists, not just celebrities. No more Chuck Norris and Shelley Long and those types. *A and E Revue*'s gonna have people on it like Edward Villella, Joan Baez, Michael Feinstein. Right up your alley. You'll also have taped pieces to intro, like a behind-the-scenes look at Harold Prince's next play and a tour of the Spoleto Festival. You've heard of that, right? They have it every summer in South Carolina, mostly classical music, I think. I'm reading from my notes here. They're also planning at least one performance segment for each show, right there in the studio, live. So far they've booked Cy Coleman and this group called the Gypsy Kings. There's also some white rock-and-roll singer from South Africa with a black band, guy with a real social conscience. I forget his name. Not that it'd mean anything to me if I did remember. Some of these acts are so esoteric even *you'll* be stumped.

"Perfect, no?

"They ought to call it *Artsy and Fartsy Revue.*

"Only problem with the show is they're doing it in New York, so you and the wife and kids'll have to move back. But you never were much of a California type anyhow. I was talking to Michael King today, just a preliminary chitchat, and I told him I didn't figure that for a major ballbuster.

"Will they pay your moving expenses?

"Every penny.

"So, the way matters stand is, I give you this call and sound you out, and if you're interested, I put you in touch with the executive producer of the show so you can ask your own questions. What exactly your duties'll be, what kind of promotional responsibilities you'll have, any travel, whatever else. You might be able to believe a little of what he says, bits and pieces. Then, if everything clicks, you get back to me and I start banging heads with the King boys and their bean counters. I don't really know what kind of money they're planning to offer, but believe me when I tell you it'll be a fortune compared to what you're getting for Latino power in the voting booth.

"What do you say?"

And this time my agent actually does want an answer, which I am able to provide promptly and with a degree of conviction that surprises even me. "It sounds good," I say. "Start banging heads."

"Think you can manage not to screw things up?"

"I'll give it everything I've got."

And we both realize the inadequacy of that.

1990   Host, *Arts & Entertainment Revue*

A&E Cable Network, New York

IT IS 8:59 ON A SUMMER NIGHT, and I am standing alone in a large, well-lighted room. In my hand is a remote control tuner that I am tapping against my thigh. On my soul is a pair of wings, ready to flap. I am waiting for a minute to pass. One more minute until it begins, sixty-one until it is over.

I flip the tuner into the air, and when it comes down, I squeeze the on button and punch in a one and a five. The television screen crackles, the picture blooms. Statistics tell us that in the average American household, a TV set is turned on for more than seven hours a day. Statistics also tell us that the average length of a scene on a program or during a commercial is three and a half seconds. So much time, so little sense.

The first thing I see on the screen is a well-known hood ornament.

"The following program," says an announcer's voice, "is brought to you in part by Mercedes-Benz and its many fine dealers in the tri-state area."

Theme music begins.

The room is too bright. There is a three-way bulb in a floor lamp next to the sofa; I switch it from the highest to the lowest wattage, then turn off a lamp on a cobbler's-bench table in the corner. Now the room is almost as dark as the fading day outside. I look through the window and see my son putting away his bicycle and waving goodnight to a friend. My daughter is sitting on the porch watching him, sucking her bedtime bottle. In a few minutes my wife will take them both upstairs, leaving me alone to ad-lib the details of this small ceremony of final disengagement.

I scuffle back to the television, remain standing, hands on hips. Too much nervous energy to sit. Besides, there is a certain attitude to the pose.

Theme music under.

Hood ornament dissolves out.
The next voice I hear is mine.

> Tonight, on Arts and Entertainment Revue, Mandy
> Patinkin tells a story with a song.

A few bars from Mandy.

> On the first anniversary of the tragedy in China's Tianan-
> men Square, a group of celebrities records a commemo-
> rative video.

A few bars from the socially conscious celebs.

> And, on this summit weekend, a look at television Soviet-
> style, with Western-style special effects.

A few moments of a Soviet version of a quiz show.
And then the theme music comes up full again, and the camera
cuts to a wide shot of a man sitting on a stool in the studio in
apparel provided by Alexander Julien and draped across his body
by a clothing consultant so that the coat doesn't bunch at the shoulders and the tie hangs straight.
Music fades.
Cut to tight shot.
Music out.

> Hello everyone, and welcome to Arts and Entertainment
> Revue. I'm—

Eric Burns.
Yes.
I've been through this before.
And something has come to me tonight with extraordinary clar-
ity, as well as with a suddenness that can only be the result of long
years of painstaking, largely subconscious preparation. The reason I
should no longer appear on television is that I am no longer willing
to tell other people's stories. Not the atypical stories of crime vic-
tims, not the romanticized stories of small-town heroes, not the
pointlessly self-serving stories of celebrities. They no longer interest
me, no longer seem worthy of either the time they demand or the
paychecks they remit.

I have reached the point in my life when I want to tell my own stories.

This is not, as it may seem, a manifestation of ego in either its superficial or virulent senses; it is, rather, the same impulse that drives the businessman to start his own company, the architect to insist on his own designs, the salesman to choose his own product, something whose virtues he can recite without duplicity. It is the impulse that compels my son to depart from the instruction booklet and build an edifice of his own devising out of Zaks, the impulse that makes my daughter switch the clothes on her stuffed animals, creating her own wardrobe combinations. It is a healthy impulse, and more than that, basic; the human being who respects himself will at some time in his life need to make up his own mind about what to say.

Not go on about Mandy Patinkin.

> We know him, first and foremost, from the musical theater. He won a Tony playing Che Guevara in *Evita*. He also starred in the highly acclaimed *Sunday in the Park with George*.

I feel like an apprentice who has been too long indentured. And to what? As a journalist, my master was random events; as a celebrity reporter, it was random individuals. People in both of these fields hold themselves in generally high regard, yet both are motivated to a large degree by sycophancy. The journalist truckles to the occurrence, the celebrity reporter to the celebrity; neither is a whole person by himself. As a result, his self-esteem is a highly unstable alloy, subject to disintegration under extreme stress.

Or perhaps not so extreme.

> Among the talented people making this musical memorial to Tiananmen Square are Roberta Flack, Ashford and Simpson, and Richie Havens.

Put it another way: I have spent too little time making decisions about the message, too much developing the skills of the messenger. Of the latter I have a fairly large supply. I enunciate clearly but without cloying overprecision. I vary my cadences so that I seem human, not metronomic. I bob my head just enough to give the impression of commitment to my topic. I have been at this, after all, for some time now.

> In fact, a spokesman for one Latino group says that the more frustrated his people become with their lack of power, the better it is for them in the long run, because they become more and more resolved to organize and fight the system that they believe is so guilty of oppressing them here in Los Angeles.

My shoulders roll slightly toward the camera so that I seem friendly, settling in to chat. They are also slanted to the camera at just the right angle. My head is angled as well, in such a way that my overbite is less pronounced.

> Righard Nixon's behavior during Watergate disqualified him from being president but has nothing to do with his views on *glasnost*, SDI, or relations with Central America.

I strike the proper balances: between blinking too much and staring wide-eyed, between smiling too much and looking dignified, between a plastered hairdo and one that is hopelessly unruly. After so many years, I could hardly be excused for continuing cosmetic shortcomings.

> But when I asked Ringwald why her character finally succumbed to the charms of Downey's character, she had a surprising answer to give.

My smile is engaging/My glasses straight.

> And so, as Pierre Francis climbs back into his boat and chugs slowly away from Wilson's Landing for yet another day ...

My aura convincing/My eye contact great.

> ... although the speculation about Hays's condition remains just that: speculation. It is beginning to seem that unless Hays himself reveals the truth, it will never be known.

My gestures are perfect/My poise of renown.

> Sharon Rainwater insists that life must go on, despite the tragedy, despite her feelings that nothing will ever be the same again.

My style is a constant/I've got myself down.

> All proceeds from this weekend's bake sale will go to the
> Parkersburg chapter of the American Red Cross.

Outside, the sky is deep purple. A streak of heat lightning runs from a star into the horizon, a jagged path. The moon is a white sliver. Clouds are gathering and just as quickly tumbling apart.

It seems to me tonight that my entire professional life has been leading to the point at which I was mature enough, free enough from the demons and insecurities and longings of childhood, to ask myself a single question: Am I better off talking to an audience of millions about subjects that do not engage me, or to a far smaller group about subjects for which I care passionately? Which serves the communicator better? Which the auditor? Which, ultimately, is the more meaningful communication? Is the measure, in other words, to be one of quantity or quality?

Maybe I'll write a book. That would allow for the passion. That would eliminate the audience of millions. There might be some things I could say about television that never occurred to the more famous memoirists, like Rather and Kuralt and Donaldson.

> *Let's go to the hop,*
> *Oh, baby,*
> *Let's go to the hop,*
> *Oh, baby,*
> *Let's go to the hop,*
> *Oh, baby,*
> *Let's go to the hop.*
> *Come …*
> *On …*
> *Let's to go the hop,*
> *Let's go!*

Let's stop.
I have been watching television long enough.
A career does not have to be a life sentence.
I cross the living room and turn off the set.
The thousands of dots that make up the hundreds of lines of resolution that make up the electronic version of my face disappear.

ACKNOWLEDGMENTS

I have changed some names and dates in the preceding pages to protect the privacy of individuals. The changes have been few, however, and none has in any way altered the point of my tales. My occasional liberties have been with literalness, not truth.

Three names are introduced here for the first time, unchanged. Without Aaron Asher and Elaine Markson I would still be singing the blues. And Joy Johannessen makes me want to polka. My gratitude is boundless.